Roseville
in all its Splendor

by

John and Nancy Bomm

Copyright 1998

Published by

L-W BOOK SALES
PO Box 69
Gas City, IN 46933

ISBN #: 0-89538-095-1

Published by: L-W Book Sales
PO Box 69
Gas City, IN 46933

Please write for our free catalog

Printed in the U.S.A. by Image Graphics

Dedication

to everyone wishing to keep alive the beauty and love of Roseville

Acknowledgements

This book may not have been completed without the generosity of the Krause family. John and Pat Krause were instrumental in this endeavor. We were missing the last nine or ten years of plates which the Ohio Historical Society did not have. We would have had to resort to regular pictures but the Krause family presented us with George Krause's personal records and there they were in living color. It really gave us the incentive to complete this book. All changes you see in the book regarding dates and patterns are the result of their wonderful gift. We cannot possibly find a way to say thank you to them. Dear Friends, Thank You!!!

We wish to thank all our friends and family who have been so supportive of us as we worked on this wonderful endeavor called a book. Many times they have given us the boost we needed to push forward and not give up.

An extra special thank you goes out to Robert Bettinger for all the knowledge and time he invested with us. His knowledge of pottery was indispensible. Without his hospitality at his home and work we would never have completed this project.

Thank you, Karin Coleman! Without all the research information she sent us, we would not have been able to complete this project. She has been sending us information for over three years and has been adopted as a part of our family.

A thank you also goes out to the Ohio Historical Society in Columbus, Ohio. Their archive division spent hours and days copying all the many pages of the Roseville Pottery Company plates.

Another thank you to Jack and Lois Emig. Lois is the granddaughter of J.F. Weaver. She has been able to document the information regarding her grandfather.

Disclaimer

All the plates in this book are from the Ohio Historical Society and the George Krause estate. We have searched across the country and have found only these specific plates. They are not a complete list of each pattern. Many have more designs than are represented.

Pricing also may vary according to location, quality, and quantity. Remember the prices are only a guide and must be used as such.

Early Period Marks: 1900-1918

During the early years, marks were very inconsistent. Many pieces had raised dishes. Some had the line name in a ribbon under the dish, while others had impressed or stamped marks in dark colors. Of course, some had no marks with just paper labels.

<u>Raised Disk with Raised Letters</u>

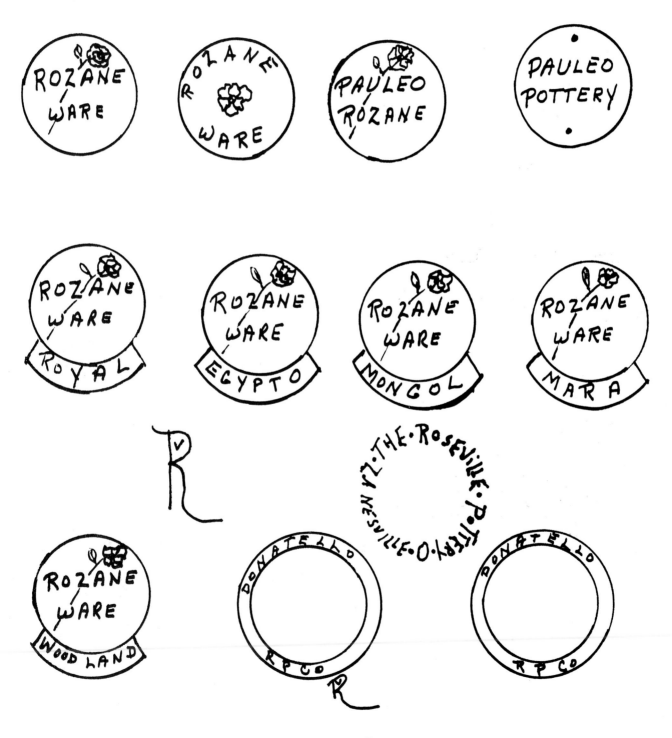

ROSEVILLE
POTTERY CO.
ZANESVILLE, O

ROZANE
"OLYMPIC"
POTTERY

Impressed

RPCo   RVPCo   ROZANE
RPCO

ROZANE
POTTERY

ROZANE
67-B
RPCo

AZUREAN   AZUREAN
RPCO

ROSEVILLE
ROZANE
POTTERY

Fugiyama   VENTIAN   Phloron
RPCo.

THE
ROSEVILLE POTTERY
CO.

-MERCIAN-
545-10.

Middle Period Marks: 1918-1935

During this time, most pottery was unmarked except with paper labels. Some patterns may have appeared marked in two or three ways.

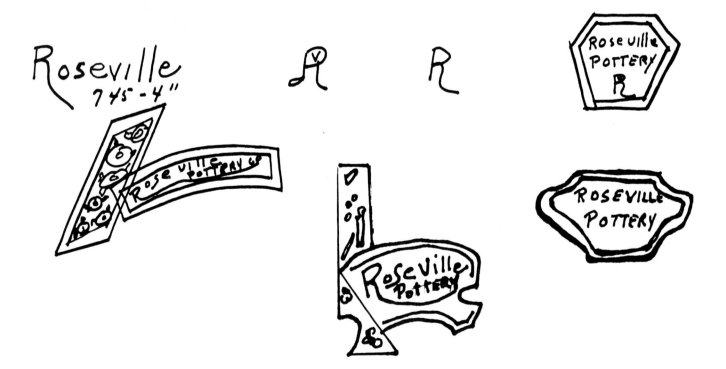

Late Period Marks: 1935-1954

"U.S.A." was added to these marks in high relief. They also carried pattern number and size.

Roseville 45-5"

Roseville U.S.A. 3/8-4"

Roseville USA 932-6" MOCK ORANGE

R USA 124-4"

R 98-5 U.S.A.

Roseville USA 1BK-8"

Lotus LL-9"

ROSEVILLE PASADENA PLANTER L-35 U.S.A

155 raymor by Roseville USA OVEN PROOF PAT. PEND.

Created for Calart by Roseville U.S.A. NO. 1507

THE BORDEN CO. Rv B2

The Hyde Park NO. 1900

The Hyde Park NO. 1905 MADE IN U.S.A.

1945 U.S.A.

NO. 1510 MADE IN U.S.A.

A Listing of Artist Names and Monograms Found on Rozane Ware:

ELIZABETH AYERS

GOLDIE

V. ADAMS

GUSSIE GERWICH

A.B.

WILLIAM HALL

M.B.

JOHN J. HEROLD

A.F. BEST

MADGE HURST

JENNY BURGOON

JOSEPHINE INLAY

ANNA DALTHERTY

HARRY LARZELERE

E. DUTRO

CLAUDE L. LEFFLER

ANTHONY DUNLAVY

A.V. LEWIS

HATTIE ELVERLEIN

L. MCGRATH

FRANK FERREL

B. MALLEN

BILL FARNSWORTH

MIGNON MARTINEAU

8

LILLIE MITCHELL

W. MIERS

HATTIE MITCHELL

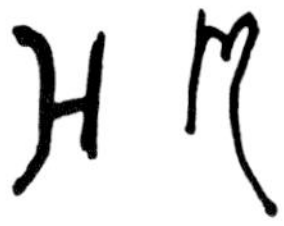

MINNIE MITCHELL

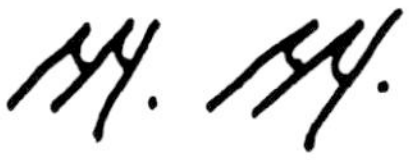

GORDEN MULL

M. MYERS

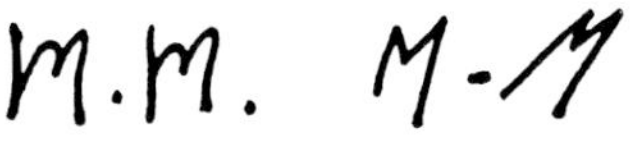

WALTER MYERS

GEORGE NEFF

MARY PIERCE

HESTER PILLSBURY

FREDERICK HURTEN RHEAD

HARRY RHEAD

R. LILLIAN SHOEMAKER

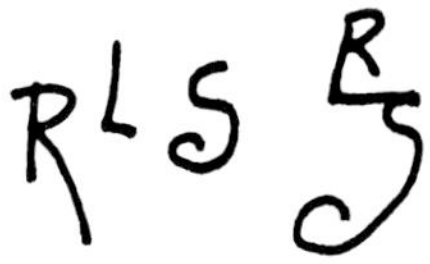

ALLEN SIMPSON

HELEN SMITH

FRED STEELE

TOT STEELE

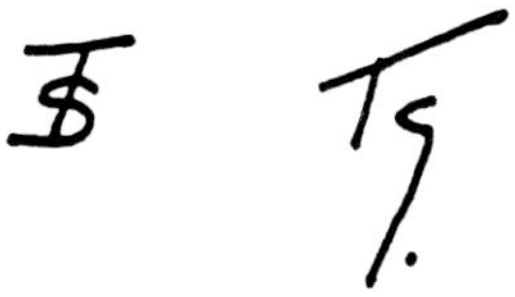

CAROLINE FRANCIS STEINLE

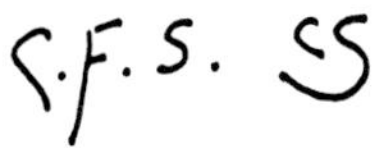

C. MINNIE TERRY

MADELINE THOMPSON

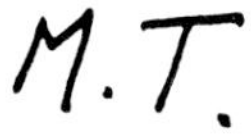

MAE TIMBERLAKE

SARAH TIMBERLAKE

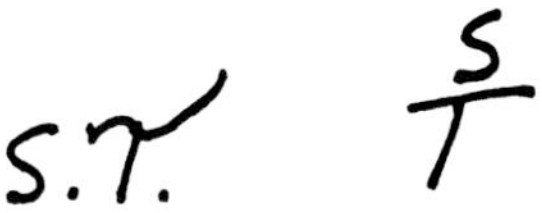

ARTHUR WILLIAMS

CLOLILDA ZANETTA

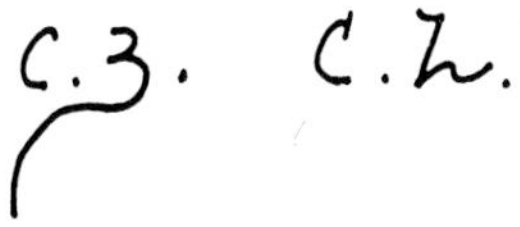

9

History of the
Roseville Pottery Company 1890-1954

The Roseville Pottery company was founded in early 1890 by J.F. (John Frederic) Weaver and three local potters and businessmen in Roseville, Ohio. Despite moving the company operation to Zanesville, Ohio just eight years later, the name continued to be used.

John Weaver was a Civil War veteran. He fought in Sherman's March to the Sea, engaged in eleven major battles and was discharged from Camp Chase in August of 1865. He was married in 1867 to former Nancy Porter and sired eleven children.

He was evidently an energetic and creative businessman. He ran a grocery on Main Street in Roseville and was also post master for four years at the same time. The post office was located in the back of the grocery. J.F. Weaver died of failing health in July 18, 1926 at the age of 70.

George F. Young

George F. Young was born February 24, 1863 in Lower Salem, Washington County, Ohio. As a son of a blacksmith from Germany, George learned the value of hard work. His early business career started as a school teacher but lasted only four years. In looking for a higher and more stable income, George tried his hand as a salesman for the Singer Sewing Machine Company.

During the depression year of 1890 George and his wife, Anna, were struggling to meet their financial obligations. Anna's millinery business failed and George found it very difficult to sell a luxury item such as a sewing machine. George could see a demand for pottery and had a desire to invest not only his time but his money in a young up and coming pottery company in Roseville. He joined the Roseville Pottery in 1891 as a salesman.

On January 4, 1892, the firm was incorporated and named Roseville Pottery Company. George Young was elected secretary and general manager. During this time, he had very limited financial interest in the company but later gained controlling interest of the companies stock.

Other officers included: C.F. Allison, President; J.F. Weaver, Vice President; Thomas Brown, Treasurer; and J.L. Pugh on the Board of Directors.

Just after the incorporation of the company, this group of far sighted businessmen purchased the old J.B. Owens plant and expanded their stoneware production. The works had three kilns and manufactured flower pots, cuspidors and painted ware. Again, in 1895, the opportunity to purchase the Midland Pottery came about and now the production was doubled. Flower pots, stoneware, bird baths, novelties, umbrella stands and cuspidors were the main business. Many of these garden items carried fine workmanship, and were created by the best potters in the field. Three more kilns were added and the total output of the two plants was valued at $100,000.00 and employed over 100 workers.

Anna M. Young

As demand continued to flourish for these products, they recognized the need for further expansion. In 1898, the acquisition of the Clark Stoneware Company on Linden Avenue in Zanesville provided the opportunity to move their office, shipping department and some of their production to Zanesville, eleven miles away. The building consisted of three kilns in a three story brick building. In 1898, a three story addition 50' x 156', was built and the following year a fourth story was added and an additional three stories were also added to the original building. The kiln shed was enlarged to accommodate 10 kilns required for the business and in 1903 a two story brick office and sample room was added.

The Linden Avenue plant was devoted entirely to the production of painted ware but in 1900-1901 Rozane was developed. The work force was approximately 200 people and the annual output was approximately $350,000.00.

In 1901, the Roseville Pottery purchased the formally owned Mosaic Tile Company plant as an auxiliary. This plant manufactured a line of German cooking ware and other similar ware. The plant employed about 50 people and had four kilns with an annual output valued at $50,000.00.

Young was appointed General Manager of the Linden Avenue plant. In 1902, another former competitor, Peters and Reed, sold the former Muskingum Stoneware plant in Zanesville to the Roseville Pottery Company. This plant was purchased to help with production of their German stone cooking ware.

George Young obtained only the best talent in hopes of becoming first in the Art Pottery business. Large numbers of his employees became famous in the pottery field. At first, the Roseville Pottery Company used only local clay but later added foreign clays to give the required strength and finish.

Most of the smaller shapes of the commercial production were made by the molding process. The larger shapes were produced by the jiggering process as none of these productions were hand turned on the potter's wheel. Each of the artists were allowed to select any available shape pottery they wished to work on. Most of the art potters wanted the public to think their art work was original; however, it is known that all the art studies on still life, animals, and portraits were purchased and then copied on the ceramic media.

In 1900, an artist, Ross C. Purdy, was hired by Young to develop an art line of pottery. This was introduced as **Rozane Royal.** *The name Rozane was formed from its roots in Roseville and their new home in Zanesville. Purdy developed the style of slip painting on the pottery under a high-gloss glaze. Many times, these subjects were as bold as oil painting, and other times, as pale as water colors. Many of these pieces were mainly brown, gray, and green in color with decorations done by hand. A clear bright glaze was then applied. Their favorite subjects were flowers, animals, and portraits. Many of the artists moved from Owens to Weller to Roseville and back again. It is possible to find signed Weller and Roseville pieces by the same artist.*

In early 1900, Young recruited John J. Herold to take over as art director and designer. Herold had worked successfully for both Owens and Weller before accepting this post. Young's foresight in hiring Herold paid off at the St. Louis Exposition in 1904, when Roseville won first prize for their Rozane Mongol style. This was a lost Chinese style of blood red coloring with a high glaze finish. It was very difficult to produce this dark red crystalline glaze, also, a long time exposure to the fumes could affect the potters lungs. On occasion, silver overlay was applied to the finished product.

Frederick Hurten Rhead was named Art Director in 1904 and held the position until 1908. Rhead was a guiding force for Roseville over these years. He over saw the production of "Mara", "Egypto", "Mongol" and "Woodland", which were introduced before his arrival in Roseville. He introduced such lines as Fudgi, Crystalis, Della Robbia, Aztec, and Olympic. Each time Weller introduced a new line, Rhead would respond with a new compatible line. He was responsible for updating the "Rozane Royal" line. He replaced the dark backgrounds of the line with a light color.

One of the earliest lines introduced by Rhead was the "Olympic". The patterns use a brick red body with a design of white or black figures. The technique of transferring printing was borrowed from early England. The design wanted is printed in clay colors on paper and then transferred to the vessel.

In 1904, Rhead began his lifelong fascination with the "Crystalline" glaze. An example of Crystalis is a web of one color against a fluid two tone dark background.

The introduction of the "Della Robbia" line in 1906, helped to establish Rhead as a major figure in American Art Pottery and helped to move Roseville ahead. The forms of "Della Robbia" were simple, with labor intense designs. Harry W. Rhead succeeded his brother Frederick as art director in 1908.

By 1914, the era of hand decorated art pottery had ended and with it the demand for Rozane ware. A new prestige line was introduced, called "Pauleo". The name was devised from a combination of Pauline, the daughter-in-law of George Young, and Rhead's daughter, Leota. The line was produced on large shapes, with no hand decoration.

Harry Rhead was instrumental in designing several less expensive and more popular lines. His most successful was "Donatello". This line was an instant success with the public and in high demand for many years. Prior to the introduction of the Donatello line, Roseville had not shown a profit for a number of years. The large success brought the company to mass production and thus reflected a profit for the Roseville Company. Over 100 shapes sold for over ten years and won national prominence for the Roseville firm.

By 1910, Young had closed both plants in Roseville, Ohio but retained the two in Zanesville. However, in 1917, the Muskingum Plant burned down and the total operation was shifted to the Linden Avenue plant.

In 1916, the production of the first Dogwood pattern started with over 75 different pieces in production and continued until 1919. The Dogwood pattern paved the way for the more than 50 floral patterns.

George Young passed down the leadership of the Roseville Company to his competent son, Russell T. Young in 1919. Russell Young continued in that position until 1932, when his mother Anna Young took charge as president of the company and incorporated the company, thus the start of Roseville Pottery, Inc.

In 1919, Frank Ferrel succeeded Harry Rhead as art director and designer. Ferrel and the technical supervisor, George Krause, teamed up to produce many a new line and glaze. A few examples of these lines are: Volpato, Dahlrose, Florentine, Tuscany, Rosecraft, Ferrella, Sunflower, Blackberry, Cherry Blossom, and Wisteria, just to name a few.

After World War I, a high-production continuous tunnel kiln was installed, however, the war had taken its toll on the pottery field. Decreasing sales and raising costs led to little or no profits for many pottery companies. Roseville was competing with Weller and was pulling out all stops to influence the pottery buyers and salesmen.

Robert P. Windisch

During Anna Young's leadership, she built a combined pottery showroom and tea room in West Zanesville to compete with the Weller retail store east of Zanesville.

By far, the most successful line created by the team of Ferrel and Krause was the Pinecone, which was designed in 1935. It proved to be the highest volume pattern created, boasting over 75 shapes in brown, blue, green, and the rarest pink. The Pinecone was later revived about 1953 in a high gloss glaze, but had no success.

When Anna Young died in 1938, the leadership was passed on to her son-in-law, F.S. Clements, who stayed with the company until 1945. He was followed by his son-in-law, Robert Windisch, who stayed with the company until the end in 1954.

During World War II, pottery reached its peak in demand, but labor and materials were limited. After the war, the competition of foreign imports and new American companies turned out cheap wares that hurt the older art potteries.

In a final attempt to increase sales, profit, and save the company, Ben Seibel was hired to produce an Oven to Table ware. New machinery was installed and the workers were trained to operate this machinery. In January, 1952, at a "Pittsburgh" pottery show, the line of Raymor was introduced and put on sale at once. This line was a gourmet dinnerware with plates, cups, saucers, coffee pot, teapot, and assorted serving pieces. Unfortunately, the mechanical equipment and employee did not adapt to this line. The public did not accept Raymor and plans were made to close the operation.

On January 2, 1954, it was announced that the Young family had sold their controlling interest in the Roseville Pottery Company to Mrs. Leota Clements. On November 15, 1954, Mrs. Clements sold the Linden Avenue plant and stock to the Mosaic Tile Company which in turn sold all dies, stock and Roseville trademark to the New England Ceramics of Connecticut.

Thus the end of a giant in the pottery field.

Pictured here is the original founder John Fredric Weaver and crew of the Roseville Plant in Roseville, Ohio.

Photo courtesy of the Weaver Collection.

Roseville Plant, Zanesville, Ohio - Photo courtesy of George Krause

Pictured here is George H. Krause (left) and Robert P. Windisch (right) with the 1950 Lotus line.

Photo courtesy of the Robert Windisch collection.

Potters using two different techniques of applying glazes at the Roseville Plant.

Photo courtesy of the George Krause Collection.

Inside photos from the Roseville Pottery Company Plant in Zanesville, Ohio.

Photo courtesy of George Krause

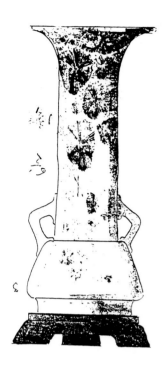

¼" Scale

just Papus & Cupid
and feather hate
instead of large heads
and I think that
it will be a big thing
and call it
MoCo-LINE
Look at this twice

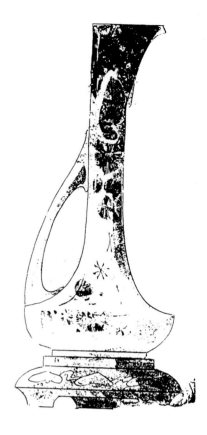

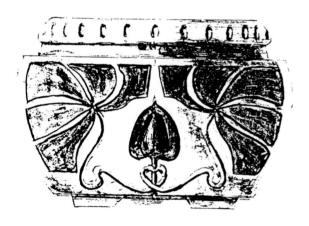

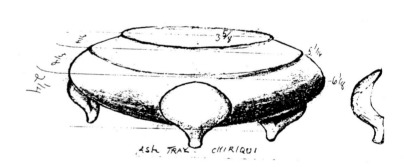

ASH TRAY CHIRIQUI

Thin-Twice Just The Same as a Liner
For a Fer and Better
Than nickle Frame

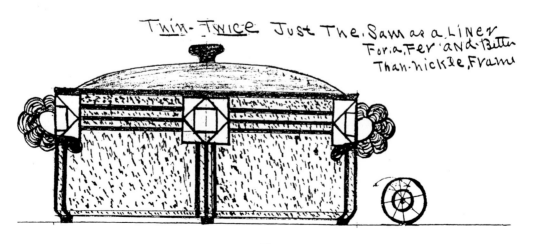

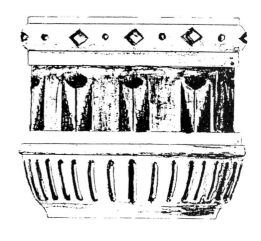

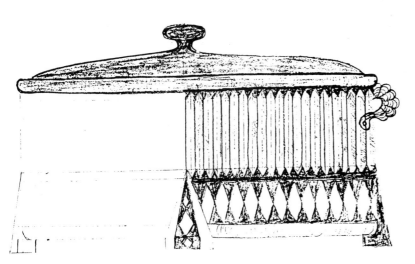

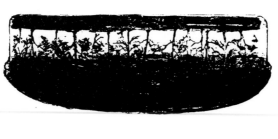

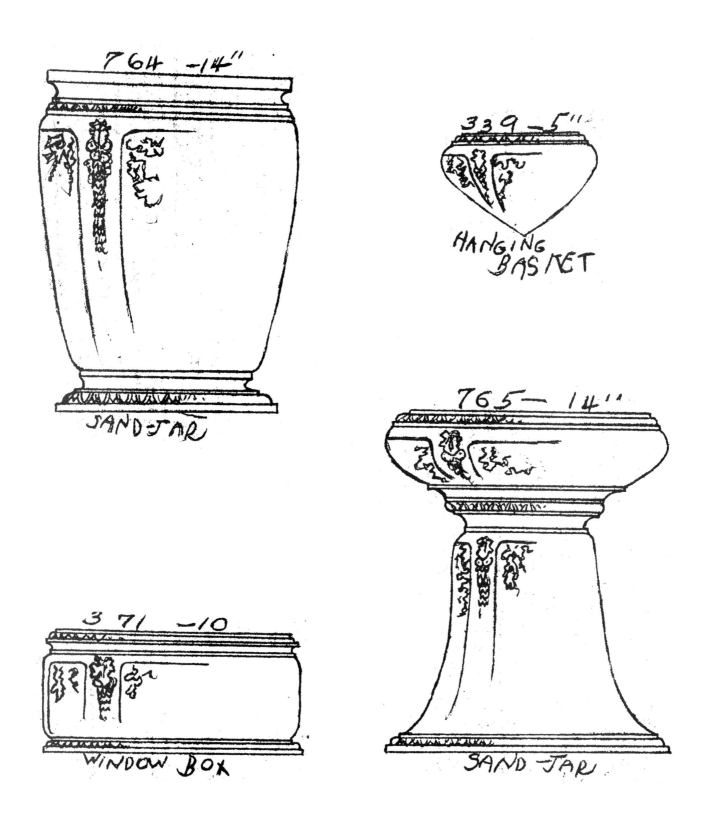

764 -14"

SAND-JAR

339 -5"

HANGING BASKET

765 - 14"

SAND JAR

371 -10

WINDOW BOX

Original art design for the Florentine Line.

ROSEVILLE POTTERY INC.   *Zanesville, Ohio*

BLEEDING HEART
Blue — Green — Red

JARDINIERES

651— 3"	$ 3.00	Doz.
4"	6.00	Doz.
5"	7.50	Doz.
6"	9.00	Doz.
7"	12.00	Doz.
8"	15.00	Doz.
10"	24.00	Doz.

JARDINIERES and PEDESTALS

651— 8"	$ 2.50	Each
10"	5.00	Each

CORNUCOPIA

141—6"	$ 6.00	Doz.
142—8"	12.00	Doz.

BASKETS

359— 8" (Oval)	$12.00	Doz.
360—10" (Oval)	15.00	Doz.
361—12" (Oval with insert)	18.00	Doz.

WALL POCKETS

1287—8"	$ 7.50	Doz.

POT and SAUCER

652—5"	$ 6.00	Doz.

GATE

140—4½"	$ 6.00	Doz.

PITCHER

1323 (Oval)	$12.00	Doz.

BOOK ENDS

6	$ 7.50	Doz.

HANGING BASKET

362—5"	$ 9.00	Doz.

ROSE BOWLS

377—4"	$ 6.00	Doz.
378—6"	12.00	Doz.

BOWLS

379— 6" (Round)	$ 6.00	Doz.
380— 8" (Round)	9.00	Doz.
381—10" (Round)	12.00	Doz.
382—10" (Oval)	12.00	Doz.
383—12" (Oblong)	15.00	Doz.
384—14" (Oval)	18.00	Doz.

INSERTS

40	$ 3.00	Doz.

CANDLE STICKS

1140 (Squat)	$ 3.00	Doz.
1139—4½"	4.50	Doz.

URNS

138—4" (Vase shape)	$ 3.00	Doz.
139—8"	12.00	Doz.

VASES

961— 4"	$ 4.50	Doz.
962— 5"	6.00	Doz.
963— 6" (Tankard)	9.00	Doz.
964— 6"	6.00	Doz.
965— 7"	9.00	Doz.
966— 7"	9.00	Doz.
968— 8" (Pocket)	9.00	Doz.
969— 8"	12.00	Doz.
970— 9" (Fan)	12.00	Doz.
971— 9"	15.00	Doz.
972—10" (Tankard)	15.00	Doz.
973—10"	18.00	Doz.
974—12"	21.00	Doz.
975—15" (Tankard)	30.00	Doz.
976—15"	24.00	Doz.
977—18"	30.00	Doz.

FLOWER HOLDER

967—7" (Bud)	$ 6.00	Doz.

No Package Charge on Orders Over $25.00

ROSEVILLE POTTERY INC.   *Zanesville, Ohio*

COSMOS
Blue — Brown — Green

JARDINIERES

649— 3"	$ 3.00	Doz.
4"	6.00	Doz.
5"	7.50	Doz.
6"	9.00	Doz.
7"	12.00	Doz.
8"	18.00	Doz.
10"	30.00	Doz.

JARDINIERE and PEDESTAL

649— 8"	250 $ 3.00	Each
10"	5.00	Each

CORNUCOPIA

136— 6"	$ 6.00	Doz.
137— 8"	9.00	Doz.

URN

134— 4"	$ 4.50	Doz.
135— 8"	12.00	Doz.

WALL POCKET

1285— 6"	$ 6.00	Doz.
1286— 8"	9.00	Doz.

HANGING BASKET

361— 5"	$ 9.00	Doz.

POT and SAUCER

650— 5"	$ 6.00	Doz.

ROSE BOWLS

375— 4"	$ 6.00	Doz.
376— 6"	12.00	Doz.

BOWLS

369— 6" (Round)	$ 6.00	Doz.
370— 8" (Round)	9.00	Doz.
371—10" (Round)	15.00	Doz.
372—10" (Oval)	12.00	Doz.
373—12" (Oval)	15.00	Doz.
374—14" (Oval)	18.00	Doz.

INSERT

39	300 $ 4.50	Doz.

GATE

133	$ 6.00	Doz.

CANDLE STICKS

1136— (Squat)	300 $ 4.50	Doz.
1137—4½" (Single)	450 6.00	Doz.

BASKETS

357—10"	$15.00	Doz.
358—12"	24.00	Doz.

FLOWER HOLDERS

959— 7"	$ 6.00	Doz.

WINDOW BOX

381—9"x3"x3½", no liner, $9.00 Doz.

VASES

944— 4"	$ 3.00	Doz.
945— 5"	4.50	Doz.
946— 6"	6.00	Doz.
947— 6"	6.00	Doz.
948— 7"	9.00	Doz.
949— 7"	9.00	Doz.
950— 8" (Pocket)	12.00	Doz.
951— 8"	12.00	Doz.
952— 9"	15.00	Doz.
953— 9"	15.00	Doz.
954—10"	18.00	Doz.
955—10" (Tankard)	15.00	Doz.
956—12"	21.00	Doz.
957—15" (Tankard)	30.00	Doz.
958—18"	30.00	Doz.

No Package Charge on Orders Over $25.00

ROSEVILLE POTTERY INC.   *Zanesville, Ohio*

FUCHSIA
Blue — Brown — Green

JARDINIERES

645—3"	$3.00	Doz.
4"	6.00	Doz.
5"	7.50	Doz.
6"	9.00	Doz.
8"	18.00	Doz.
10"	30.00	Doz.

JARDINIERES and PEDESTALS

645— 8"	250 $3.00	Each
10"	5.00	Each

WALL POCKETS

1282—8"	$7.50	Doz.

HANGING BASKETS

359—5"	$9.00	Doz.

POTS and SAUCERS

646—5"	$6.00	Doz.

BASKETS

350— 6" (with insert)	$12.00	Doz.
351—10"	15.00	Doz.

CORNUCOPIA

129—6"	$6.00	Doz.

ROSE BOWLS

346—4"	$ 6.00	Doz.
347—6"	12.00	Doz.

PITCHER

1322—6 Pint	$12.00	Doz.

BOWLS

348— 5" (Round)	$ 6.00	Doz.
349— 8" (Round)	9.00	Doz.
350— 8" (Round)	12.00	Doz.
351—10" (Oval)	12.00	Doz.
352—12" (Oval)	15.00	Doz.
353—14" (Oval)	18.00	Doz.

INSERTS

37	300 $4.50	Doz.

CANDLE STICKS

1132— (Squat)	300 $4.50	Doz.
1133—5" (Single)	450 6.00	Doz.

VASES

891— 6"	$ 6.00	Doz.
892— 6"	6.00	Doz.
893— 6"	6.00	Doz.
894— 7"	7.50	Doz.
895— 7"	7.50	Doz.
896— 8" (Pocket)	12.00	Doz.
897— 8"	9.00	Doz.
898— 8"	9.00	Doz.
899— 9"	12.00	Doz.
900— 9"	12.00	Doz.
901—10"	15.00	Doz.
902—10" (Tankard)	15.00	Doz.
903—12"	18.00	Doz.
904—15"	24.00	Doz.
905—18"	30.00	Doz.

No Package Charge on Orders Over $25.00

ROSEVILLE POTTERY INC. · · · · *Zanesville, Ohio*

IRIS
Coral — Brown — Blue

JARDINIERES

647— 3"	$ 3.00	Doz.
4"	6.00	Doz.
5"	7.50	Doz.
6"	9.00	Doz.
8"	18.00	Doz.
10"	30.00	Doz.

JARDINIERES and PEDESTALS

647— 8"	250 $ 3.00	Each
10"	5.00	Each

FLOWER HOLDER

918—7"	$ 6.00	Doz.

CORNUCOPIA

131—6"	$ 6.00	Doz.
132—8"	7.50	Doz.

BOOK ENDS

5	$ 7.50	Doz.

URNS

130—4"	$ 4.50	Doz.
923—8"	12.00	Doz.

WALL BRACKET

2	$ 9.00	Doz.

WALL POCKET

1284—8"	$ 7.50	Doz.

HANGING BASKET

360—5"	$ 9.00	Doz.

POT and SAUCER

648—5"	$ 6.00	Doz.

VASES

914— 4"	$ 3.00	Doz.
915— 5"	4.50	Doz.
916— 6"	6.00	Doz.
917— 6"	6.00	Doz.
919— 7"	7.50	Doz.
920— 7"	9.00	Doz.
921— 8"	12.00	Doz.
922— 8" Pocket	12.00	Doz.
924— 9"	15.00	Doz.
925— 9"	15.00	Doz.
926—10" Tankard	15.00	Doz.
927—10"	18.00	Doz.
928—12"	21.00	Doz.
929—15"	30.00	Doz.

ROSE BOWLS

357—4"	$ 6.00	Doz.
358—6"	12.00	Doz.

BOWLS

359— 5" (Round)	$ 4.50	Doz.
360— 6" (Round)	6.00	Doz.
361— 8" (Round)	9.00	Doz.
362—10" (Oval)	12.00	Doz.
363—12" (Oval)	15.00	Doz.
364—14" (Oval)	18.00	Doz.

INSERT

38	300 $ 4.50	Doz.

CANDLE STICKS

1134—(Squat)	300 $ 4.50	Doz.
1135—4½"	450 6.00	Doz.

BASKETS

354— 8"	$12.00	Doz.
355—10"	18.00	Doz.

No Package Charge on Orders Over $25.00

PINECONE

Green — Blue — Brown

JARDINIERES

632— 3"	$ 3.00	Doz.
4"	6.00	Doz.
5"	7.50	Doz.
6"	9.00	Doz.
7"	12.00	Doz.
8"	18.00	Doz.
10"	30.00	Doz.

JARDINIERES and PEDESTALS

632— 8"x16"	2.50 3.00	Each
10"x18"	5.00	Each

FLOWER HOLDERS

112—7" Novelty	$ 7.50	Doz.
121—7" Pocket	7.50	Doz.
124—5"	6.00	Doz.

ROSE BOWLS

261—6"	$12.00	Doz.
278—4"	6.00	Doz.

BOWLS

279—9"x6" Oval	$12.00	Doz.
321—9" Round	12.00	Doz.
322—12" Oval	15.00	Doz.
323—15" Oval	18.00	Doz.
354—6" Round	6.00	Doz.
355—8" Round	9.00	Doz.

HANGING BASKETS

352—5"	$9.00	Doz.

ASH TRAY

25—	$3.00	Doz.

SAND JAR

776—10"x14"	$2.50	Each

UMBRELLA STAND

777—8½"x20"	$3.00	Each

CANDLE STICKS

1099—4½" Single	4.50 6.00	Doz.
1106—5½" Triple	12.00	Doz.
1123— Squat	3.00 4.50	Doz.

NOVELTY WINDOW BOXES

379—9"x3"x3½" (No liner)	$ 9.00	Doz.

BASKETS

338—10"	$15.00	Doz.
352— 8" (With Insert)	15.00	Doz.
353—12"	15.00	Doz.

PITCHER

1321—6 Pint	$12.00	Doz.

CORNUCOPIA

126—6"	$ 6.00	Doz.
128—8"	12.00	Doz.

POTS and SAUCERS

633—5"	$6.00	Doz.

BOOK ENDS

1—4¾"	$7.50	Doz.

INSERTS

32—Round	3.00 4.50	Doz.
33—Oval	3.00 4.50	Doz.

VASES

712—12"	$21.00	Doz.
747—10"	15.00	Doz.
838— 6"	6.00	Doz.
839— 6"	6.00	Doz.
841— 7"	7.50	Doz.
842— 8"	9.00	Doz.
843— 8"	12.00	Doz.
844— 8"	12.00	Doz.
845— 8" Pocket	15.00	Doz.
848—10"	18.00	Doz.
850—14"	30.00	Doz.
906— 6"	6.00	Doz.
907— 7"	7.50	Doz.
909—10" (Tankard)	15.00	Doz.
910—10"	18.00	Doz.
913—18"	42.00	Doz.
960— 4" (To match pitcher)	3.00	Doz.

URNS

908— 8"	$12.00	Doz.
912—15"	30.00	Doz.

WALL BRACKETS

1—5"x8"	$9.00	Doz.

WALL POCKETS

1273—8"	$7.50	Doz.

No Package Charge on Orders Over $25.00

POPPY

Gray — Green — Coral

JARDINIERES

642— 4"	$ 6.60	Doz.
5"	9.00	Doz.
6"	12.00	Doz.
7"	15.00	Doz.
8"	21.00	Doz.
9"	30.00	Doz.
10"	36.00	Doz.

JARDINIERES and PEDESTALS

642— 8"	$3.00	Each
10"	6.00	Each

VASES

866— 6"	$ 7.50	Doz.
867— 6"	7.50	Doz.
868— 7"	9.00	Doz.
869— 7"	9.00	Doz.
870— 8" (Pocket)	12.00	Doz.
871— 8"	12.00	Doz.
872— 9"	15.00	Doz.
873— 9"	15.00	Doz.
874—10"	18.00	Doz.
875—10"	18.00	Doz.
876—10" (Tankard)	15.00	Doz.
877—12"	21.00	Doz.
878—15"	30.00	Doz.
879—18"	45.00	Doz.
880—18" (Tankard)	45.00	Doz.

WALL POCKETS

1281—8" (Combination Candle Stix)	$12.00	Doz.

HANGING BASKETS

358— 5"	$ 9.00	Doz.

POTS and SAUCERS

643— 5"	$ 9.00	Doz.

BOWLS

336— 5" (Round)	$ 6.60	Doz.
337— 8" (Round)	12.00	Doz.
338— 8" (Oval)	12.00	Doz.
339—12" (Oval)	18.00	Doz.
340—14" (Oval)	21.00	Doz.
341— 7" (Combination Candle Stix)	18.00	Doz.

INSERTS

35 (Round)	$ 4.50	Doz.

CANDLE STICKS

1129— (Squat)	$ 4.50	Doz.
1130—4½" (Single)	6.00	Doz.

ROSE BOWLS

334— 4"	$ 6.60	Doz.
335— 6"	12.00	Doz.

BASKETS

347—10"	$15.00	Doz.
348—12"	15.00	Doz.

No Package Charge on Orders Over $25.00

WHITE ROSE

Brown — Coral — Blue

JARDINIERES

653— 3"	$ 3.00	Doz.
4"	6.00	Doz.
5"	7.50	Doz.
6"	9.00	Doz.
7"	12.00	Doz.
8"	15.00	Doz.
10"	24.00	Doz.

JARDINIERES and PEDESTALS

653— 8"	$ 2.50	Each
10"	5.00	Each

BASKETS

362— 8"	$12.00	Doz.
363—10"	15.00	Doz.
364—12"	18.00	Doz.

GATE

148	$ 6.00	Doz.

CORNUCOPIA

143— 6"	$ 6.00	Doz.
144— 8"	9.00	Doz.
145— 8" (Double)	12.00	Doz.

TEA SET

No. 1 Tea Pot (with lid)	$12.00	Doz.
No. 1 Creamer	4.50	Doz.
No. 1 Sugar	4.50	Doz.

PITCHER

1324	$ 9.00	Doz.

INSERT

41	$ 3.00	Doz.

CANDLE STICKS

1141—Squat	$ 3.00	Doz.
1142—4½" Single	4.50	Doz.
1143—Double	9.00	Doz.

ROSE BOWLS

387— 4"	$ 6.00	Doz.
388— 7"	12.00	Doz.

VASES

978— 4"	$ 3.00	Doz.
979— 6"	6.00	Doz.
980— 6"	6.00	Doz.
981— 6" (Tankard)	7.50	Doz.
982— 7"	9.00	Doz.
983— 7"	9.00	Doz.
984— 8" (Pocket)	12.00	Doz.
985— 8"	12.00	Doz.
986— 9"	15.00	Doz.
987— 9" (Fan)	15.00	Doz.
988—10"	18.00	Doz.
990—10" (Tankard)	18.00	Doz.
991—12"	21.00	Doz.
992—15"	24.00	Doz.
993—15" (Tankard)	30.00	Doz.
994—18"	30.00	Doz.

FLOWER HOLDER

995— 7" (Bud)	$ 6.00	Doz.

BOWLS

389— 6" (Round)	$ 6.00	Doz.
390— 8" (Round)	9.00	Doz.
391—10" (Oval)	12.00	Doz.
392—10" (Round)	12.00	Doz.
393—12" (Oblong)	15.00	Doz.
394—14" (Oblong)	18.00	Doz.

BOOK END

7	$ 7.50	Doz.

HORN OF PLENTY

1 (with insert)	$15.00	Doz.

URNS

146— 6"	$ 6.00	Doz.
147— 8"	12.00	Doz.

WINDOW BOX

382— 9"	$ 9.00	Doz.

WALL POCKET

1288— 6"	$ 6.00	Doz.
1289— 8"	9.00	Doz.

POT and SAUCER

654— 5"	$ 6.00	Doz.

HANGING BASKET

463— 5"	$ 9.00	Doz.

No Package Charge on Orders Over $25.00

ROZANE

Brown — Green — Blue — Ivory

VASES

1— 6"	$ 6.00	Doz.
2— 6"	6.00	Doz.
3— 8"	12.00	Doz.
4— 8"	12.00	Doz.
6— 9" (Oval)	15.00	Doz.
7— 9"	15.00	Doz.
8—10"	18.00	Doz.
9—10"	18.00	Doz.
10—12"	21.00	Doz.
11—15"	30.00	Doz.

ROSE BOWLS

398—4"	$ 6.00	Doz.
6"	9.00	Doz.
8"	18.00	Doz.

BOWLS

395— 9" (Round)	$15.00	Doz.
396—10" (Round)	15.00	Doz.
397—14" (Oblong)	18.00	Doz.
407— 6" (Scalloped) (Oblong)	6.00	Doz.
408— 8" (Odd) (1¼" deep)	9.00	Doz.
409—12" (Odd) (Oblong decoration inside)	12.00	Doz.

HORN OF PLENTY

2 (No insert)	$18.00	Doz.

INSERT

44—6"	$ 4.50	Doz.

FIGURINES

1—5" (Fish)	$ 4.50	Doz.
2—5½" (Flame)	4.50	Doz.

CANDLE STICKS

1144—3"	$ 4.50	Doz.

COCKLE SHELL

410	$12.00	Doz.

URN

5—8"	$ 9.00	Doz.

CORNUCOPIA

159—6"	$ 6.00	Doz.

No Package Charge on Orders Over $25.00.   Terms: 2% 15 Days, Net 60

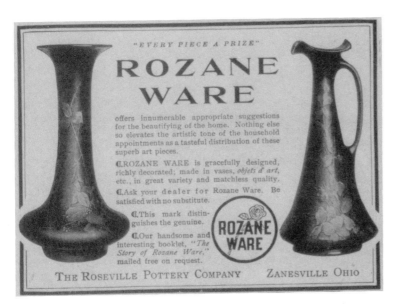

1904 Harper's Bazar Magazine Ad for the Rozane Ware Line

*1904 Harper's Bazar
Magazine Ad for
Rozane Ware Line*

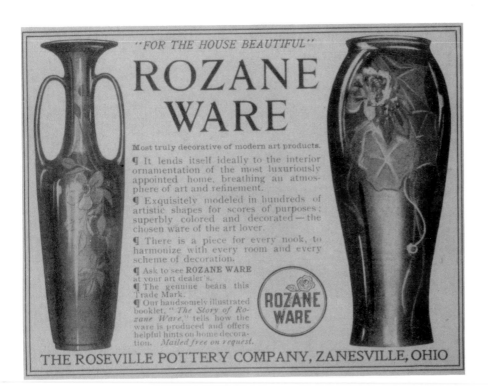

*April 1904 Ad for the Rozane Ware Line from
The Ladies Home Journal Magazine*

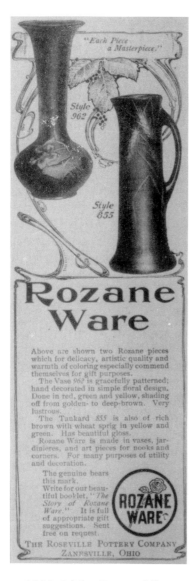

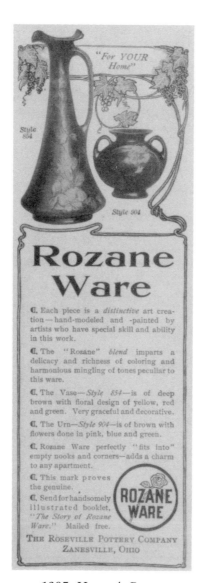

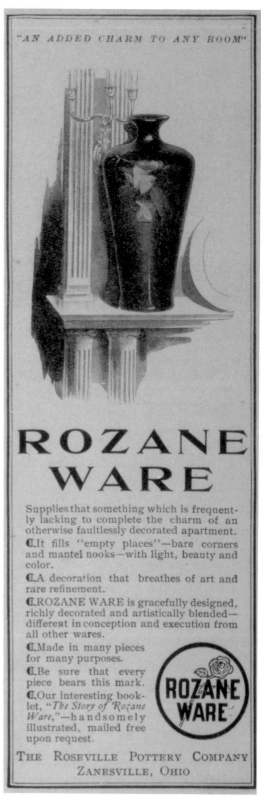

*1904 Ad for Rozane Ware
from Harper's Bazar
Magazine*

*1905 Harper's Bazar
Magazine Ad for
Rozane Ware*

*June 1904 Ad for the Rozane Ware Line
from Harper's Bazar Magazine*

1906 Ad for Rozane Ware Line from Harper's Bazar Magazine

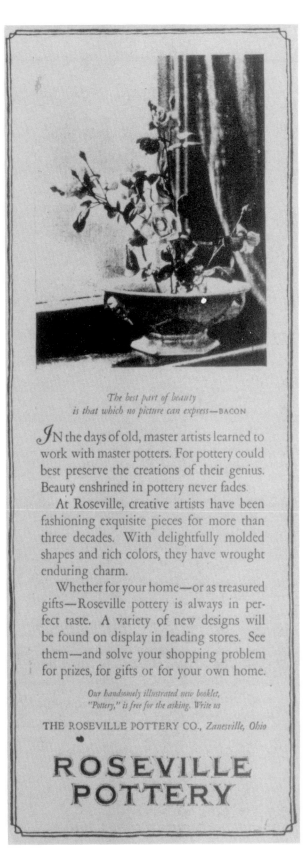

September 1927 Ad for the Tuscany Line from The House Beautiful Magazine

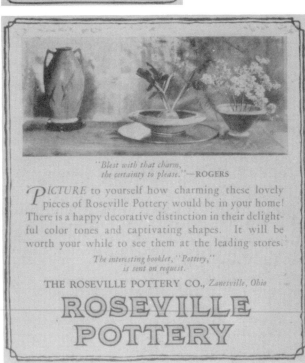

May 1928 Ad for the Cremona Line from Good Housekeeping Magazine

A FEW art objects, discreetly placed, add so much to a home! Not the hit-and-miss massing of Victorian days, but the tasteful arrangement of 1928.

And just here it is that Roseville serves so incomparably! Charming Roseville Pottery, created with that touch of genius by men and women who love their craft.

Beauty that grows as you live with it, such is the essence of Roseville Pottery. For instance, the jar and vases pictured here. Adorable they are, in delicate tints, daintily decorated with arrowheads.

These pieces and a diversity of other designs... bowls, jars, vases, candlesticks in a wide selection of sizes, shapes and colors . . . can be seen at good stores. For the home or as gifts they have a distinction of their own.

You will want a copy of the interesting booklet, "Pottery." Write for it.

THE ROSEVILLE POTTERY CO., *Zanesville, Ohio*

ROSEVILLE POTTERY

*March 1928 Ad for the Cremona Line from
the House Beautiful Magazine*

LET INDIVIDUALITY be your slogan this year when it comes to the giving of gifts. Let your gifts be such as inspire delight at your thoughtfulness—and originality of choice.

An achievement to be striven for! And it is yours to fulfil, simply by a wise selection of the fascinating *Futura* pottery by Roseville.

Yes, this year give Futura. What personality there is in these modernistic shapes! With charming artistry they speak the bold language of today —these dashing vases, flower bowls, candlesticks, wall-pockets, jardinieres and hanging baskets.

The lucky receivers of such gifts will revel in their exquisite, soft tints and their interesting flares and angles. And perhaps you will want a vase or two or a bowl for your own! A selection awaits you at leading stores. Remember, it is Futura pottery by Roseville.

If you want to know the story of pottery, ask us to send you a copy of the free, illustrated booklet, "Pottery".

THE ROSEVILLE POTTERY CO., *Zanesville, Ohio*

ROSEVILLE POTTERY

*December 1928 Ad for the Futura Line from
the House Beautiful Magazine*

*"Ever-varying features of the
enrapturing spirit of beauty."* —ANON

YOU WILL LOVE these new creations of the
Roseville potteries in the delightful *Futura* design.
Done in the modern manner, they exhibit the vogue
of today and breathe the spirit of tomorrow.

In this Futura pottery by Roseville, there is an abun-
dance of sizes and shapes to choose from, scarcely
any two alike. There are vases, bowls, candlesticks,
wall-pockets, jardinieres, hanging baskets—all with
the youthful verve and daring of these our times.

And how exquisitely colored! Blue, gray, tan,
rose, green—harmonies of pleasing, soft tints that
render more fascinating the flares, curves and angles
of Futura.

Picture to yourself the charm of Futura in your
home. Futura pottery brings the tang of the modern,
strikes the key of the recent in decorative schemes.
And nothing could be more original or intriguing
for gifts. Ask to see the displays in leading stores.

*For the interesting story of pottery,
write us to send you a free copy of the
profusely illustrated booklet, "Pottery".*

THE ROSEVILLE POTTERY CO., *Zanesville, Ohio*

ROSEVILLE POTTERY

*"The expression of the beauti-
ful is a chief means in art."* —BECKWITH

BEAUTY imprisoned and preserved in imperishable creations! That is the accomplish-
ment of charming Roseville Pottery.

It is beauty that ever lasts, adorning the
home with subtle distinction. Or as gifts, expressing sentiment and appreciation in a manner always to be treasured.

Lovers of good pottery find delight in such
forms as are pictured here...in the delicate lines
and graceful curves...in the soft, pleasing colors.

These and other pieces in entrancing variety are obtainable at good stores. They are
the fruition of more than three decades of
Roseville master artisans.

*Write for a copy of the illus-
trated booklet, "Pottery."*

THE ROSEVILLE POTTERY CO., *Zanesville, Ohio*

ROSEVILLE POTTERY

*November 1928 Ad for the Futura Line from
the House Beautiful Magazine*

*April 1928 Ad for the Tuscany Line from
the House Beautiful Magazine*

"Beauty is its own excuse" — WHITTIER

*I*N GRACEFUL candlesticks...in vases daintily modelled ... artistic creations of Roseville Pottery express in your home an unerring charm of beauty.

Or perhaps you wish a flower bowl ... a jar ... a wall pocket...a jardiniere. Many indeed are the pieces, shapes and designs in which Roseville Pottery comes...in pleasing, delicate colors...in the modernistic or in the more conservative patterning.

Truly, you will find fascination in the deft artistry of Roseville craftsmen. How effective are these Roseville pieces! How decorative!...They are meant for gay flowers and gleaming candles...They are meant to be possessed and cherished.

For more than a generation Roseville Pottery has served to bring delight to those who purchase for themselves, or as exquisite gifts ... And, so it serves today...Take a few minutes to visit the interesting displays at leading stores...Surely, it will be worth while.

A profusely illustrated booklet, "Pottery" gives the interesting history of pottery. Write for your free copy.

THE ROSEVILLE POTTERY CO., *Zanesville, Ohio*

ROSEVILLE POTTERY

April 1929 Ad for the Savona Line from the American Home Magazine

"Blest with that charm, the certainty to please." — ROGERS

*P*ICTURE to yourself how charming such lovely pottery would be in your home! What an effective setting for flowers and foliage! Perhaps just the thing you need for that odd corner or table.

That is the function of Roseville Pottery — to bring exquisite beauty to the home. And you will adore these new Roseville designs. There is a happy decorative distinction in their delightful color tones and captivating shapes.

They are in soft, fascinating tints, with embossed modernistic floral designs, all gracefully modelled. Here is true artistry — revealing the fine craftsmanship of more than three decades of Roseville potters.

Vases, flower holders, bowls, candlesticks — there is a wide choice for gifts or for yourself. See them at the leading stores.

"Pottery" is the title of a delightfully illustrated twenty-four page booklet which will be sent gladly upon request.

THE ROSEVILLE POTTERY CO., *Zanesville, Ohio*

ROSEVILLE POTTERY

May 1928 Ad for the Cremona Line from the House Beautiful Magazine

Pottery that you will love as the years come and go is so enticingly created by Roseville master craftsmen.

How graceful are the curves, the angles, the proportions and the exquisite modeling! The colors are delightful, too . . . and tastefully rich! You will be glad that you knew about this wonderful pottery.

Fascinating and adorable . . . Roseville Pottery is always new, unusual, distinctive. Into your home these lovely pieces bring a beauty that never ceases to be admired . . . and you will find they are wonderfully appreciated as gifts.

Vases, flower bowls, jars, candlesticks, wallpockets . . . mighty interesting selections await you at leading stores. Ask to see the displays of Roseville Pottery.

A copy of the richly illustrated booklet,
"Pottery," will be mailed you free on
request. Write for your copy.

THE ROSEVILLE POTTERY COMPANY, Zanesville, Ohio

ROSEVILLE POTTERY

If you love good pottery you will find keen moments of joy in these richly delightful, happily distinctive creations of Roseville master craftsmen.

Here are lines and curves and angles that have sprung right out of a many-sided spirit of artistry. Roseville potters live their craft and for more than a generation their handiwork has won the favor of those who appreciate charming things.

And exquisite indeed are the colors of these beautiful pieces. Subtle harmonies of pleasing tints and blending tones. Blue, gray, tan, rose, green . . . soft as the hues of twilight.

In Roseville Pottery there is a wealth of fascinating objects . . . for you to choose for yourself . . . or as a gift to someone near. There are flower bowls, vases, jars, candlesticks, wall pockets, jardinieres . . . in many sizes and shapes. You will enjoy seeing them at the leading stores, where they are on display.

The story of pottery is interestingly told
in the booklet, "Pottery". . . A free
copy is awaiting you . . . Write for it

THE ROSEVILLE POTTERY COMPANY, Zanesville, Ohio

ROSEVILLE POTTERY

October 1929 Ad for the Imperial II Line from
the House Beautiful Magazine

November 1929 Ad for the Futura Line from
the House Beautiful Magazine

GIFTS with a rich personality! Gifts that are so distinctive, so much in good taste . . . that charmingly express your sentiment, in a manner always to be treasured!

If you wish to achieve the unusual in gift-giving, then choose remembrances of Roseville Pottery . . . beautiful tokens like the delightful new Roseville creations pictured here.

Here are pieces in the spirit of today's fine artistry . . . exquisite vases, ever lovely. How enchanting! Curves and flares . . . interesting, intriguing contours. Adorably shaped, daintily decorated . . . in soft, pleasing color tones. And there are many other captivating items . . . candlesticks, wall pockets, jars and flower bowls.

Roseville Pottery is to be seen at leading stores. You will enjoy making your selection now, for fine original gifts superbly in vogue.

There are many gift suggestions in
the attractive little booklet, "Pottery."
Write for your free copy.

THE ROSEVILLE POTTERY CO., Zanesville, Ohio.

"Appeal effectively
to the higher aesthetic tastes"— BECKWITH

A TRULY delightful means of expressing your personality in the home is afforded by such intriguing designs as these in the Futura patterns by Roseville. Bold and dashing in conception, they express the beautiful in modern art. Many different Futura items in several colors await you at leading stores.

The abundantly illustrated booklet,
"Pottery," is sent free on request.

THE ROSEVILLE POTTERY CO., *Zanesville, Ohio*

March 1929 Ad for the Futura Line from
the Good Housekeeping Magazine

"Beauty is its own excuse"—WHITTIER

YOU will find fascination in the charming creations of Roseville Pottery craftsmen. . . . How effective are these pieces! How decorative in the home! . . . They are meant for gay flowers and gleaming candles, meant to be possessed and cherished. . . . There is a delightful variety of designs. Visit the displays at leading stores.

Write for a copy of the illustrated
booklet, "Pottery". It is free on request.

THE ROSEVILLE POTTERY CO., *Zanesville, Ohio*

December 1929 Ad for the Futura Line from
the House Beautiful Magazine

April 1929 Ad for the Savona Line from
the Good Housekeeping Magazine

*"Beauty is created
by the emotion of the artist"*—SCHOEN

INTRIGUING, modern, is this fascinating window box . . . lovingly wrought by Roseville craftsmen. How delightful with gorgeous tulips! There are many other pieces, too—vases, jars, bowls, candlesticks. Exquisitely fashioned, in soft color harmonies, with delicately modeled decorations. See them at leading stores where many selections await you.

Write for a free copy of the beautifully illustrated booklet, "Pottery".

THE ROSEVILLE POTTERY CO., *Zanesville, Ohio*

ROSEVILLE POTTERY

*May 1929 Ad for from the
Good Housekeeping Magazine*

CHARM . . . is in many things . . . gay sunlight on southern seas . . . irresistible strains of a Wagnerian symphony . . . cozy nook by the fireside when the wind is blustering · · · In Roseville Pottery there is a charm that endures . . . permanently wrought by artists who love their craft. Glorious shapes, soft blending of twilight tints, subtle beauty of heirlooms . . . these are the charm of Roseville bowls, jars, vases and candlesticks · · · For the home, for gifts or prizes, see them at leading stores.

*Write for the interesting booklet,
"Pottery." Free on request.*

THE ROSEVILLE POTTERY COMPANY, Zanesville, Ohio.

ROSEVILLE POTTERY

*March 1930 Ad for the Imperial II Line from
the Ladies Home Journal Magazine*

SMART...

We like to possess things that are smart . . . voguish . . . correct . . . beautiful. We like to enjoy them.

The recent Roseville Pottery designs meet these ideals, with classic and Early American distinctiveness. In lovely colors: vases, bowls, jars and candlesticks that are treasured through the years.

And exquisite pieces that are made into lamps, like the one on the right in the picture. It is smart now to have table lamps of pottery . . . See Roseville Pottery displays at the leading stores soon.

*Write for your free copy of the
interesting booklet, "Pottery."*

THE ROSEVILLE POTTERY COMPANY, Zanesville, Ohio.

ROSEVILLE POTTERY

*April 1930 Ad for the Imperial II Line from
the Good Housekeeping Magazine*

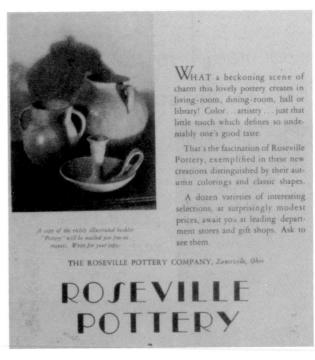

WHAT a beckoning scene of charm this lovely pottery creates in living-room, dining-room, hall or library! Color . . . artistry . . . just that little touch which defines so undeniably one's good taste.

That's the fascination of Roseville Pottery, exemplified in these new creations distinguished by their autumn colorings and classic shapes.

A dozen varieties of interesting selections, at surprisingly modest prices, await you at leading department stores and gift shops. Ask to see them.

*A copy of the richly illustrated booklet
"Pottery" will be mailed you free on
request. Write for your copy.*

THE ROSEVILLE POTTERY COMPANY, Zanesville, Ohio

ROSEVILLE POTTERY

*November 1930 Ad for the Windsor Line from
the Good Housekeeping Magazine*

A free copy of the illustrated booklet, "Pottery", will be gladly sent on request.

Gifts of pottery inspire delight at your thoughtfulness and the good taste of your choice.

Particularly fascinating are the new Roseville creations. Charm of contour and beauty of color impel one to choose these bowls, jars, vases and candlesticks. And the loving craftsmanship with which they are fashioned captures, as surely as the holiday season comes, the heart of the recipient.

There is an entrancing variety of sizes, shapes and designs in Roseville Pottery . . . and the prices are so modest! Ask to see the Roseville displays at leading gift shops and department stores.

THE ROSEVILLE POTTERY COMPANY
ZANESVILLE, OHIO

ROSEVILLE POTTERY

December 1930 Ad for the Ferrella Line from the Good Housekeeping Magazine

Warm colors, exquisite proportions, a touch of unmistakable artistry, in a wide variety of shapes and sizes . . . . at leading dealers everywhere.

ROSEVILLE POTTERY
Zanesville, Ohio

October 1931 Ad for the Windsor Line from the House Beautiful Magazine

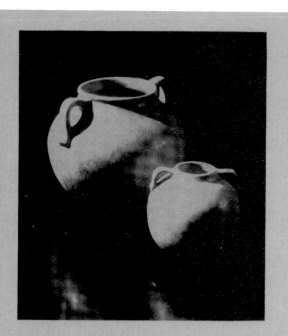

IN the spring of the year we bring the fascination of the out-of-doors into the home. Then we delight in forsythia sprays, pussy willows, and the gay and scented beauty of flowering bulbs.

Roseville Pottery provides the perfect setting for spring flowers. Its lovely texture and exquisite coloring blend with a wide variety of blossoms; and the wealth of designs offered by Roseville makes graceful display possible with all sorts and types of growing things.

Because of its beauty of form, texture and color, Roseville Pottery is appropriate as a permanent part of your decorative scheme. It is "livable" pottery, and has the true distinction of a charming and usable creation.

Bowls, jars, vases and candlesticks of many sizes and shapes are fashioned for you by Roseville craftsmen. You may see them at leading gift shops and department stores. Ask for them by name so you may be sure of genuine Roseville quality.

Write, and a copy of the interesting, illustrated booklet, "Pottery," will be sent you free.

THE ROSEVILLE POTTERY COMPANY, Zanesville, Ohio

ROSEVILLE POTTERY

March 1931 Ad for the Windsor Line from the House Beautiful Magazine

FASCINATING for gifts and bringing warmth of color and beauty of proportion into your home. Delightful variety of shapes and sizes. Write for free booklet, "Pottery."

ROSEVILLE POTTERY
Zanesville, Ohio

December 1931 Ad for the Montacello Line from the House Beautiful Magazine

YOU will revel in the exquisite beauty of Roseville Pottery, the soft texture and lovely coloring.

A profusion of adorable pieces awaits your selection, for your home or as gifts.

Tall vases for majestic blooms, low bowls for pert little flowers, the right jar for the stairway niche, candlesticks to grace the table.

See this delightful pottery at leading stores. Simply fascinating for gifts. Write for free booklet, "Pottery".

THE ROSEVILLE POTTERY CO., ZANESVILLE, OHIO

ROSEVILLE POTTERY

December 1931 Ad for the Montacello Line from the Ladies Home Journal Magazine

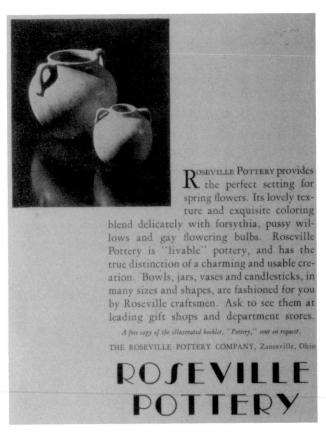

ROSEVILLE POTTERY provides the perfect setting for spring flowers. Its lovely texture and exquisite coloring blend delicately with forsythia, pussy willows and gay flowering bulbs. Roseville Pottery is "livable" pottery, and has the true distinction of a charming and usable creation. Bowls, jars, vases and candlesticks, in many sizes and shapes, are fashioned for you by Roseville craftsmen. Ask to see them at leading gift shops and department stores.

A free copy of the illustrated booklet, "Pottery," sent on request.

THE ROSEVILLE POTTERY COMPANY, Zanesville, Ohio

ROSEVILLE POTTERY

March 1931 Ad for the Earlam Line from the Ladies Home Journal Magazine

July 1940 Ad for a Free Book from Roseville

October 1940 Ad for the
White Rose Line from the
American Home Magazine

December 1940 Ad for the
White Rose Line from the Better
Homes & Garden Magazine

May 1941 Ad for the
Clematis Line from the
American Home Magazine

June 1941 Ad for the Columbine Line
from the American Home Magazine

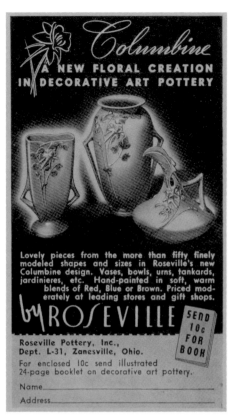

March 1941 Ad for the Columbine Line from the Ladies Home Journal Magazine

September 1941 Ad for the Bushberry Line from the Better Homes & Garden Magazine

November 1941 Ad for the Bushberry Line from the American Home Magazine

A 1941 Ad for the Bushberry Line

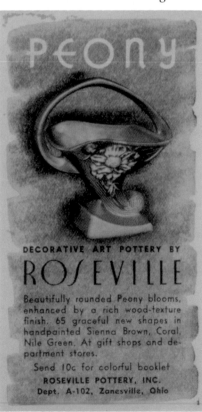

October 1942 Ad for the Peony Line from the Good Housekeeping Magazine

April 1942 Ad for the Foxglove Line from the Better Homes & Gardens Magazine

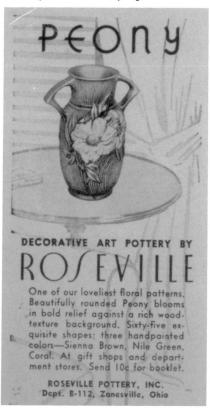

*November 1942 Ad for the
Peony Line from the
Better Homes & Gardens Magazine*

*December 1942 Ad for the
Peony Line from the
Ladies Home Journal Magazine*

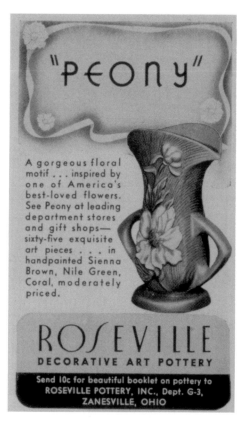

*January 1943 Ad for the
Peony Line from the
Good Housekeeping Magazine*

*March 1943 Ad for the
Water Lily Line from the
American Home Magazine*

*March 1943 Ad for the
Water Lily Line from the American
Home Magazine*

*April 1943 Ad for the
Water Lily Line from the
American Home Magazine*

WATER LILY

Beautiful new decorative art pottery that will distinguish your loveliest setting. Fifty graceful shapes —choice of exquisite, hand-painted colors — Rose, Ciel Blue or Walnut Brown. Modestly priced at department stores and gift shops.

Send 10c for pottery booklet
ROSEVILLE POTTERY, INC.
Dept. B-43, Zanesville, Ohio

ROSEVILLE
DECORATIVE ART POTTERY

*May 1943 Ad for the
Water Lily Line from the
American Home Magazine*

BEAUTY TO ENTHRALL YOU
MAGNOLIA

A charming floral pattern sculptured on fascinating new art shapes. 65 pieces — hand-painted Tan, Blue or Green. At dep't stores, gift shops.

Send For Free Magnolia Folder
ROSEVILLE POTTERY, INC.
Dept. A-73, Zanesville, Ohio

ROSEVILLE
DECORATIVE ART POTTERY

*July 1943 Ad for the
Magnolia Line from the
American Home Magazine*

MAGNOLIA

A charming floral pattern sculptured on fascinating new art shapes. 65 pieces—hand-painted Tan, Blue, Green finishes. At dep't stores, gift shops everywhere.

Send For Free Magnolia Folder
ROSEVILLE POTTERY, INC.
Dept. B-93, Zanesville, Ohio

ROSEVILLE
DECORATIVE ART POTTERY

*July 1943 Ad for the Magnolia
Line from the Better Homes
& Garden Magazine*

Give
ROSEVILLE
DECORATIVE ART POTTERY

"Magnolia"

So graceful in contour, so lovely in color, exquisite Roseville pottery inspires lasting joy and appreciation. Select now from a variety of charming shapes and sizes — at department stores and gift shops.

Send for free Magnolia folder
ROSEVILLE POTTERY, INC.
Dept. HG-123, Zanesville, Ohio

*December 1943 Ad for the
Magnolia Line from the Better
Homes & Garden Magazine*

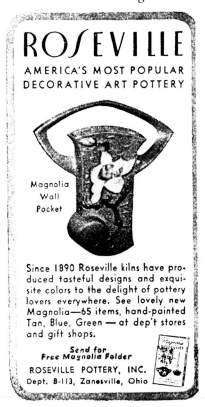

ROSEVILLE
AMERICA'S MOST POPULAR DECORATIVE ART POTTERY

Magnolia
Wall
Pocket

Since 1890 Roseville kilns have produced tasteful designs and exquisite colors to the delight of pottery lovers everywhere. See lovely new Magnolia—65 items, hand-painted Tan, Blue, Green — at dep't stores and gift shops.

*Send for
Free Magnolia Folder*
ROSEVILLE POTTERY, INC.
Dept. B-113, Zanesville, Ohio

*December 1943 Ad for the
Magnolia Line from the
House Beautiful Magazine*

ROSEVILLE
DECORATIVE ART POTTERY

"Magnolia"

Beautiful new art forms combined with exquisite raised floral design and rich color tones distinguish this charming new "Magnolia" pattern by Roseville. 65 items—hand-painted Tan, Blue, Green. At department stores and gift shops everywhere.

Send for free Magnolia folder
ROSEVILLE POTTERY, INC.
Dept. A-24, Zanesville, Ohio

*February 1944 Ad for the
Magnolia Line from the Better
Homes & Garden Magazine*

*May 1945 Ad for the
Clematis Line from the Better
Homes & Garden Magazine*

*July 1945 Ad for the
Freesia Line from the Better
Homes & Garden Magazine*

*October 1945 Ad for the
Freesia Line from the Better
Homes & Garden Magazine*

*March 1946 Ad for the
Freesia Line from the
American Home Magazine*

*May 1946 Ad for the
Freesia Line from the Better
Homes & Garden Magazine*

*October 1946 Ad for the Zephyr
Lily Line from the Better
Homes & Garden Magazine*

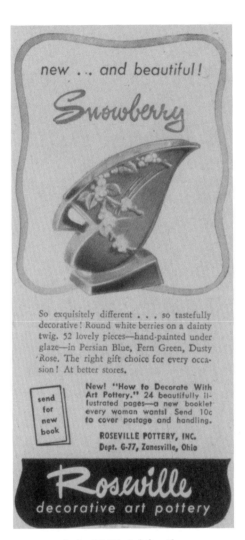

new . . and beautiful!

Snowberry

So exquisitely different . . . so tastefully decorative! Round white berries on a dainty twig. 52 lovely pieces—hand-painted under glaze—in Persian Blue, Fern Green, Dusty Rose. The right gift choice for every occasion! At better stores.

New! "How to Decorate With Art Pottery." 24 beautifully illustrated pages—a new booklet every woman wants! Send 10c to cover postage and handling.

send for new book

ROSEVILLE POTTERY, INC.
Dept. G-77, Zanesville, Ohio

Roseville
decorative art pottery

*July 1947 Ad for the
Snowberry Line from the
Good Housekeeping Magazine*

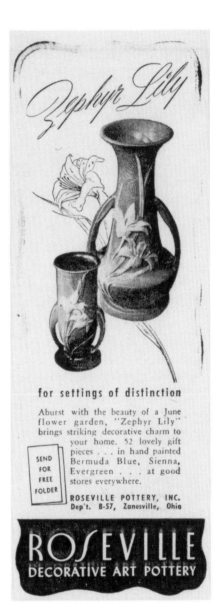

Zephyr Lily

for settings of distinction

A burst with the beauty of a June flower garden, "Zephyr Lily" brings striking decorative charm to your home. 52 lovely gift pieces . . . in hand painted Bermuda Blue, Sienna, Evergreen . . . at good stores everywhere.

 SEND FOR FREE FOLDER

ROSEVILLE POTTERY, INC.
Dep't. B-57, Zanesville, Ohio

ROSEVILLE
DECORATIVE ART POTTERY

*May 1947 Ad for the
Zephyr Lily Line from the Better
Homes & Garden Magazine*

Zephyr Lily

enhances the decorative charm of the home

Enchantingly beautiful with its rich, hand-painted colors and graceful art shapes, "Zephyr Lily" by Roseville provides decorative distinction to the loveliest setting. 52 charming gift-pieces in Bermuda Blue, Sienna, Evergreen . . . at good stores everywhere.

SEND FOR FREE FOLDER

FREE! Send for Zephyr Lily folder showing interesting selection of new items.

ROSEVILLE POTTERY, INC.
Dept. B-27, Zanesville, Ohio

ROSEVILLE
DECORATIVE ART POTTERY

*July 1947 Ad for the
Zephyr Lily Line from the Better
Homes & Garden Magazine*

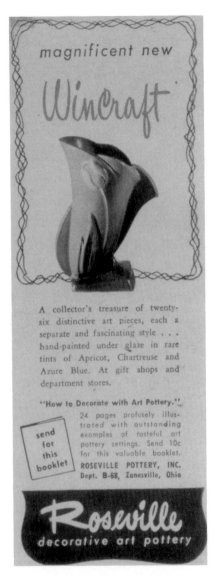

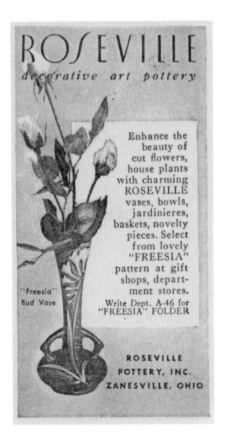

June 1948 Ad for the Wincraft Line from the Better Homes & Garden Magazine

November 1948 Ad for the Freesia Line from the American Home Magazine

November 1948 Ad for the Wincraft Line from the Better Home & Garden Magazine

July 1949 Ad for the
Ming Tree Line from the
Good Housekeeping Magazine

December 1949 Ad for the
Ming Tree Line from
Better Homes & Garden Magazine

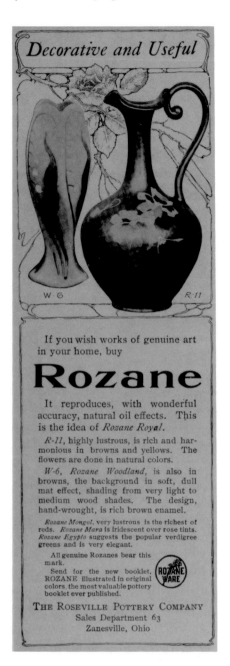

If you wish works of genuine art
in your home, buy

Rozane

It reproduces, with wonderful
accuracy, natural oil effects. This
is the idea of *Rozane Royal*.

R-11, highly lustrous, is rich and harmonious in browns and yellows. The
flowers are done in natural colors.

W-6, Rozane Woodland, is also in
browns, the background in soft, dull
mat effect, shading from very light to
medium wood shades. The design,
hand-wrought, is rich brown enamel.

Rozane Mongol, very lustrous is the richest of
reds. *Rozane Mara* is iridescent over rose tints.
Rozane Egypto suggests the popular verdigree
greens and is very elegant.

All genuine Rozanes bear this
mark.

Send for the new booklet,
ROZANE illustrated in original
colors, the most valuable pottery
booklet ever published.

THE ROSEVILLE POTTERY COMPANY
Sales Department 63
Zanesville, Ohio

*An ad from the 1905
Harper's Bazar Magazine.*

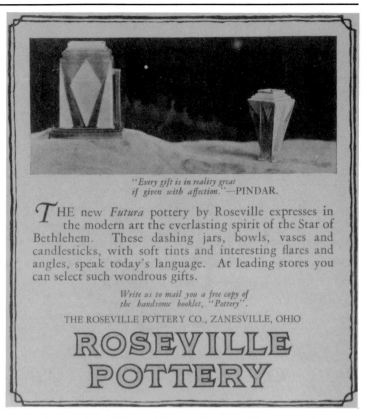

*"Every gift is in reality great
if given with affection."*—PINDAR.

THE new *Futura* pottery by Roseville expresses in
the modern art the everlasting spirit of the Star of
Bethlehem. These dashing jars, bowls, vases and
candlesticks, with soft tints and interesting flares and
angles, speak today's language. At leading stores you
can select such wondrous gifts.

*Write us to mail you a free copy of
the handsome booklet, "Pottery".*

THE ROSEVILLE POTTERY CO., ZANESVILLE, OHIO

ROSEVILLE
POTTERY

*December 1928 Ad for the Futura Line from the
Good Housekeeping Magazine*

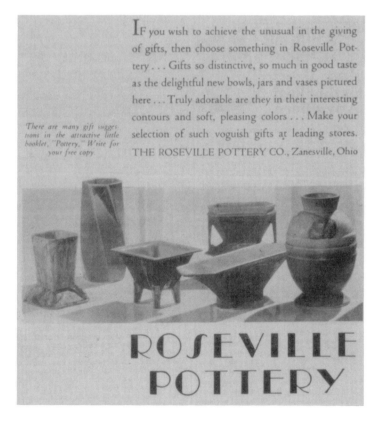

IF you wish to achieve the unusual in the giving
of gifts, then choose something in Roseville Pottery . . . Gifts so distinctive, so much in good taste
as the delightful new bowls, jars and vases pictured
here . . . Truly adorable are they in their interesting
contours and soft, pleasing colors . . . Make your
selection of such voguish gifts at leading stores.
THE ROSEVILLE POTTERY CO., Zaneville, Ohio

*There are many gift sugges-
tions in the attractive little
booklet, "Pottery," Write for
your free copy.*

ROSEVILLE
POTTERY

*December 1929 Ad from the
Good Housekeeping Magazine*

When the fireplace is not in use, a pair of tall vases or tankards filled with green foliage, flowers, or dried grasses will effectively enhance the hearth. For this arrangement, a pair of Roseville tankards are used. Three branches of huckleberry have been placed in each vase so that the highest branch stands above the vase rim, one-and-a-half times the container's height.

Bookcases are usually secondary to the fireplace in room interest. Therefore their decoration can be more casual and not so carefully balanced. For example, groups of small pottery objects such as a jardiniere on the top shelf, an ash tray or candy dish on the second shelf and a pottery basket for flowers or plants on the third shelf. It is best to select objects of different heights and keep the number limited to three to avoid a cluttered effect. A fan-shaped bowl like the Roseville style pictured at the top of the page is ideal for flowers or vines atop a narrow bookcase between two picture groupings.

On your buffet, a bowl of fruit with candlesticks is appropriate, like the Roseville Art Pottery group pictured above. A shallow leaf bowl for passing sweetmeats and sandwiches is likewise both useful and decorative. (Shown at top of picture, right.)

1947 Brochure on "How to decorate with art pottery" published by Roseville Pottery, Inc., Zanesville, Ohio

The buffet is an ideal place

for your coffee and tea service, candlesticks,

a leaf-shaped plate for fruit,

sandwiches or teacakes, and a vase for flowers.

A pair of Roseville Art Pottery
wall pockets filled with real or artificial ivy
enriches the narrow wall area that may be
too dark or small for a picture.

Bring that dark corner to life
by using a tall floor vase. It is important
enough to use decoratively without anything
in it. It is also effective when filled
with flowers or greens — real or artificial —
as pictured here. Notice that the highest
stalk of flowers has a stem about two-and-a-
half times the height of the vase. This
allows the stem to reach the holder at the
bottom of the vase and still have enough height
above the vase top to have good balance.

Avoid the monotony of having the dining
room table always look the same. Variety through
the use of changing bowls of flowers, fruit,
candles and plants furnish ever-fresh interest. If
the dining table is nicely finished there is no
need for a cover between meals. A center
decoration like this Roseville Art Pottery ensemble of
autumn corn, grasses and gourds flanked
by candlesticks is sufficient.

A pair of art pottery pots planted with
real or artificial geraniums is particularly pleasing on
an early American maple table, or in any
provincial dining room. A dining table center
decoration should be lovely to look at from all sides.
Also, it should not be higher than 14'' maximum,
to allow for the unobstructed flow
of conversation and view across the table.

1947 Brochure on "How to decorate with art pottery" published by Roseville Pottery, Inc., Zanesville, Ohio

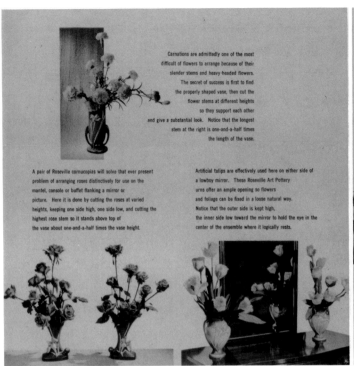

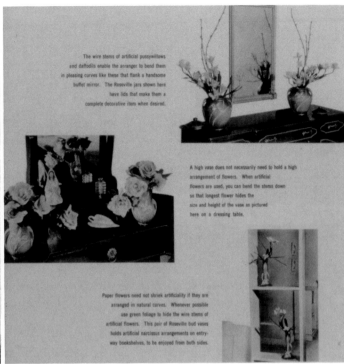

1947 Brochure on "How to decorate with art pottery" published by Roseville Pottery, Inc., Zanesville, Ohio

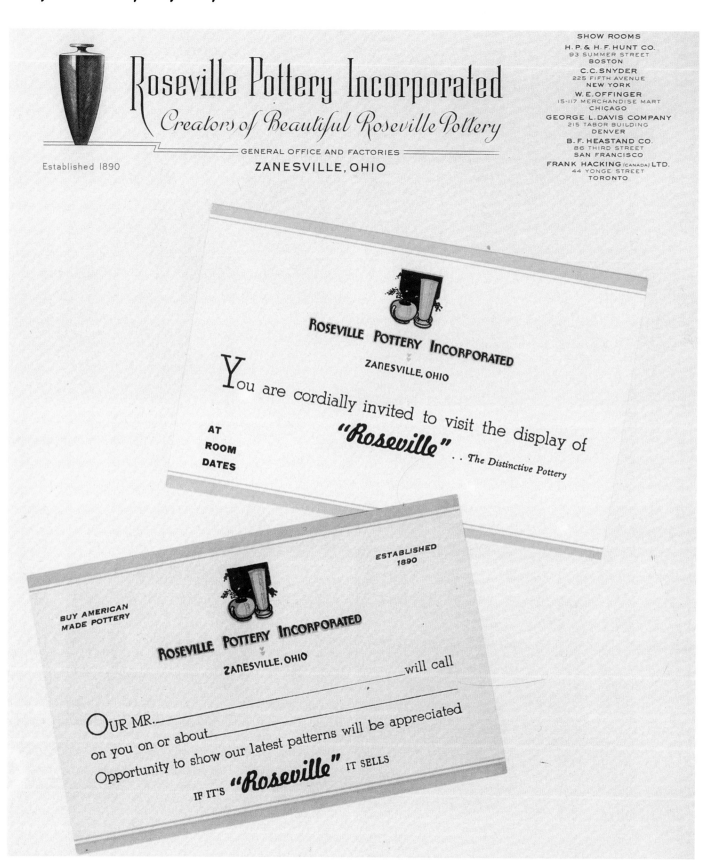

Original Letterhead and Calling Cards for the Roseville Pottery Company, Zanesville, Ohio

Roseville Pottery charted history dated May 15, 1944

Compliments of the Ohio Historical Society

Antique Matt Green 1910-1914

A very rustic looking plain shape of matt green glaze with darker tones coming through. Plates from the Ohio Historical Society reflect seven different shapes ranging in size from 4-5-6-7-8-9-10" and a 12". They also came in two or three legged stands, both plain in design with no decoration or flair. It is unknown if they made these stands for each of the different jardinieres. Information would lead us to believe that this is true. All pieces are unmarked.

Compliments of the George Krause collection.

Apple Blossom 1948

This line displays opened apple blossoms with brown branches winding through the blossoms and into the handles. The backgrounds were pink, green and brown and came in a satin glaze. Green is the highest in demand.

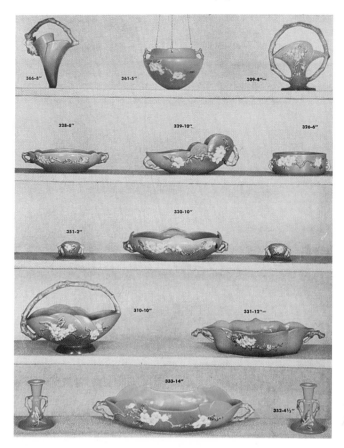

*Both top photos are compliments
of the George Krause collection.*

Roseville... Lovely Art Pottery

Use small vases on your
coffee table, bookcase or
dresser ... tall vases by
your fireplace ... and
matching pieces on mantle,
dining table, and buffet to
make your house a home.

Make your home lovely and livable with decorative
Roseville pottery. These beautifully designed pieces
are all creations of Roseville Pottery, Inc., well-
known makers of fine pottery. The craftsmen who produced them have devoted a lifetime to the art of
pottery making. The enthusiasm and ability they have
for their chosen work is reflected in the infinite care,
profound skill, and originality of each exquisite piece.
The design on this satin-textured, hand-fired pottery
is as gay as Spring itself. Each piece is carefully
hand-painted under multi-color glaze; attractively
decorated with dainty sprays of apple blossoms.
Handles simulate apple branches. The shapes of these
vases lend themselves readily to a variety of attractive
floral arrangements for every room in your home. Nature's own soft colors are harmonious with every color
scheme. Choose the pieces you want in coral, aqua blue,

or apple green, for your own home or for gifts to others.

(A) C-SH218	Lip-Top Vase	10" high	$4.25
(B) C-SH219	Column Vase	9" high	3.95
(C) C-SH220	Window Box	4" high; 12" long	4.50
	(flowers not included)	
(D) C-SH221	Basket	7¼" high	5.25
(E) C-SH222	3-Piece Set		5.75
	Candle Holders 2" high	
	(candles not included)	
	Bowl 10" long	
(F) C-SH223	Floor Vase	14" high	8.25
(G) C-SH224	Cornucopia Vase	7" high	pt. 5.25
(H) C-SH225	Rose Bowl	6" high	3.25

Colors shown match actual colors as closely as
modern high-speed printing permits.

page 58

*This ad is from the 1952 Spring and Summer
Catalog of the Jewel Tea Company, Inc.
Pictured are pieces from the Apple Blossom Line.*

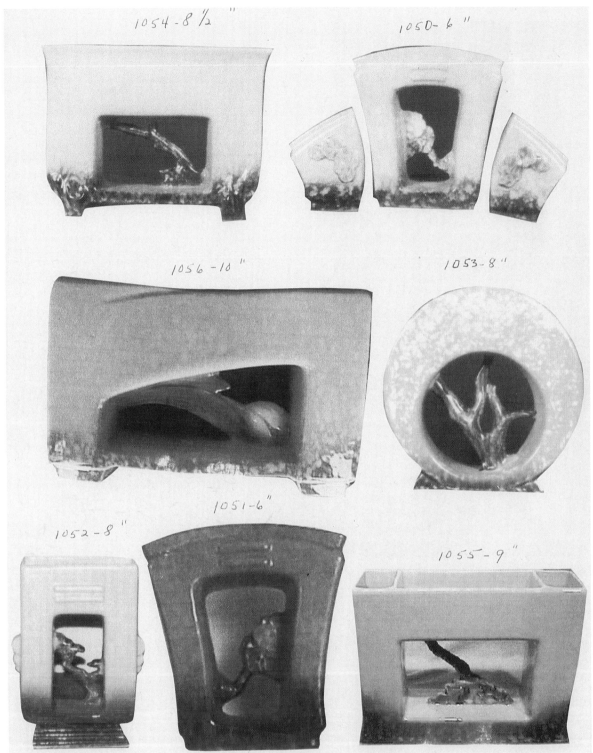

1054-8½"

1050-6"

1056-10"

1053-8"

1052-8"

1051-6"

1055-9"

Artwood January 1951

A traditional 50's line which premiered at the Pittsburgh show on July 4, 1951. Artwood came in variable shapes and sizes. Many of the single shapes had a window effect in the middle with a tree branch climbing from one side to the other. Several shapes were divided into two independent pieces but are joined by a tree branch clinging to both sides. The third shape had one big unit and two smaller units with the larger one having a window effect with the branch climbing through, while the smaller units had tree or leaf designs on them. They came in a very smooth high gloss finish with a variety of colors: emerald green, poppy yellow, and stone gray. Marked clearly with Roseville U.S.A.

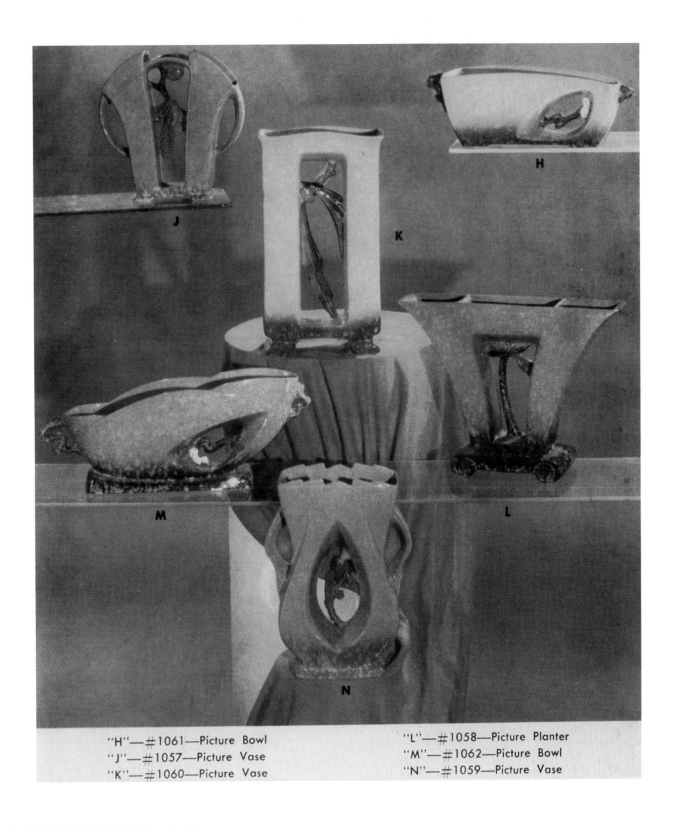

"H"—#1061—Picture Bowl
"J"—#1057—Picture Vase
"K"—#1060—Picture Vase

"L"—#1058—Picture Planter
"M"—#1062—Picture Bowl
"N"—#1059—Picture Vase

Compliments of the George Krause collection

Compliments of the Ohio Historical Society

Autumn - Circa 1910

Often described as a light color background with dark trees and country side in foreground. Part of creamware line with high gloss glaze. Often seen in yellow to orange, pink to red, light blue to dark blue, light green to dark green. Beside a complete toilet set in several colors, there were 7-8-9-10" jardinieres and 7-8-9-10" footed jardinieres.

Compliments of the Ohio Historical Society

Aztec Art - Introduced in 1904

   The Aztec Art had no reflection on the Aztec Indian styles. If any kinship it would be to the American Indians before Columbus. Styles most used were tall vases ranging to over 14-16" in height. One of the most common finds today is the water pitcher in three different designs. Simple shapes, molded with smooth surfaces and hand decorated with a squeezed bag pattern. Simple yet stylish forms in azure blue, olive green, soft white, teal, gray, beige, and brown. Mostly unmarked but a few have been found with paper labels or an Rv on the bottom.

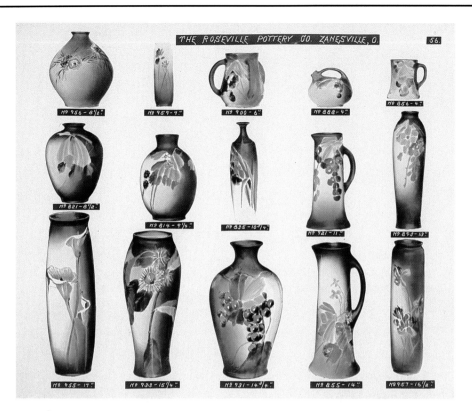

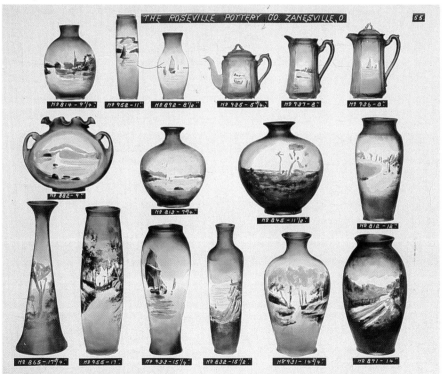

Compliments of the Ohio Historical Society

Azurean Introduced around 1902

This top of the line item was done solely in Azure blue and white with hand painted trim. A high gloss glaze over hand painted landscapes, seascapes or floral designs. Many of the original Rozane shapes were used. Many are artist signed. Marked with Azurean or RPCo die stamp. Shapes vary from a 4" mug, 4" water jug, 5 3/4" teapot, 8" pitchers, 8" chocolate pot to 15 1/4" and 17 3/4" tall vase. Many older shapes such as a 9" pillow vase and 11" tanker were used.

Compliments of the Ohio Historical Society

Azurine-Orchid-Turquoise 1920-1921

Similar to the Rosecraft line with simple shapes and tall peaked handles, some as high as 13". No fancy design under the high gloss glaze. The same blue was used for the Azurean items. Soft pastel rose would describe Orchid while light blue/green would best describe Turquoise, no markings.

600-15" 594-9" 596-9" 598-12"

605-6" 233-8" 603-4"

604-7" 590-7" 626-4" 588-6" 592-7"

Compliments of the George Krause collection

Baneda 1933

Produced in several colors and shades of green, red and the rarest of all blue backgrounds. Decorated with a band of leaves, vines and pods completely around the vessel. The green backgrounds are covered with a matt glaze while the red and blue background are covered with a high gloss glaze.

Mrs. Anna Young was responsible for naming this line. She was aware that the company needed a new line to stimulate sales. The name Baneda was derived from the fact that a wide band encompassed all the shapes. Common shapes had handles either in rounded knobs or open cut styles. Believed to have been produced in about 36 different styles. Marked with a gold triangular Roseville sticker.

Compliments of the Ohio Historical Society

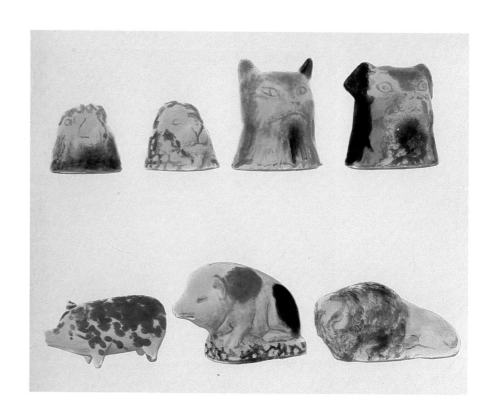

*Both photos are compliments of
the Ohio Historical Society*

Banks and Novelties Produced in the early 1900's

Often produced very poorly, molds were bad, the painting was done by hand and often in a hurry with little care or pride. Many examples reflect poor glazing. These catalog pages show busts of Uncle Sam, cats, bald eagles and other birds. Sitting, standing, or lying down buffalo, pigs, bee hives were also manufactured. Other novelty items were "Ye Olden Times" jug, and the monkey bottles. Unfortunately, none of these banks or novelties were marked and they come in a wide variety of color, green-blue, blended, brown, black and spongeware. Earlier banks manufactured before 1900 included apples and oranges, and were also unmarked and had the same problems with production. Since the banks were made to be handled by children and broken when filled, there are few examples available today.

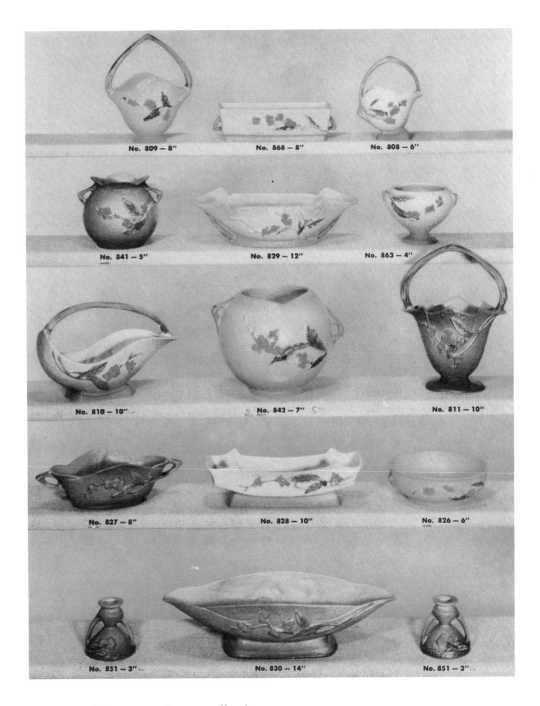

No. 809 — 8"   No. 868 — 8"   No. 808 — 6"

No. 841 — 5"   No. 829 — 12"   No. 863 — 4"

No. 810 — 10"   No. 842 — 7"   No. 811 — 10"

No. 827 — 8"   No. 828 — 10"   No. 826 — 6"

No. 851 — 3"   No. 830 — 14"   No. 851 — 3"

Compliments of the George Krause collection

Bittersweet - Circa January 1951

Orange pods or berries with green leaves winding across the vessel with brown branches as handles. They came in a soft light background of terra cotta, rose or green with a soft satin matt glaze. Many unusual shapes were designed for this line: baskets, ewers, and even a tea set.

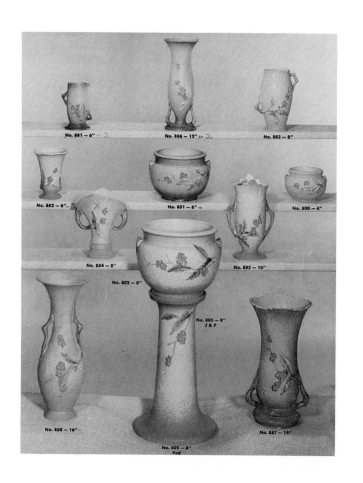

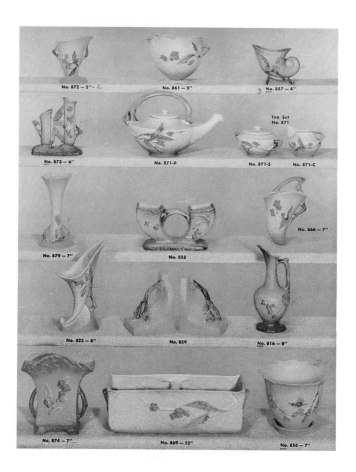

Compliments of the George Krause collection.

Compliments of the Ohio Historical Society

Blackberry - Circa 1932

A band of blackberries hanging from heavy vines and leaves. Usually but not necessarily . . . light green and yellow leaves against a light brown background which turns to a darker green around the rim. Half way down the vessel the surface becomes heavy with leaves showing through the satin matt glaze. Most shapes were rounded and traditional with small handles. Twenty-eight shapes are displayed in plates from the Ohio Historical Society but it is believed there were a total of thirty-five different styles. If any can be found marked, they would have a triangular paper label.

61

BLEEDING HEART   1607·T

964 ~ 6"
380 ~ 8"
1287 ~ 8"
1140
1139 ~ 4½"
362 ~ 5"
359 ~ 8"
966 ~ 7"
968 ~ 8"
970 ~ 9"
377 ~ 4"
379 ~ 6"
1323
651 ~ 5"
971 ~ 9"
361 ~ 12"
384 ~ 14"
40
961 ~ 4"
142 ~ 8"
381 ~ 10"
138 ~ 4"
967 ~ 7"
651 ~ 3"
976 ~ 15"
974 ~ 12"
973 ~ 10"
972 ~ 10"
975 ~ 15"
977 ~ 18"

Compliments of the George Krause collection

Bleeding Heart - Circa January 1940

    A row of heart shaped pink blossoms spreading across the vessel which are sheltered under a spray of green leaves. Backgrounds are pink, blue and green with a soft matt glaze. There are forty-eight different shapes displayed in the Ohio Historical Society catalog, but there are more known to be in existence. Many of the vases have six sided rims and are unique in shape and design. They are marked with raised "Roseville U.S.A."

Compliments of the George Krause collection

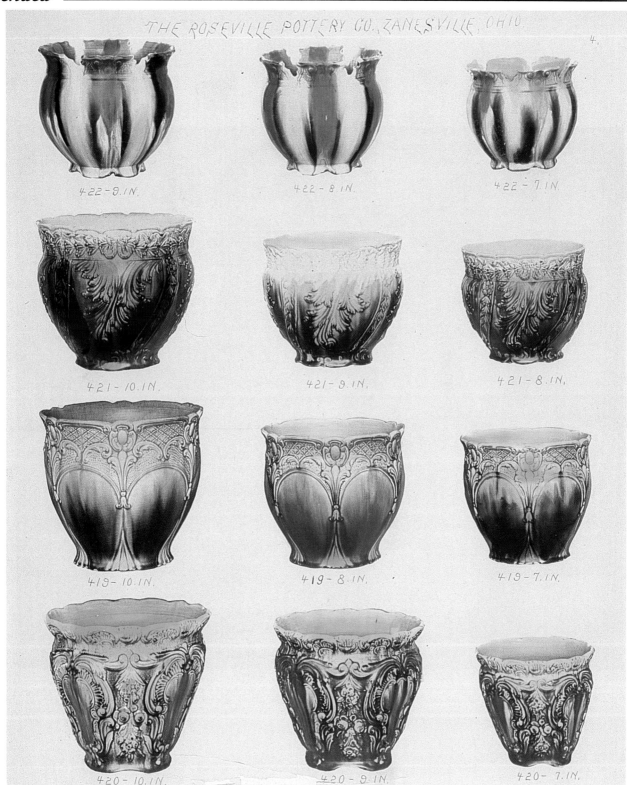

THE ROSEVILLE POTTERY CO., ZANESVILLE, OHIO.

4.

422 - 9.IN.   422 - 8.IN.   422 - 7.IN.

421 - 10.IN.   421 - 9.IN.   421 - 8.IN.

419 - 10.IN.   419 - 8.IN.   419 - 7.IN.

420 - 10.IN.   420 - 9.IN.   420 - 7.IN.

Compliments of the Ohio Historical Society

Blended - Circa early 1900's

Described as a style of blending or flowing more than one color into another. In some cases three or more colors were blended into one design of a jardiniere and pedestal or umbrella stand. Covered with a high gloss glaze it is often referred to as Majolica ware. Most of this line was hand painted with a large variety of sizes and shapes. Believed to have been marked with an oblong paper label but as time goes on . . . no label . . . no mark. It is rare to find one that is marked.

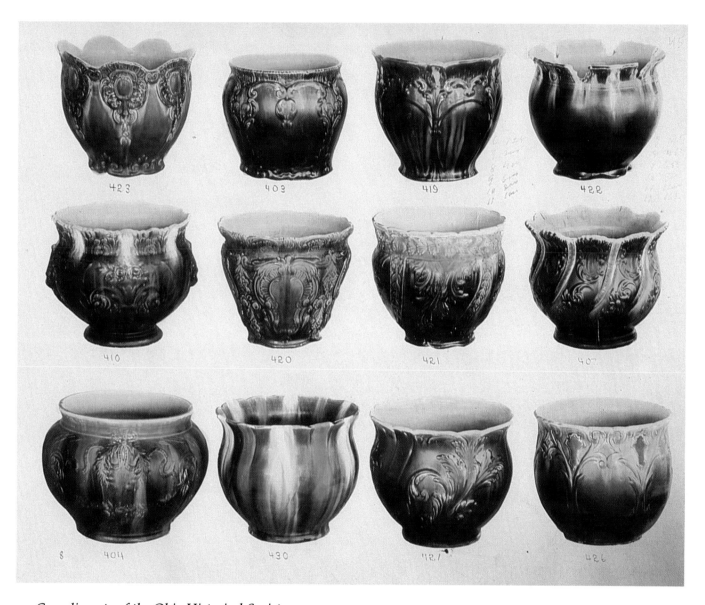

Compliments of the Ohio Historical Society

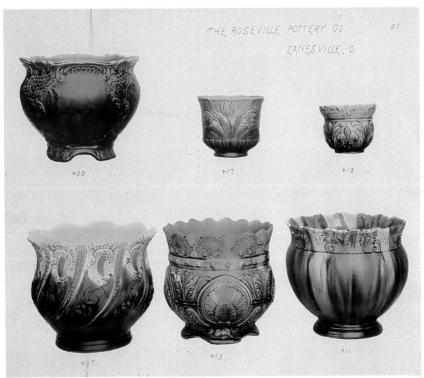

Compliments of the Ohio Historical Society

Compliments of the Ohio Historical Society

701—10"X21"   706—8"X21"   719—8½"X21"

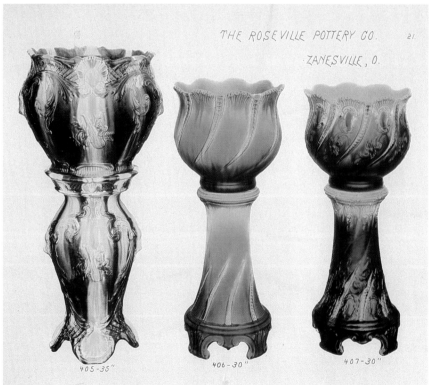

THE ROSEVILLE POTTERY CO.
ZANESVILLE, O.

405—35"   406—30"   407—30"

Compliments of the Ohio Historical Society

Compliments of the Ohio Historical Society

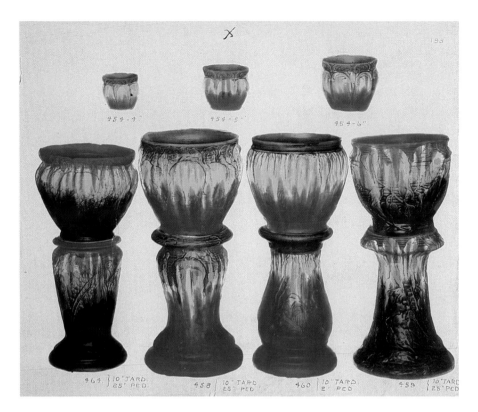

Compliments of the Ohio Historical Society

#422-7-8-9-10-11-12 IN
J&P 10"X24"-10 X 29

#404-8-10-12 IN
J&P 12X27½

#437-12-13 N
J&P 13X27

THE ROSEVILLE POTTERY CO. ZANESVILLE OHIO.

425-44"

410-37"

414-33"

Compliments of the Ohio Historical Society

Compliments of the Ohio Historical Society

Compliments of the Ohio Historical Society

Blue/Black Teapots - Circa 1920's

Teapots were very successful with Roseville. Often they would take out a particular style or color and promote it. They did this with both black and blue teapots. Black teapots were plain, untrimmed, round and fat with a high gloss glaze. They were made from red clay which Roseville seldom used. Blue teapots were shiny with metallic gold or white decals. Shapes were original and varied in size, handles, spouts and height. These were all unmarked.

Compliments of the Ohio Historical Society

Blue/Green/Red and Gold - Circa early 1900's

Floral designs outlined with gold trim on a solid background of royal blue or forest green covered with a high gloss glaze. Cuspidors, small jardinieres and toilet sets have been found. We can only guess on the number of items manufactured.

Compliments of the George Krause collection

Burmese - Circa July 1950

A head of a male figure wearing a ceremonial hat and a female head wearing a flower behind her right ear are used to highlight this style. Used as bookends, candle holders, and just as figures. Also included is a 10" planter which came in the same color and satin matt glaze. Most common colors are green metal black, ivory, and antique copper green. They are usually marked with Roseville in relief and a number or with a simple R.

Compliments of the George Krause collection

Bushberry - Circa July 1941

Very creative styles were used for this line. The body of each is designed to resemble the bark of a tree with large maple like shaped leaves across the vessel. Clusters of berries hang from the leaves. The handles are designed as tree branches in very original shapes. The background comes in blue, terra cotta and green. A satin matt glaze was used. Believed to come in over 60 shapes. Marked with a Roseville in relief and style numbers.

Compliments of the George Krause collection

Cal Art - Circa early 1950

Cal Art was a ceramic company that petitioned Roseville to produce a line of pottery. The line included different size trays and several planters in plain shapes with little or no embossed designs on basic colors; white, pale green, yellow, blue, or gray. Several planters have frosting or an overglaze on them, while the trays may have a very soft blending of colors such as pink blended with white. Both a matt glaze and a high gloss glaze were used. Marked "Created for Cal Art by Roseville U.S.A." and a style number or Cal Art Creation and a style number. Very few designs have surfaced.

Cameo - Circa 1910

Sometimes called a Ceramic but listed on Ohio Historical Society plates as Cameo. There is a dark band and different size dark blocks around the top of each jardiniere. Girls with hands joined running through the forest or a peacock in a vertical panel are embossed on dark green or cream background with a matt glaze. The plates show a flower pot design and four different size round jardinieres. Most of the pedestal bases for the cream design are tri-footed, while the pedestal for the peacock jardiniere has a rounded base, unmarked.

Photo's compliments of the Ohio Historical Society

Compliments of the George Krause collection

Capri - Circa late line-1950

Introduced when the company was feeling a need for another line to save the company. What did the buyers want? Many modernistic designs with bright colors and low prices were the norm for this line. Designs included ashtrays, shells, vases, baskets, planters, and window boxes. Marked with Roseville in relief and came in a wide variety of colors which were produced in a high gloss glaze.

Top - Compliments of the George Krause collection.

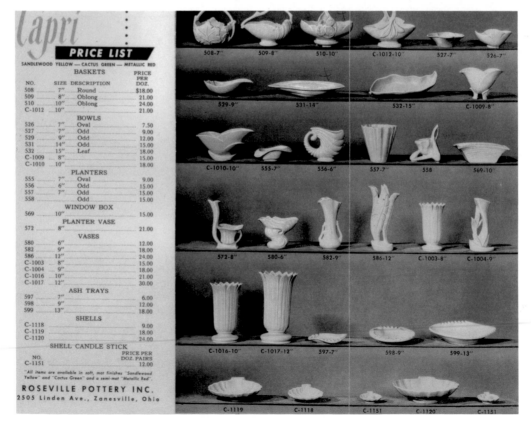

Compliments of the George Krause collection

Carnelian I - Circa 1915-1927

This pattern has a blending or layering of colors, some dripping while others overlap. There was a strong use of handles and many special designed shapes. They were a lot more ornate than Carnelian II. Many of the larger shapes have a heavy look about them. Between Carnelian I and II, there were 110 different styles produced. Several Carnelian I styles were marked in an ink stamp R, but not all pieces. A matt glaze was used throughout this line.

Compliments of the George Krause collection

Compliments of the George Krause collection

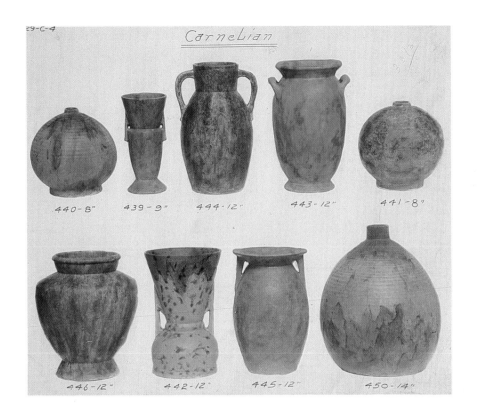

29-C-4
Carnelian

440-8" 439-9" 444-12" 443-12" 441-8"

446-12" 442-12" 445-12" 450-14"

Compliments of the George Krause collection

Carnelian II - Circa 1915-1931

   This pattern has a blending or layering of colors. In the beginning of this pattern most of the Carnelian I molds were used. In most cases, they would take an already finished Carneliam I piece and blend it with other colors. This can be seen by checking the bottoms of the Carnelian I green or blue - not matching the colors on the outside. Roseville produced a total of 87 pieces under the Carnelian I and II patterns. Then after the Futura line was introduced and turned out to be a success they produced #439 to 461, which some collectors call Carnelian III. They were molds created only for Carnelian II and were more daring and larger than before. Many of these shapes have a heavy appearance and were a lot more ornate than Carnelian I. Both matt and satin glazes were used on this line. Many of the Carnelian I and II were used later in Imperial II, Rosecraft Black and Earlam. When marked, they used paper stickers which were lost over time. Evaluation of this line is mainly in the eyes of the purchaser. Decisions are made depending on crispness of mold and blending of one color with another.

Compliments of the George Krause collection

Compliments of the Ohio Historical Society

Ceramic Design - Circa early 1900

A line believed to be heavily embossed in a light pale background. This line was, in most cases, heavily decorated with wide rims and legs. All varieties of planters, with or without liners, from several major groups, Perisan, Ivory, Matt, and Tints were used. These range from 3" to 16" and came in a matt to high gloss glaze finish on a variety of jardinieres and planters with a basic ivory color. Wall pockets and cemetery vases were a last minute thought. The line is mostly unmarked but a few have been found with an ink stamp of "Roseville Pottery Co., Zanesville, O."

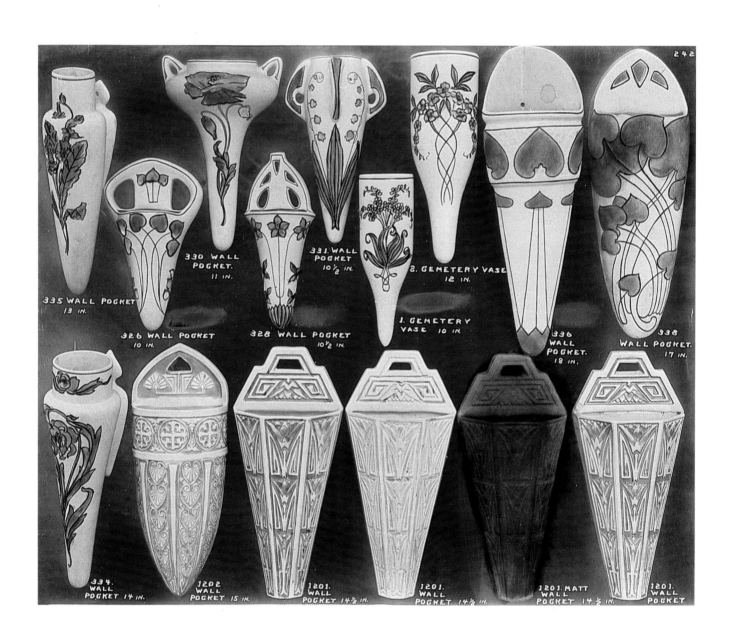

Compliments of the Ohio Historical Society

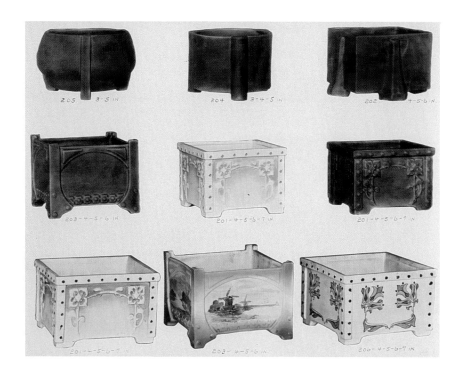

Compliments of the Ohio Historical Society

Compliments of the Ohio Historical Society

Cherry Blossom - Circa 1932

Pattern displayed vertical running slits that encompass two-thirds of the vessel. Clinging to the top of the slits is a vine of fully open white cherry blossoms entangled with brown vines and green leaves. Backgrounds vary from a full terra cotta to a pale pink or cherry tint leading to a dark green. Small handles are displayed throughout the line with a satin matt glaze. There are approximately 26 different styles in the line, but there may be more. Usually marked with a black paper triangular sticker.

Cherry Jubilee - Circa early 1900

A creamware line of ivory colored styles displaying a large decal of a cluster of cherries hanging from a branch with green leaves overlapping the cherries. A large variety of styles were included: mugs, teapots, coffee pots, trivets, pitchers, tankers, sugar and creamers. Many of the Dutch ware line were reproduced as the Cherry Jubilee. A matt to high gloss glaze covered the decals. The older pieces used piping around the edge of the mugs, while the later line did not. The later lines of the teens used larger decals on a wider variety of styles, with no markings.

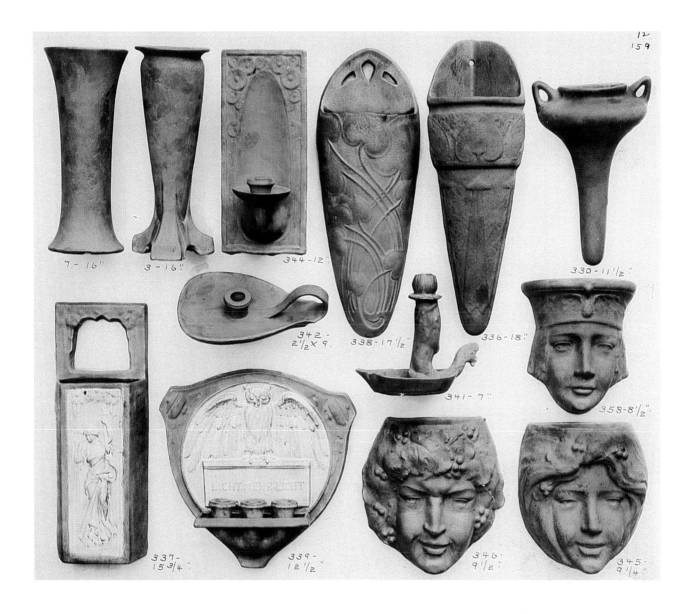

12
159

7 - 16"   3 - 16"   344 - 12"   338 - 17½"   336 - 18"   330 - 11½"

342 - 2½ x 9.   341 - 7"   358 - 8½".

337 - 15¾"   339 - 12½"   346 - 9½: 345 - 9¼"

Compliments of the Ohio Historical Society

Chloron - Circa 1907

   Manufactured about two years after the Rozane Egypto line, this pattern was very similar in color and style to its sister, but most Chloron pieces display "pepper" dots throughout and have a thin matt glaze. Several pieces have ivory centers, such designs are wall pockets, plaques and sconces. The easiest way to differentiate Chloron from Egypto or Matt Green is to check catalog reprints, but this is not always correct. Many of the same molds were used in all three lines of Chloron, Matt Green and Egypto. Most of the line is unmarked, however, several pieces have Chloron stamped in ink on the bottoms. Forty-seven different styles appear on the catalog pages.

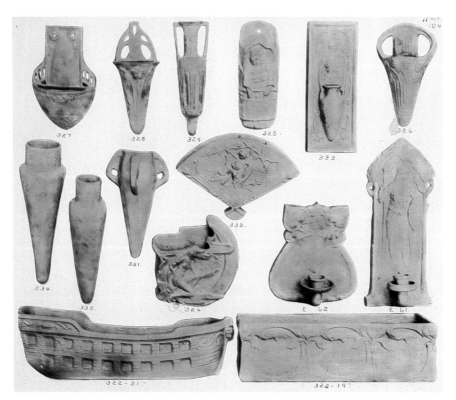

Compliments of the Ohio Historical Society

Compliments of the Ohio Historical Society

Chocolate Pot or Chocolate Sets - Circa 1910's

These pieces were produced about the same time as the creamware designs. The chocolate pots came in a variety of shapes and designs. One common trait on all the styles were the large open type handles. The spouts varied from short and stubby to the most common, a large snake appearing design.

The chocolate sets, consisted of a large chocolate pot (2 qt.), milk pitcher (2 qt.), and teapot with sugar and creamer. Popular designs included the Cherry Jubilee, Plum, Wheat Grain and several florals. The most popular color was white, but all basic tableware colors were produced, (blue, yellow, tan, green).

Designs were transfers with a high gloss glaze and were unmarked.

Compliments of the George Krause collection

Clemena - Circa January 1934

These styles were produced with white smooth embossed flowers embellished in a basket weave with vines and leaves encompassing the style. Small handles protrude from the sides. Colors vary from a beige with a white or light yellow design to a blue with white middle and a green with a lighter color center. Nineteen different designs appear in the catalog pages but there are several more available. All are marked with Roseville impressed and the style number.

Compliments of the George Krause collection

Clematis - Circa July 1944

A large open flower is embossed in the center of a massive looking creation. The flower is joined with thick clusters of leaves and foliage on a very uneven bold background. Flowers of pink with yellow centers against a forest green background, a yellow flower with a brown center is displayed in the middle of a shaded green to a brown background, an ivory flower with a big yellow center and green leaves enhance the blue backgrounds. A soft satin finish covers the designs. The colors tend to darken as they approach the base and handles. Marked with Roseville in relief and a style number.

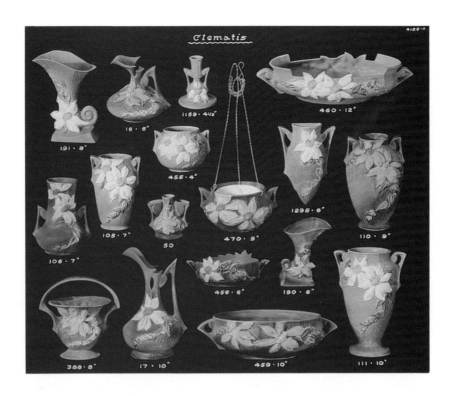

Compliments of the George Krause collection

Compliments of the Ohio Historical Society

Colonial - Turn of the Century

Large embossed shells or leaf designs coming down from the sides were almost hidden in this sponge ware. A strong use of metallic gold emphasized the rim and shells or leaves. The gold is even followed through to the inside of the rim. Brown branch looking handles were incorporated on all the pitchers and lids. Came in a variety of colors: green, blue, brown, yellow, and an almost white with blue and yellow sponge lines. A complete toilet set was offered in this design but other utility ware pieces are possible. A high gloss glaze was used and all items were unmarked.

Compliments of the George Krause collection

Columbine - Circa January 1941

A large open floral design branching out from thin vines with unopen buds and green leaves attached, which flow through a blending of colors as blue to almost black, pink to brown, and brown to green. Over 40 different designs were featured in this pattern. Many had wide pointed handles, baskets with wide spread handles, and a wall pocket with a curled under tail. Glazed in a matt style and marked with a raised "Roseville U.S.A."

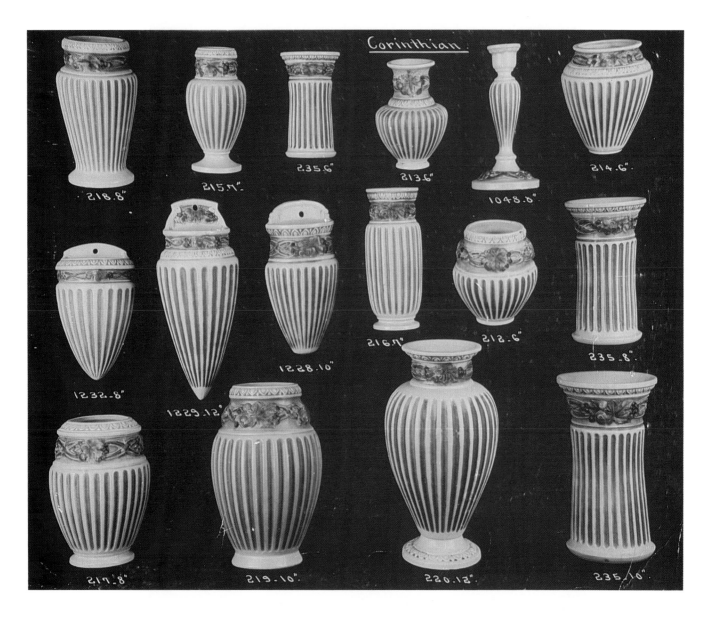

Compliments of the Ohio Historical Society

Corinthian - Circa 1923

At this time, Roseville was looking for a successor to the Donatello line. Thus the Corinthian Line, produced in the same styles with the same blending of ivory and green combinations. It was embossed with a bunch of grapes, small yellow and red blossoms intermingled with berry vines and green leaves. The pattern offered a formal appearance with fluted rims and a matt to satin glaze. Usually marked with an ink stamped Rv. A wide variety of styles were offered, which included several size wall pockets, two hanging baskets, two gates, and four different size jardinieres and pedestals. Over 40 different styles were included in the pattern.

Compliments of the Ohio Historical Society

"THE CORNELIAN TOILET SET."

30.

SOAP DISH.   SHAVING MUG.   BRUSH HOLDER.   MOUTH EWER.

CHAMBER.

EWER & BASIN.   COMBINETTE.

Compliments of the Ohio Historical Society

Cornelian Cooking Ware - Circa 1900

This group contained a large group of embossed pieces on spongeware. The spongeware was made in a Victorian style with sponging over the top of the designs; ivory over blue, and yellow over brown sponged with gold throughout. A few pieces had fluted edges around the pouring spout. The embossed pieces were mainly pitchers or large items with enough room to display such items as: wheat, poppy, ears of corn, or wild rose, mainly with yellow, green, or blue backgrounds and a high gloss glaze finish. Produced in 8 different pitchers, tobacco jars, bread and milk set and a complete berry set. All are unmarked.

"THE CORNELIAN COOKING UTENSILS."

31.

6 PTS.   3 PTS.   2 PTS.   1 PT.   CRACKER JAR.   OAT MEAL.

PITCHERS.

CUSTARD CUP.   SHIRRED EGGS. 4"-5"   BUTTER.   FRUIT DISH.

MIXING BOWLS. 7"-8"-9"-10"-12"-14".   PUDDING DISHES. 4"-5"-6"-7"-8"-9"-10"-12".   PUNCH BOWL.

47.

E.1.   E.2.   E.3.   E.4.   E.5.

Compliments of the Ohio Historical Society

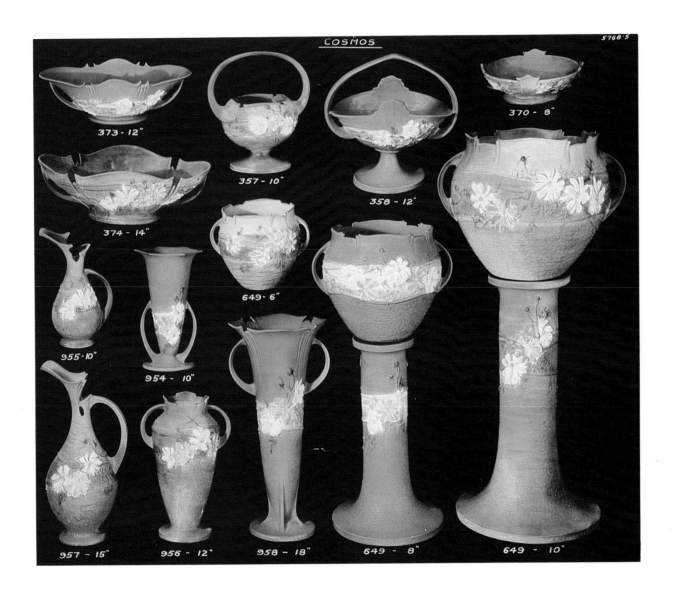

COSMOS

5768·5

373 - 12"

357 - 10"

358 - 12"

370 - 8"

374 - 14"

649 - 6"

955 - 10"

954 - 10"

957 - 15"

956 - 12"

958 - 18"

649 - 8"

649 - 10"

Compliments of the George Krause collection

Cosmos - Circa July 1939

All three colors of solid blue, green or earth tone brown backgrounds have natural blending throughout. They are accented with a green band and life like cosmos of orchid or ivory with green leaves have natural blending throughout. Deep cut out rims are common in this pattern. Almost 50 styles are displayed in the catalog sheets. Large handles are also common on many of the vases, including the jardinieres. A matt glaze was used and the entire pattern is marked with Roseville impressed and the style number.

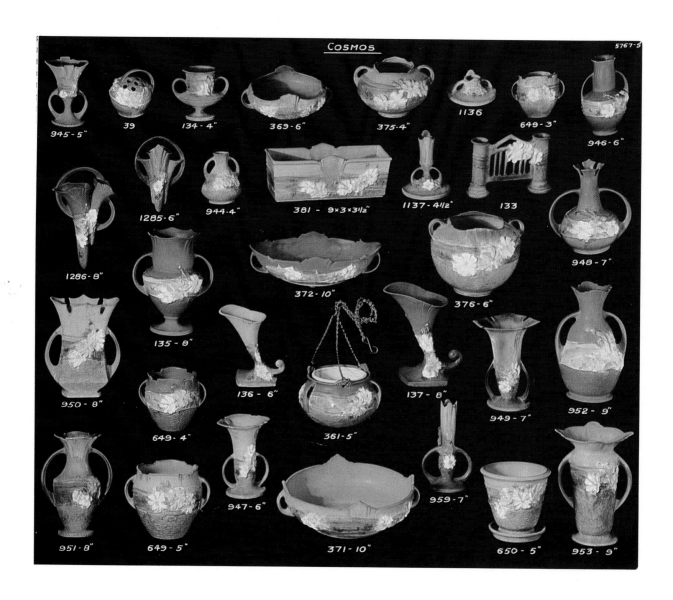

Compliments of the George Krause collection

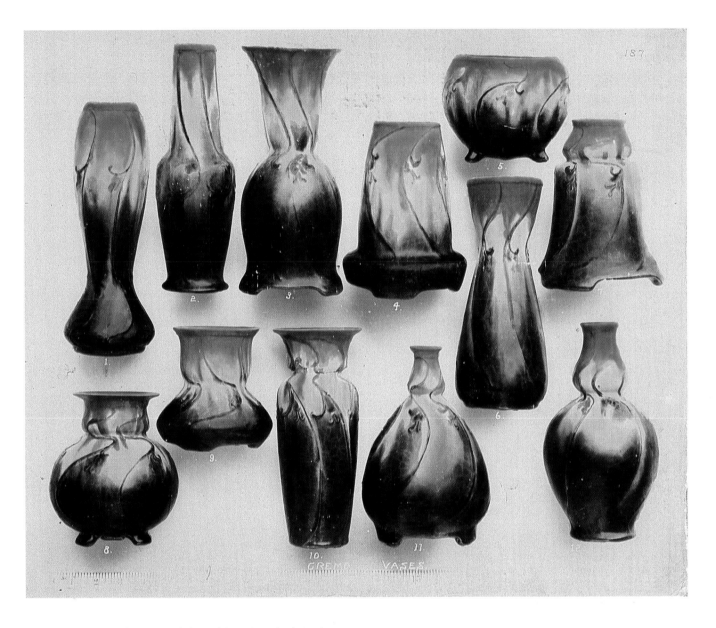

Compliments of the Ohio Historical Society

Cremo - Circa early 1910's

Produced in the early teens with a very distinguished looking style. About a dozen styles are pictured in the old catalog pages. Half of them have footed bases with wide lipped rims. The colors start with a dark green, almost black base, blending into lighter green to a pale yellow and topped off with a bright rose at the rim. Very small blue like flowers are almost hidden in the yellow sections. A bright satin glaze tops off this exquisite design, no marks are known.

CREMONA WARE

353/5 72/4 3.51/4 176/6 74/6

75 352/5 177/8 73/5 356/8

357/8 355/8 1068/4 178/8 354/7

360/10 361/12 362/12 358/10 359/10

Compliments of the George Krause collection

Cremona - Circa 1927

This design features a very soft almost misty tone with a flower, leaves and branches hidden under the satin glaze. Colorful designs include a pink background with pale blue or green flowers, pale green with shade darker green and blue flowers and a yellow or white background with blue flowers. Twenty styles are shown in catalog pages. Most of the styles are copies of early lines, Cornellian I and Tuscany are examples. Only four styles are pictured with handles. Plain and simple were the key to this pattern. Several are marked with paper labels but the majority are found unmarked.

Compliments of the Robert Bettinger collection

Crocus - Between 1910 to 1914

    Emerging around the same time as Aztec, with one major difference, the squeeze bag technique was not used. Instead, impressed hand painted designs were used under a high gloss glaze. Similar creative designs were used in both the Aztec and Crocus lines. Very few styles were exclusive to this line. Many were artist signed but no other markings.

Compliments of the Ohio Historical Society

Cuspidors - Circa late 1800's to the 1920's

Roseville produced many different styles, small, big, high, plain, decorated, spongeware, banded, embossed, from other patterns, and from one of a kind. Some were made with no glaze, some with a matt glaze, and others with a high gloss glaze. The combination was endless and what the public wanted was produced.

Compliments of the Ohio Historical Society

Compliments of the Ohio
Historical Society

Dahlrose - Circa mid 1920's

A rough texture body in terra cotta with a band of ivory looking flowers tied together with green leaves and stems winding around the top of each style. Terra Cotta turns into darker brown and dark green as it approaches the thick rounded lip of the rim. The darker tones are carried over the small handles and around some of the very unusual bases. Black and silver paper labels were used to mark this pattern, however, most are found unmarked.

Several pieces are found in lighter shades than the normal coloring. Matt glaze covered these traditional shapes. Approximately 30 different shapes have been identified. Several unusual shapes were created by the art department for this line . . . a seven inch candle holder and a flowing design on a double bud vase were among these.

DAWN
142-R

No.1121 ~ 2"
No.4 ~ 5"
No.31 ~ 3×4"
No.345 ~ 8"
No.319 ~ 6"
No.830 ~ 8"
No.315 ~ 4"
No.828 ~ 8"
No.829 ~ 8"
No.318 ~ 14"
No.831 ~ 9"
No.827 - 6"
No.826 ~ 6"
No.317 ~ 10"
No.834 ~ 15"
No.316 ~ 6"
No.832 ~ 10"
No.833 ~ 12"

Compliments of the Ohio Historical Society

Dawn - Circa April 1937

This pattern boasts a thin long pointed leaf design with a berry center impressed into a soft almost pastel like shape. The leaf design is painted a soft blue or yellow on pale pink, yellow or blue matt glaze. The rounded shapes on square pedestal-like bases leave a hint of the Art Deco times. Handles are no more than a square peg sticking out of the side. Less than 20 pieces are displayed in the Roseville catalog. Marked with an impressed Roseville and style number.

Plate 1

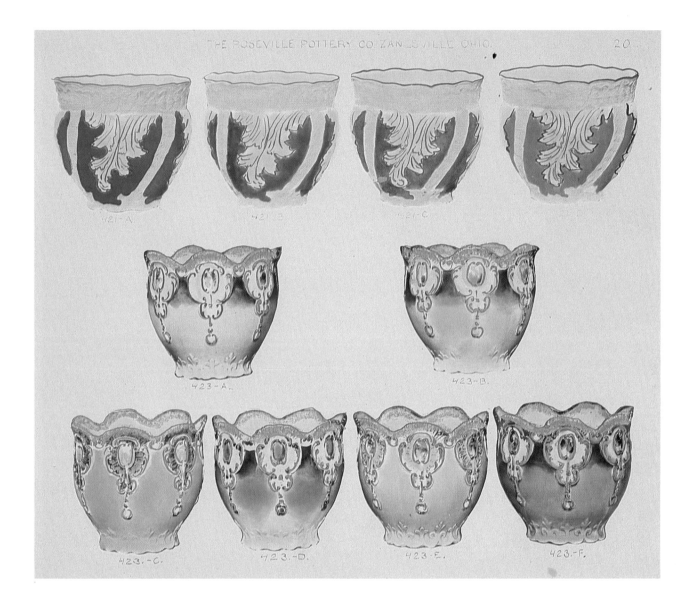

Compliments of the Ohio Historical Society

Decorated Art - Turn of the Century

Roseville used the name Decorated for many lines in the early years. Around 1900, they produced jardinieres, vases, and umbrella stands that were decorated in a Victorian style. They had a look of hand painted china, not pottery. Large displays of fruit and flowers were highlighted on legged vases and pedestal like jardinieres. The inners were not forgotten in this line, a very shiny glaze of ivory was used. Late in 1903, they again used a decorated line of creamware. This line consisted of mugs and tankers. Large decals of fruit and berries were glazed over with a high gloss glaze. A generous dusting of gold around the decal and on the handles highlighted this line. A ring of gold piping was used to highlight the lip of the mugs. Unfortunately, no markings or paper labels were used. Many of these styles were used for the Rozane Royal Line.

Plate 2

Plate 3

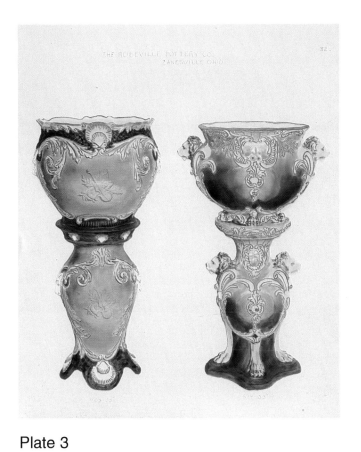

Plate 3

Plate 3

Plate 4

Plate 5

Plate 6

Plate 7

Compliments of the Ohio Historical Society

Compliments of the Ohio Historical Society

Decorated Landscape - Circa 1900

Both sgraffito (**Sgraffito-decoration by cutting away part of the surface layer of clay to expose a different color**) and squeeze bag technique were used in this line. A lost line since no marks are available to identify pieces as Roseville. Designs were produced on highly decorated vases, jardinieres and pedestals, umbrella stands and other styles which displayed scenes of trees, shrubs, vines, birds and flowers. Dark colors; brown, burnt orange, dark blue, black, yellow and gray were used.

Many of the jardinieres and pedestals have wide lips on both pieces. Insides of the jardinieres and umbrella stands are lighter than the outside. A very high gloss glaze was used over the entire line.

Compliments of the Ohio Historical Society

Decorated Matt - Circa early 1900's

A very heavy appearing line. The base of the jardiniere and umbrella stands are flat with a stylish three footed design. Belts of highly embossed designs flow around the upper portion and around the lip of the rim. A strong use of gray, light blue and other soft background colors with white and orange were used to highlight the design. Flowers, birds and trees were common. Usually a brighter color was used inside with a matt to satin glaze overall. Unmarked but often found artist signed.

Compliments of the Ohio Historical Society

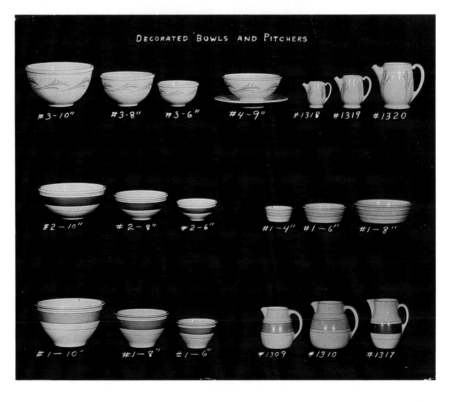

Decorated Utility Ware - late teen and 1940's

A very high gloss creamy white kitchen ware. The main backbone of this line were pitchers and assorted size mixing bowls. Pitchers with extended spouts and tea/coffee pots were common. A few styles available beside pitchers were: mixing bowls, plates, salad bowls, bake pans and mugs. One style of pitcher and bowls had small orange dots and gray or aqua leaves flowing around the circumference of the piece. Others had black and orange strips encompassing the pitchers, bowls and mugs, while others used bands of different sizes in blue, gray and green with one or two bands of black piping. A majority of the line is marked with Rv in ink stamp. However, a few pieces have been found unmarked.

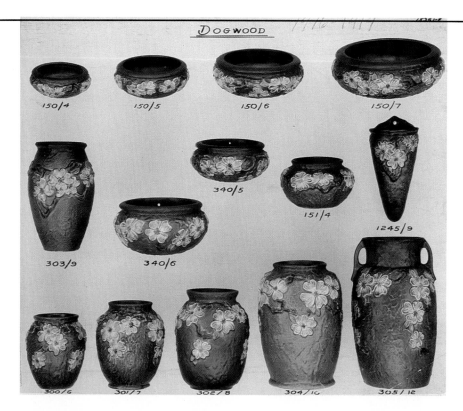

Compliments of the George Krause collection

Dogwood I - Circa 1916-1919

Developed by Frank Ferrel with a far Eastern influence. It was manufactured with a rough textured background of dogwood blossoms weaving across light brown branches and among the green leaves. They contained a strong definition on the branches and flowers. The background is a dark blend of green and brown. There was much more definition on the pedals of the flower than in Dogwood II. Most of the line was rounded with no handles. They also had a wide rounded lip on the edge of each vase and jardiniere. This was the first matt glazed floral line produced by Roseville. It set the stage for the many florals to come. Most of the line is ink stamped with an Rv.

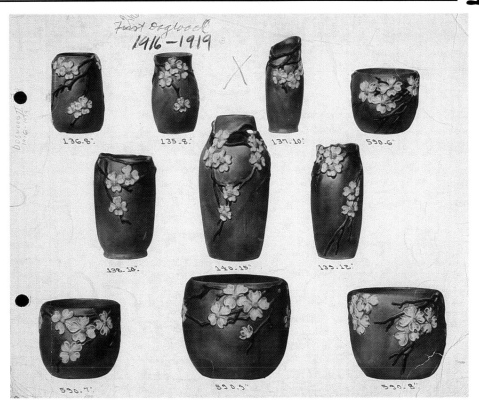

Compliments of the Ohio Historical Society

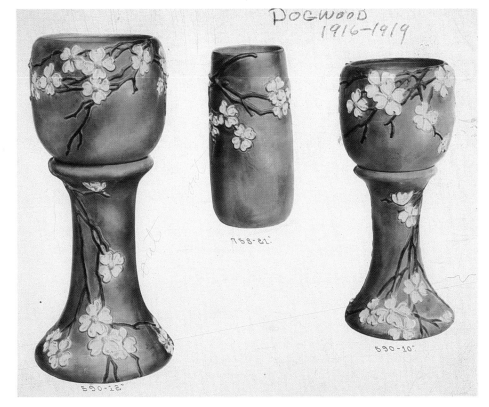

Dogwood II

There is a discussion on the time the line was started. The catalog pages are dated 1916-1919, while most written articles acknowledge the start as between 1924-1928. This version shows a much deeper olive green with an almost ivory looking dogwood. The blossoms are clinging to black vines that are often dripping over the entire smooth textured surface. On several styles, the vines actually climb over the rim, thus rendering it very unevenly shaped. The color starts off at the bottom with a dark terra cotta and blends to an olive green as the color flows to the top. These came in a matt glaze and they are unmarked.

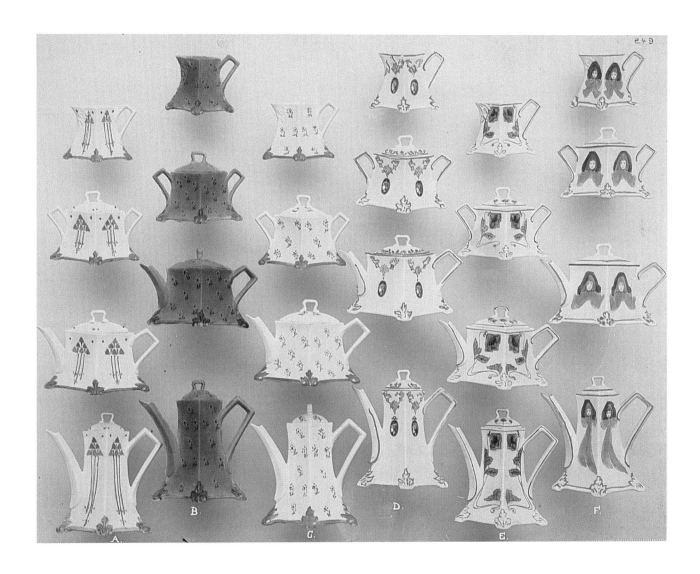

Compliments of the Ohio Historical Society

Donatella Tea Sets - Circa 1912

First introduced around 1912 to 1915 along with other forms of creamware such as: Indian, Dutch Tanker, Holland sets and the Landscape line.

Designed to be much taller than the every day tea sets of that era. They were geometric in design with rectangular handles and long shapely pointed spouts. Each piece came with open squared handles on each lid.

Each set consists of a tall coffee pot, smaller tea pot, sugar and creamer. Various designs have been found including Medallion, Tulip, Tree appearing designs, Persian as well as several other conventional patterns.

Perhaps this is the reason this line was referred to as Conventional as well as Donatella. As most of the lines of this period, they were unmarked.

Donatello - Circa 1915

A product of Harry W. Rhead, this pattern was Roseville's first major success. Produced for a decade with as many as a hundred different shapes and sizes consisting of ivory and green vertical fluting with a band of cherubs in a wide variety of scenes separated by trees on a light brown background. Several rows of white piping are used to emphasize the rim, base and the band of cherubs. The first line had a matt glaze while the later productions were semi-gloss to glossy glaze. Other color combinations have been found, ivory, brown, and a lavender-gray with brown and ivory bands. Most of the line was unmarked, however, ink impressed Rv and impressed "Donatello R. P. Co." have also been found.

Compliments of the Ohio Historical Society

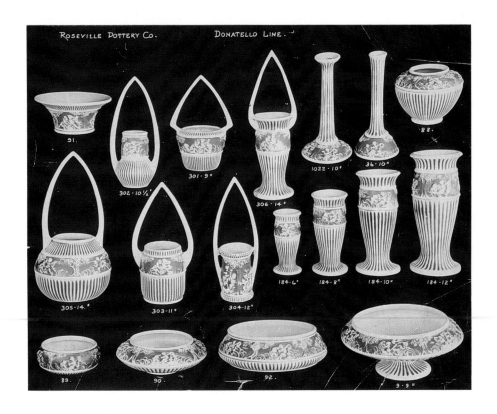

Compliments of the Ohio Historical Society

Compliments of the Ohio Historical Society

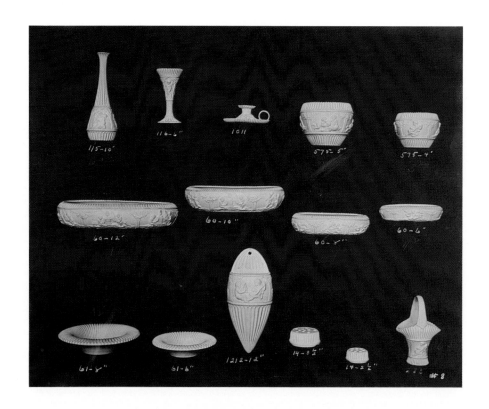

Compliments of the Ohio Historical Society

Compliments of the Ohio Historical Society

Dresser Sets - Early teens

A line of creamware, designed to appeal to the women of the house. Complete sets were decorated with desirable looking decals and usually a ring of dark piping around the rims. The set included a tray, ring tree, pin holder and a powder jar. Favorite styles included Medallion, Forget-Me-Not, Persian, Gibson Girl, Dutch, Landscape, and several combinations in different color strips. Possibilities were unlimited with the use of decals. Matt glaze was used first and later the satin high gloss glaze became more popular. The complete sets were unmarked.

DUTCH TOILET.

166.

Compliments of the Ohio Historical Society

Dutch - Before 1916

The Dutch design was very popular and inspired a separate line of its own. Yet another part of the creamware line, it had decals installed on ivory colored designs with a number of different Dutch scenes. They were over glazed and trimmed in blue and green, and often done free hand. The line consisted of tea sets, tanker sets, smoker sets, pitchers and complete toilet sets. All were unmarked.

Dutch Tea Pots.

199

Jnd Tea Pot.   № 5.   № 3.   № 2

№ 1   № 15   № 17.   № 6

№ 13 Conventional.   № 13 Dutch.   № 14.   № 4

Compliments of the Ohio Historical Society

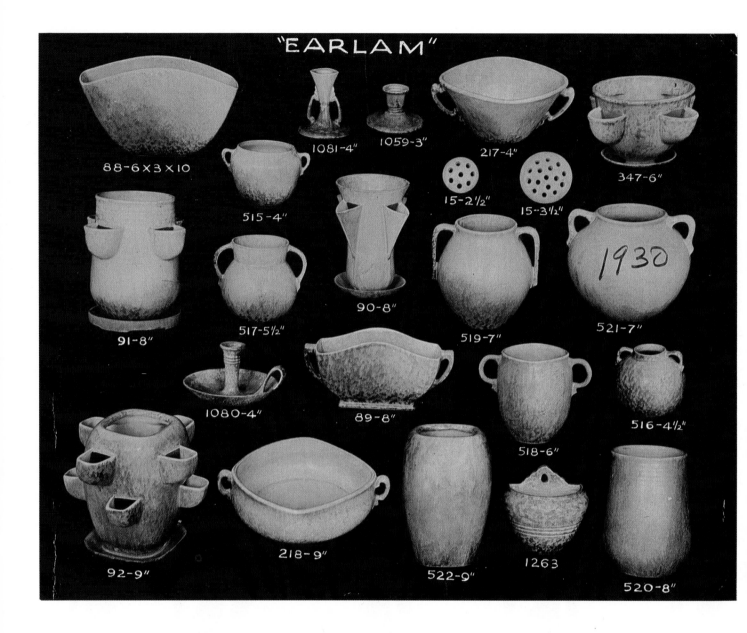

"EARLAM"

88-6 X 3 X 10
1081-4"
1059-3"
217-4"
347-6"
515-4"
15-2½"
15-3½"
91-8"
517-5½"
90-8"
519-7"
521-7"
1080-4"
89-8"
518-6"
516-4½"
92-9"
218-9"
522-9"
1263
520-8"

1930

Compliments of the Ohio Historical Society

Earlam - Circa 1930

This pottery was a two toned (usually green, tan, or blue) design with the darker color fading to a lighter at the top of the vessel. Usually came in a brighter color inside with a matt or satin glaze. Most of the design has a slightly incised ridge around the neck. Catalog pages reflect a wide variety of styles, including frogs, vases, bowls, planters, candlesticks, and unusually designed planters. Mostly marked with a gray or black paper label, if still attached.

Compliments of the Ohio Historical Society

Early Pitchers - Before 1916

A part of the old utility line, they were embossed with a high gloss glaze. The pitchers came unmarked and in a large variety of styles and sizes. In most cases, the scenes were hand painted. Among the most popular are "The Bridge", two different sizes of "Cow" pitcher, "Bull", "The Boy", "Golden Rod", "Wild Rose", "Mill", "Grapes", "Landscape", "Teddy Bear", "Owl", "Iris", "Tulip", "Tourist", and two different "Holland" scenes.

Compliments of the Ohio Historical Society

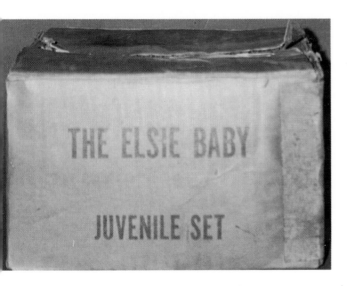

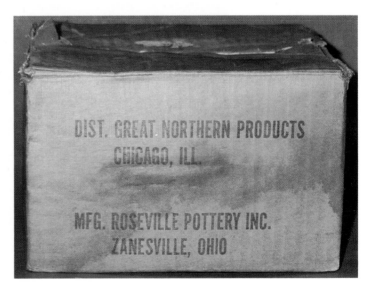

Compliments of the Hardy Hudson collection

Elsie the Cow - After World War II

After the war, Roseville produced a line of juvenile ware for the "Borden Co." The line consisted of plates, cups and cereal bowls with Elsie the Cow and her calf, Beauregard embossed on a plain smooth background. A special mark was created for this line with "The Borden Co.", a small Rv plus the letter "B" at the beginning of each shape number.

Compliments of Mike Nickel, Cynthia Horvath, Len Boucher collections

Experimental Creations of Master Potters and Artists

Many unfamiliar designs, colors, glazes and decorations were tested before they were accepted for production. Most are one of a kind and generally they are very expensive. These one of a kind shapes have a name, style, special glazing, and tint used, carved into the back or bottom of the vessel. Several still have Roseville in relief and a size number on the bottom. Unlimited styles and designs have been found. These vases are very rare and priceless.

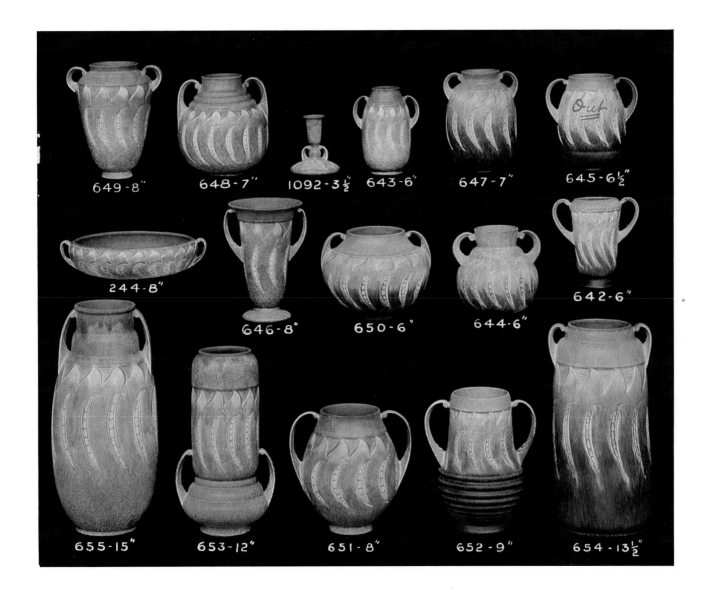

Compliments of the Ohio Historical Society

Falline - Circa 1933

This pattern contained many original designs, candle holders, bowls, and a large variety of exquisitely designed vases with creatively displayed handles. Catalog pages show 16 different styles. Often described as the pea pod pattern, vessels are encircled with a pea pod like decoration below a row of waves. Backgrounds range from dark blue or brown (from the bottom up) to lighter brown, beige, or green to a top of terra cotta or light brown, and glazed over with a satin matt finish. Usually found marked with a silver paper label.

Fatima/Rayman Club Whiskey - (Promotional Line) Teens

Another promotional line of creamware. Liggett and Myers Tobacco Company enticed Roseville to produce grosses of special ashtrays to use as a promotion for their Fatima Turkish cigarettes. Decals were used on these ashtrays as well as other ashtray promotions for companies such as the Rayman Club Whiskey Company and the Kaiserhof Hotel-Cafe of Chicago. The line had a matt glaze and was unmarked.

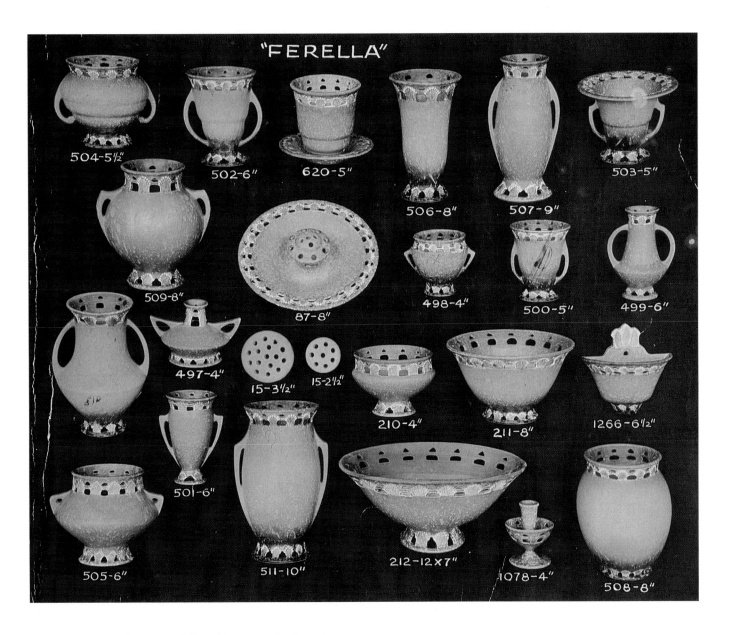

Compliments of the Ohio Historical Society

Ferella - Circa 1931

By far, the most popular line of this period. This pattern was named after Frank Ferrell who was the top designer at Roseville during this period. This design shows a mottled body with window cuts completely around the base and rim. These windows separate small clusters of tall stemmed flowers. Stems are green and lavender with pink and lavender blooms. Entirely confined in a matt glaze. Raspberry background color is blended into a band of dark green on the rim while a soft terra cotta background has a darker almost black base and darkens slightly at the rim. Usually marked with a paper label or found unmarked.

Compliments of the Ohio Historical Society

Fern Dish - Circa 1900

This pattern came in several different designs of a shallow piece used to display a small fern assortment. Often only several inches high but came in a variety of lengths (6"-7" and 8"). Embossed with designs of leaves and florals, usually in bright colors, and covered with a satin or high gloss glaze. Several designs included heavy blending of colors. Most were footed and unmarked.

Another design was heavily embossed with bands of ribbon around the rim with a raised ribbon bottom and came in a variety of washed colors over the embossed designs. The second design came with an inner liner made in light colors.

A third design appeared as a goblet designed as a tree. The base was flat with the trunk of the tree rooting from the base, and climbing up the goblet with branches protruding from the sides and blending back into the cup. Leaves and florals encompass the top of the goblet.

Compliments of the Ohio Historical Society

Fleur Delis - Circa early 1900's

A line of jardinieres and pedestals designed to appeal to the family that did not have room to display a large typical jardiniere and pedestal. Pieces came in a twenty inch height on ivory or white background. Styles have an indented rim with a ribbon of red dots spaced evenly around the ribbon. There are wide bands in assorted colors around the base plus a lily-like emblem used as a coat of arms by the King of France which was embossed in a staggered design on both pieces. A satin or high glaze was used to highlight this combination. They were unmarked.

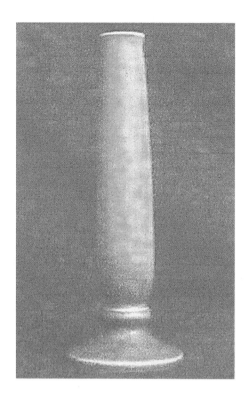

Florane - Circa 1920

Shapes of this pattern used the old Rosecraft molds: undecorated, no piping, small handles and rolled rims. Bases are dark brown or dark green, almost black, blended into a terra cotta. On the bowls, the darker section was usually around the rim, not the base. Matt glazed and marked with an Rv.

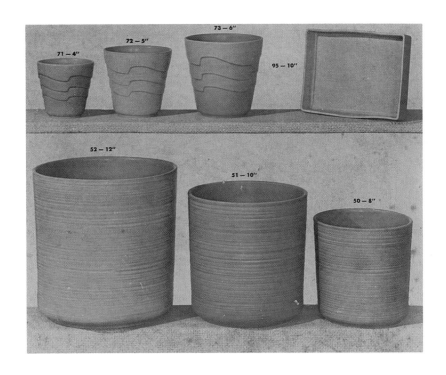

Compliments of the George Krause collection

Florane II (Etruscan) - Circa July 1949

A reproduction of the earlier Florane line of the 1920's. This design shows the free flowing shapes to capture the contemporary style of the 1950's ranging from planters to cornucopias. The basic colors of tan, green, and blue were used with a brighter color on the inner liner to provide contrast. Often referred to as the Etruscan Line. These catalog pages display 24 shapes of which only one, the candlestick was used in Florane I. This free style was characteristic of this contemporary period. Several size fluted vases (9", 12" and 14") were available. Three large sand jars were produced in this line for the first time. The pattern had no fancy designs or blending of colors and came in a plain matt glaze. Marked in relief with an R or Roseville and a style number.

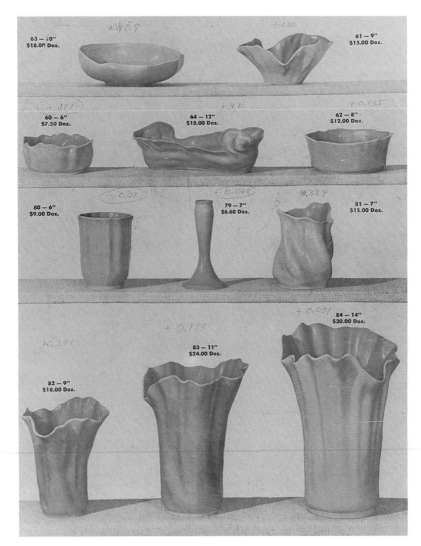

Compliments of the Ohio Historical Society

Floor Vases - Turn of the Century

Many different patterns of floor vases were produced around this time. They were designed as a vase, not an umbrella stand, with tapered sides, small necks, expanded bottoms or bases, and ranged in sizes from 20" to 30". Even the Rozane line had several. After Rozane, there came a flood of embossed designs with a matt glaze and even several high gloss glazes. Many were hand painted and artist signed only. Florals and forest scenes were the most popular. Most of the designs were numbered on the plates but were unmarked when produced.

142

Compliments of the Ohio Historical Society

Compliments of the Ohio Historical Society

Florentine I - Circa 1924

Very similar to the pattern "Panel". It was the most popular line of its time, second only to the Donatello Line. Designed in panels of rough mottled flowers separated by a draping cluster of berries and fruit on blue and green backgrounds. It came in white or ivory with light brown panels and green cluster, beige background with dark brown and green plus dark brown with beige and green clusters. This pattern was ink stamped Rv with a matt glaze. Catalog pages display over 70 styles of this line.

Compliments of the Ohio Historical Society

FLORENTINE

1062 - 4"
6 - 4"
339 - 5"
602 - 6"
602 - 5"
130 - 4"
322 - 8"
321 - 7"
1238 - 7"
126 - 7"
231 - 8"
255 - 8"
252 - 6"
233 - 10"
232 - 10"
234 - 12"
763 - 20"
602 - 9

Compliments of the Ohio Historical Society

Florentine II - Circa 1940

    Although similar in design to Florentine I, there were several major differences. Florentine I was a very successful line and Roseville hoped this new line would re-capture the previous success. The backgrounds were much lighter than Florentine I and had less decorations. The brown and green clusters were not used to separate the panels. There were also less decorations on the rim of each base. It is believed to have been manufactured for commercial use since there was less emphases on the smaller shapes. Marked with a raised Roseville U.S.A. in a satin matt finish.

Compliments of the Len and Terry Senior collection

Forest (Vista) - Circa 1920

This pattern has been described as an earth tone body with raised forest scenes, but very little additional information is mentioned in the old records. Visually it is described as a cluster of large green trees encompassing the vessel. The trees are rooted in water appearing at the bottom and travel upward toward the top of each piece. Highlighting the large green mass of leaves are a red or lavender flower or berry hidden among the leaves. The background is usually a gray wash but a few blue pieces have been found. The unique shaped vases have small blocks of clay attached almost as a second thought while the baskets have tall slender shaped handles. A satin matt glaze was used and most pieces have been found unmarked. A few have been found with an ink Rv. Several publications have not listed Forest as a pattern but picked up on a description as a vista surrounding both sides. All records indicate Vista and Forest to be one in the same pattern.

Note: This is a unique line in which every piece must be evaluated on several important factors: the success of the firing, glaze application and the artistry work. Each of these denotes the real value of each piece.

Compliments of the Charolotte Buchanan collection

Forget-Me-Not - Circa 1915

A pattern of creamware showing tiny blue and lavender flowers with green leaves encircling the piece. Gold trim was used to edge most of the line which included a dresser set, pitcher, teapot, sugar, creamer and candlesticks. Mostly glazed with a matt to shiny finish and unmarked.

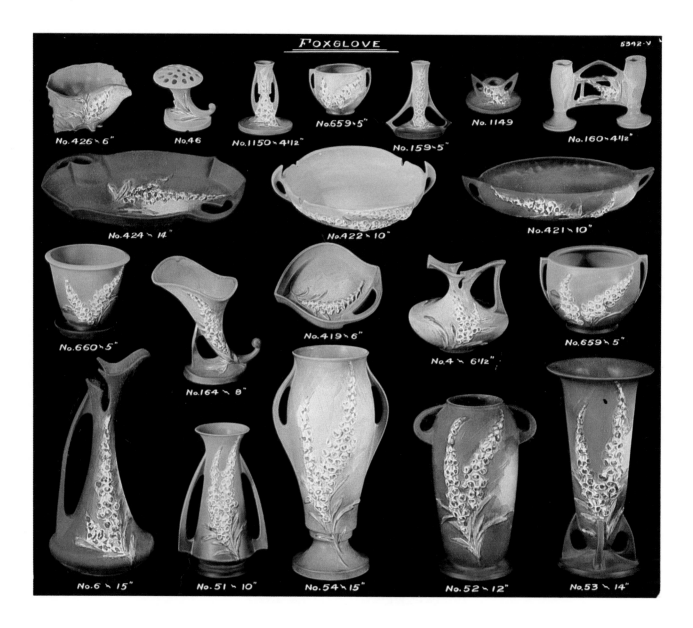

Compliments of the George Krause collection

Foxglove - Circa January 1942

A natural pattern of tall stocks of white or pink foxglove in deep relief climbing through a cluster of long green leaves on a smooth matt finish. Pale blue blending into a dark blue or black at the base, soft forest green shading to pink and light pink highlighted into tan or brown were used. Several styles had flared lips and curved struts as stabilizers, while most handles are pointed and baskets had large open handles. Flat bases are the norm in this pattern. The catalog pages show over 50 styles, but there are additional styles not displayed. Most of the pottery is marked with a raised "Roseville U.S.A." and the style number.

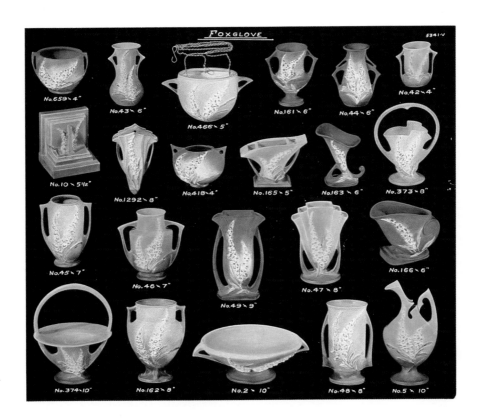

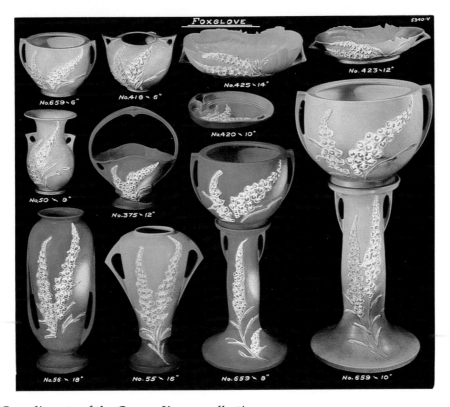

Compliments of the George Krause collection

151

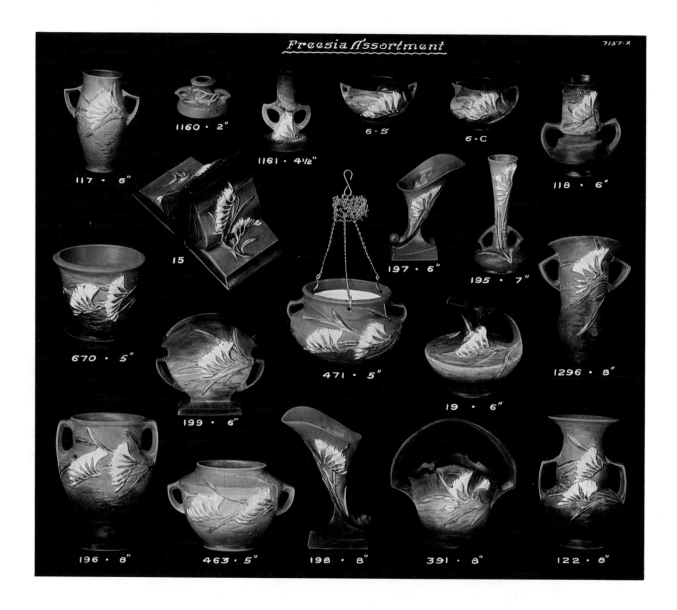

Compliments of the George Krause collection

Freesia - Circa January 1945

A floral cluster of trumpet shaped white, yellow and lavender Freesia climbing across and up each shape. Long stems and long slender leaves protrude from under and around each flower with patches of ivory indentations highlighting each shape. Pattern basically came in three different colors; tropical green blending to a dark green, sky blue to an almost blue or royal blue, and terra cotta to a dark brown. The darker colors usually highlight the base, rim, lid or handle. The background and handle are done in a similar matt glaze. Although the Roseville catalog pages display over 45 different styles, most of these are not original to this line. Many of the styles are common with the garden line. Marked with the impressed "Roseville U.S.A." and style numbers.

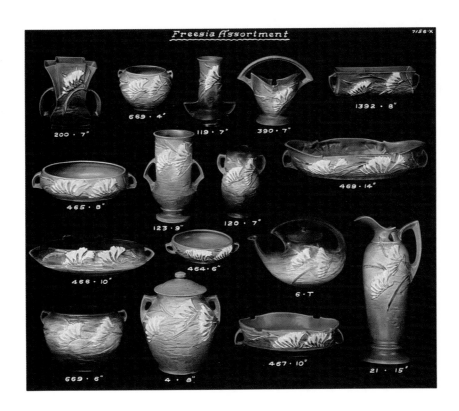

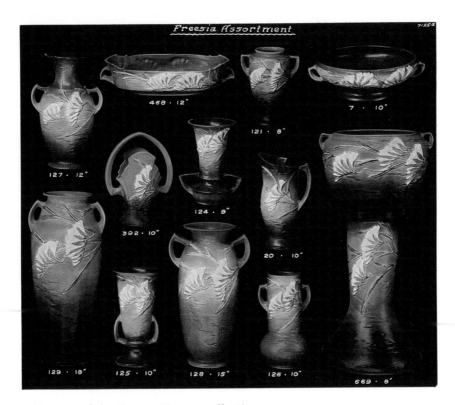

Compliments of the George Krause collection

Fuchsia - Circa July 1938

A mottled background of pink, white and yellow fuchsia blossoms dangling from branches with wide round leaves. A cascade appearance is significant in the background of these arrangements. The background colors seem to fade in and out. The blue fades into a white or yellow, green fades into a terra cotta, and terra cotta fades into a pale yellow. Most of the styles are traditional with one unique difference, the handles are wider than normal and rounded. The catalog pages display 39 different styles all in a satin matt glaze. Marked with an impressed "Roseville" and style number.

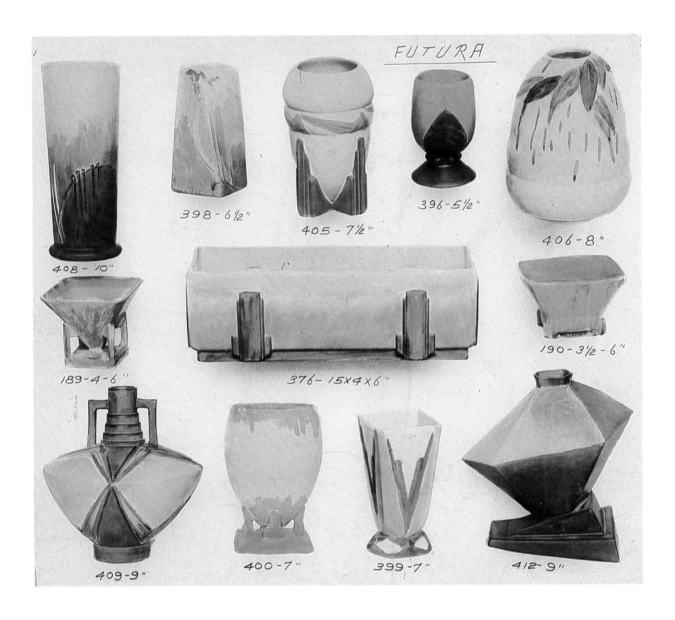

FUTURA

398 - 6½"

405 - 7½"

396 - 5½"

406 - 8"

408 - 10"

189-4-6"

376 - 15x4x6"

190-3½-6"

409-9"

400-7"

399-7"

412-9"

Compliments of the Ohio Historical Society

Futura - Circa 1924

   A step into the future. A design of things to come. Very creative and open minded shapes from the Roseville craftsman. Round, square, oblong and angular shapes with melting and blending of colors were common in this design. These patterns would fit into the Modern Times, The Art Deco Period, and even the past. Mostly unmarked or marked with a paper label and covered with a matt or high gloss glaze. Over 75 styles are shown on the catalog pages but remember any shape was possible. More and more shapes have been discovered.

Compliments of the Ohio Historical Society

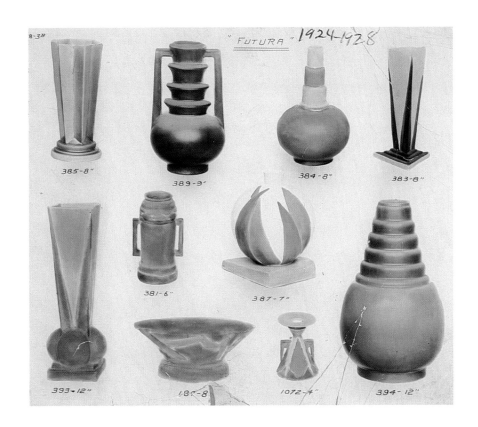

Compliments of the Ohio Historical Society

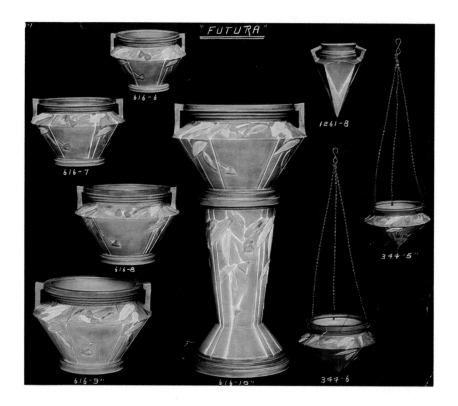

Compliments of the Ohio Historical Society

Compliments of the Ohio Historical Society

Garden Line - Turn of the Century

One of the first lines for Roseville. Produced in molds with a rough clay look and were often unglazed. The Roseville catalog pages show bird baths, urns, jardinieres, and assorted designed flower pots. Basically, plain looking with limited embossing or ribbon styles. Some fluting was common. A large variety of sizes were available both in bird baths and pots. A hard to identify line since nothing was marked. Later designs were in more detail, brighter colors and different glazes. Some were even hand painted but were also unmarked.

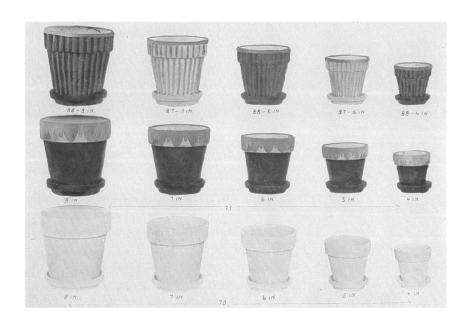

Compliments of the Ohio Historical Society

Compliments of the George Krause collection

Gardenia - Circa January 1950

These smooth lines are highlighted by a large open white gardenia which is suspended from branches and pointed green leaves on a band that wraps completely around the shape. The handles are of a rounded nature with a darkening of colors to highlight them and the base. They came in colors of silver haze gray, golden tan, and seafoam green. They were produced in a matt glaze and marked with an impressed "Roseville U.S.A." and style number.

Compliments of the George Krause collection

Compliments of the Ohio Historical Society

German Cooking Ware - Circa 1902

First oven proof cookware made by Roseville. A total of 30 pieces were included in this line; two cocortes 3" and 3 1/2" (included baker) with handles, two bowls 5" and 6", four pudding dishes 3 1/2"- 4 1/2" - 5 1/2" and 6 1/2", deep pudding dish, bowl, shirred egg dish, pie pan, casserole, covered casserole with lid, two deep bakers, egg cocortes, custard dish, cream pitcher, water pitcher, teapot with lid, and coffee pot with lid. They were produced in the Victorian style with little trim only a brief border and came in a soft green or red tint with a bright cream liner.

Believed also, to have been produced in several other colors. The handles on the coffee pot, teapot and two pitchers had a knob at the top and another more than half way down the handle. They were produced in a very bright high gloss glaze finish and were all unmarked.

This line was mass produced for a Chicago company called the Romafin Pottery Company. It offered a 21 piece starter set for $3.50. For a limited time, they would also pay shipping to anywhere in the U.S. For .10¢, a customer would receive a custard cup or a cocorte to inspect before purchasing the complete set.

Compliments of the Ohio Historical Society

German Farm Ware - Before the Turn of the Century

Not to be confused with the German Cooking Ware of 1902, in fact, a complete opposite. This design was a simple shape with handles and a high gloss salt glaze. It came in a variety of kitchen ware; pitchers, coffee and teapots, butter dishes, oatmeal sets and preserve canning and fruit jars. The coffee and teapots were highly decorated, on a light background and decorated with gold lettering - personalized from the giver to a person as a gift. The canning and fruit jars were plain in design but came in cream as well as split in cream and brown. These canning jars were reusable and were sealed with hot wax to preserve the product. They were unmarked.

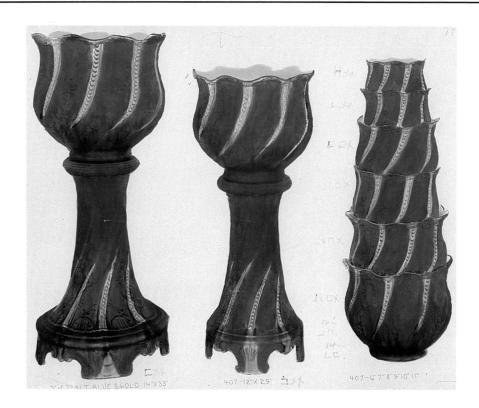

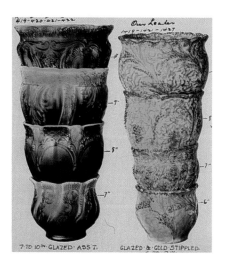

Compliments of the Ohio Historical Society

Glaze - Turn of the Century

This is the description given to a line of jardinieres and pedestals that were produced in late 1890. Both pieces were heavily embossed. The jardiniere had uneven lips around the rim. The pedestals were on feet and had ribbons of flowers and birds encompassing the pattern. Gold tints were added to the glaze to give it a rich elegant look. Animal heads or clusters of flowers with a blending of colors and designs highlighted this pattern. Many of the jardinieres had a French decor look while others were more of a colonial design. All were unmarked.

Compliments of the Ohio Historical Society

Compliments of the Ohio Historical Society

Gold Traced - Circa Early Teens

A line of early ivory candlesticks, spittoons, wall pockets and planters with very little decoration. The simple design used gold lines with black piping. The top of the candlesticks were flat and sprayed with gold traces, while wall pockets and spittoons had gold trim around the rim. Most of the line is unmarked and has a matt glaze finish. There has been one candlestick found marked Roseville Pottery Co., Zanesville, O in a circle.

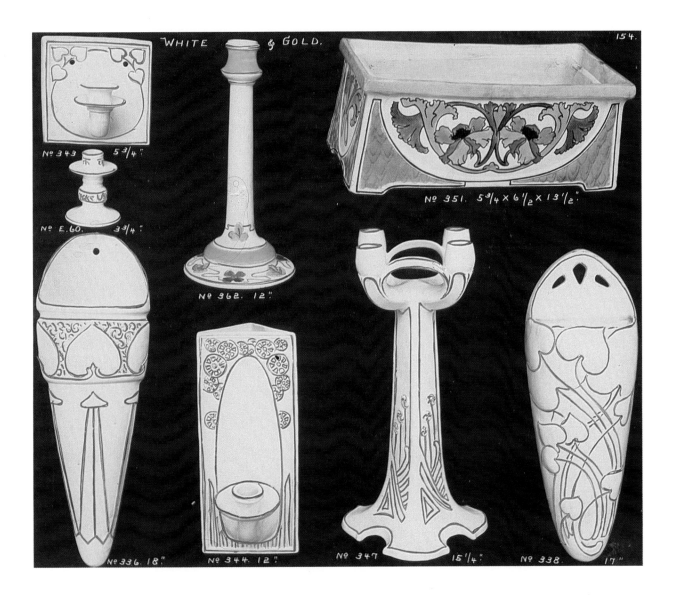

Compliments of the Ohio Historical Society

Gold & White Traced - Circa Early Teens

    This pattern has a more ceramic appearance with more detail than the Gold Traced line. Generously decorated in a multitude of colors with gold and silver lines surrounding flowers or fern like designs. The line is similar to Persian, unmarked and has a satin or shiny glaze. This style was used on a wide variety of candlesticks, wall pockets, planters, wall plaques, and hanging baskets.

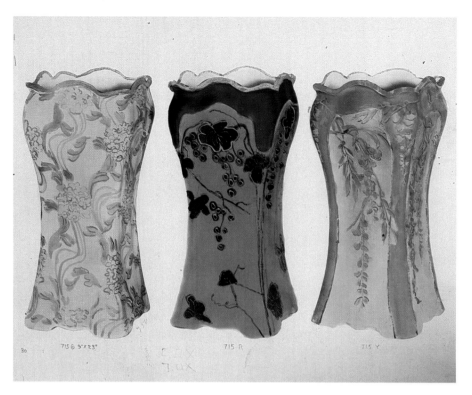

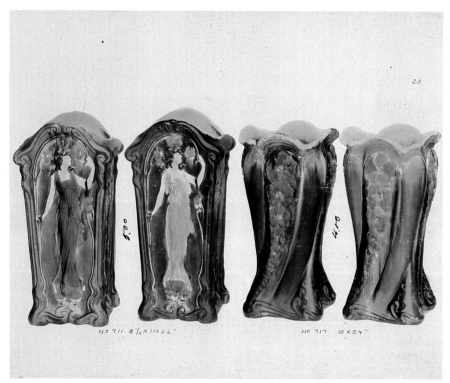

Compliments of the Ohio Historical Society

Gold and Silver Decorated - Circa 1910

A line of decorated umbrella stands that had floral designs hand painted in gold and silver, which added a rich appearance to the common household item. Usually they had a solid background color of tan, olive green, or dark blue. Designs ran the entire length of the style with decorations wrapping totally around or covering both sides of the stand. Uneven rims and bases were the norm. This line was endless in patterns, as new styles came out, gold and silver were tried. All are unmarked.

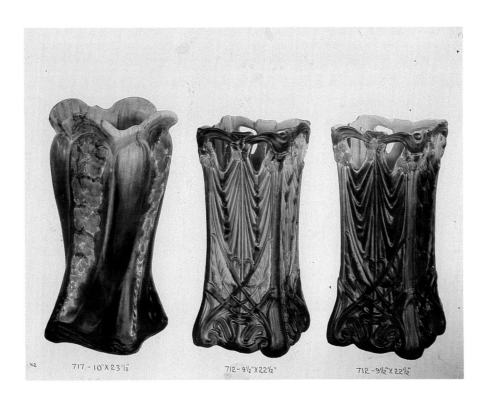

42   717 - 10"X 23½"   712 - 9½"X 22½"   712 - 9½"X 22½"

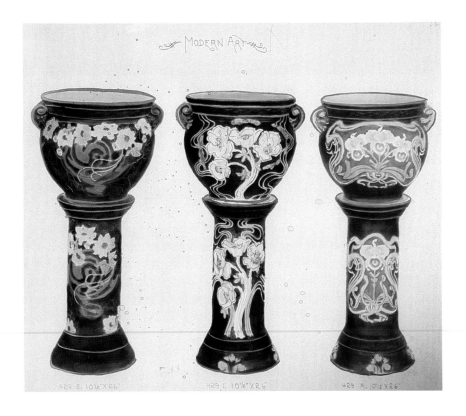

MODERN ART

429 B. 10½"X R6"   429 E. 10½"X R 6   429 R. 10½"X R6

Compliments of the Ohio Historical Society

Compliments of the Steve Schnock collection

Good Night Candlesticks - Circa 1910's

According to Roseville records another line of creamware was started in the teens referred to as "Candlesticks". One example is a candle holder encircled halfway with a shield to reflect the light of the candle and a handle with which to carry it. The decal of a child going to bed is on the inside of the reflector with dark piping around the edge of the creamware. Vines of climbing leaves enhance the front and side of the piece. A matt glaze encompasses the candle holder and no mark is found for identification. Other styles of the creamware line do have similar candle holders.

Compliments of the Ohio Historical Society

Green - Circa 1910

A line of heavily embossed designs of "Victorian" style cuspidors, umbrella stands, jardinieres and pedestals. This term was used several times in the Roseville catalog pages to describe those items which the predominant color was green. It was unmarked and covered with a shiny glaze. Wide lip edges were also predominant at this time. Fancy handles helped to give this line that "Victorian" appearance. Often mistaken for the Matt Green Line.

Compliments of the Ohio Historical Society

Holland - Before 1900

A very popular pattern of colorful Holland painted figures of men in a variety of different scenes. The paintings were all hand done. They were produced on a natural or oatmeal background with a green or gray band at the top and bottom in a high gloss glaze. A variety of cups, pitchers, tobacco jars, and toilet set complete this line. All are unmarked.

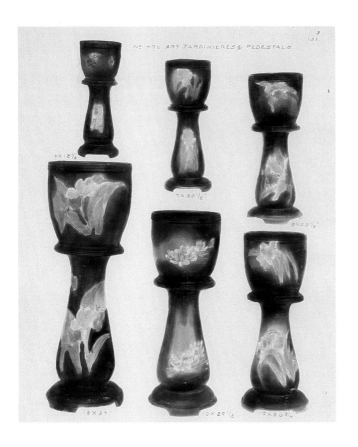

Compliments of the Ohio Historical Society

Home Art - Circa 1908

Believed to be a do-it-yourself or customize your own pottery line which featured oversized floral designs. Many different flowers with stems and leaves were produced in decal forms. The individual would purchase the basic pottery; a jardiniere and pedestal in seven or more shapes and sizes, large jardiniere, umbrella stand and/or even a 3" flower pot. Once a choice was made, the individual could select from a large variety of the flower decals which would best suit their home decor. The factory would charge a fee to apply the decals or the individual could do it at home. The shapes had a shiny glaze and came in brown only. All are unmarked.

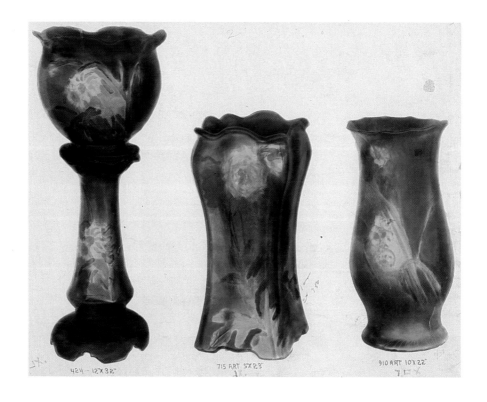

Compliments of the Ohio Historical Society

Hyde Park - Circa late 1940 to 1954

The Hyde Park Company was one of several companies for which Roseville manufactured products. Roseville produced the pottery and impressed the name "The Hyde Park" and a style number or year on the bottom. This company then sold and distributed the line of ashtrays and cigarette boxes. Most of the line was tailored to individuals, companies, or organizations by attaching a metal disk. Initials were used for the individuals last name. Colors varied from bright red with black shading, yellow and green speckled, gray, green and yellow shaded around the edges, solid black, orange or any color requested. "The Hyde Park" Company apparently sold these to companies or organizations in large bulk quantities to be used as awards. One such was presented 2 years after the close of the Roseville plant. The disk, a special campaign award, read "Combined Jewish Appeal of Greater Boston" 1956. Very little is known about the "Hyde Park" Company after the close of Roseville.

Compliments of the Ohio Historical Society

Ideal Pitchers - Circa 1920's

This was the first line of pitchers produced by Roseville. As the name implies, there was a pitcher for every purpose. The sizes varied from a 5oz. to an almost two gallon and came in a solid pink, green and ivory with gold piping. Also, it came in two tone pitchers with gold bands dividing the colors. All were unmarked.

"IMPERIAL" 424-12" X 32"

"IMPERIAL" 444-8"-9"-10"-12"

Compliments of the Ohio Historical Society

Imperial - Circa 1905

First produced around 1905 as a decorated design to enhance an oriental motif. It was designed with a circle of stars surrounding a Lion standing on its hind legs. Similar to other designs, as an example, the Fleur de Luer. The pattern came in jardinieres and pedestals, as well as, a variety of jardiniere sizes. Some had handles, while others had scalloped feet or rims, possibly both. They were produced in assorted colors of solid royal blue and dark green with gold like figurals and designs. All were unmarked.

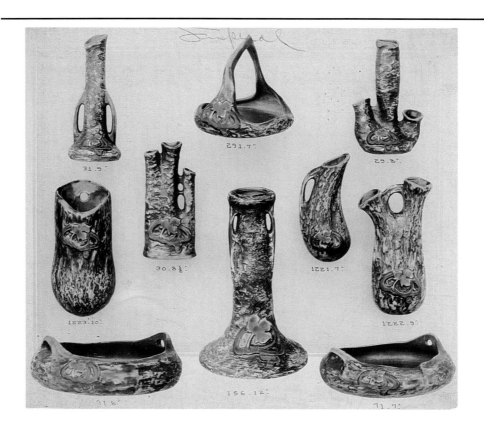

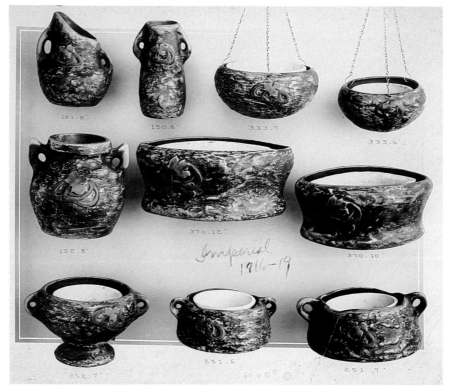

Compliments of the Ohio Historical Society

Imperial I - Circa 1916-1919

A tree bark design with a pretzel appearing vine in the middle of a large green leaf and a small cluster of blue berries give this design a unique pattern. The rough wood appearance is blended with green, brown and beige. The lips and handles are rounded, even the baskets have rounded handles. Pieces were manufactured in a satin finish and are unmarked. Thirty different styles are pictured in the Roseville catalog pages, but at least that many more have been found.

Compliments of the Ohio Historical Society

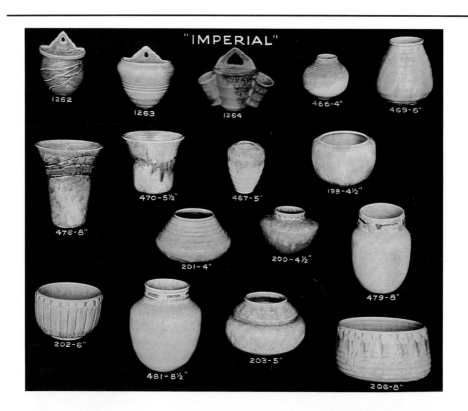

Compliments of the George Krause collection

Imperial II - Circa 1924

This pattern was a textured matt or satin glaze over a wide variety of shapes. It came in an assortment of blending and dripping glazes over running each other and forming a crystallization around the rims and into the lining. Other pieces are smoothly designed with a glossy glaze. Several shapes had a band of small flowers around the rim, while others had a ring completely around the shape. A wide variety of color combinations, plus a blending of light and dark colors were included. The line is mostly unmarked but several have been found with a black paper label. The Roseville catalog shows 33 different shapes.

INDIAN N° 1. TANKARD SET. A. FINISH.   INDIAN N° 1. TANKARD SET. B. FINISH.

Compliments of the Ohio Historical Society

Indian - Circa early Teens

Brightly colored decals of Indian chiefs and warriors were shown on smooth ivory creamware. The catalog pages show only one page of Indians, two large 10 1/2" tankers and six different 5" mugs.

Other Indian decals have been found on the same size tankers and mugs. The shapes were the same as the Dutch Line, even as far as blue piping around the rim to add that finished look. A clear matt glaze protected the decals. All are unmarked.

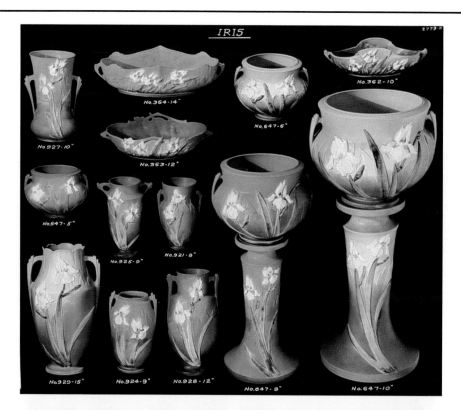

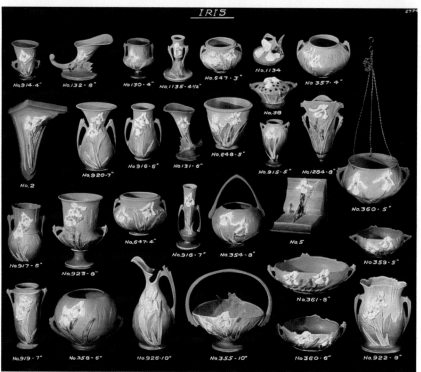

Compliments of the George Krause collection

Iris - Circa January 1939

    A natural looking iris flower embossed on traditional shapes. The large flower had either white or yellow blossoms with pale green stems and leaves. It came in three basic color combinations of a pale pink shading into a pale green; a light blue shading to a darker blue; and a soft yellow shading to a brown. The leaves that are attached to the iris blossom are green, but there are traces of leaves blending into the colored background. The shapes are reused molds from other earlier lines, as an example: the Thornapple. They were impressed with "Roseville" and a shape number and were glazed in a satin matt finish. Approximately 43 styles known

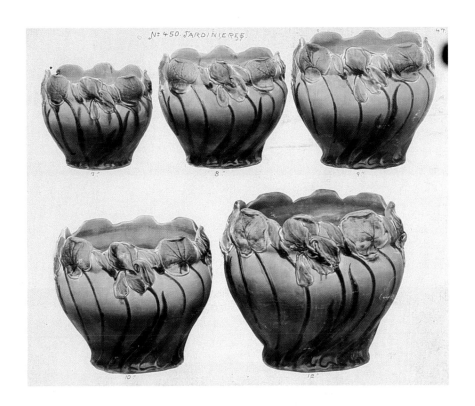

Compliments of the Ohio Historical Society

Iris - Turn of the Century

A line of jardiniere and pedestal with large embossed iris blossoms extending above the rim to form scalloped edges. The blossoms are suspended by a long stem and pointed leaves. Leaves and stems were a brown/green while the background came in red, blue, green, brown or orange in a matt glaze. Several jardinieres and pedestals were made in this iris pattern. In the Roseville catalog pages a 12" x 36" jardiniere and pedestal is displayed plus five different size jardiniere ranging from 7" to 12". The iris pattern has been reproduced on different style jardinieres.

Compliments of the Ohio Historical Society

Ivory (Old) - Circa 1910

Often referred to as Old Ivory and very unlike the Ivory Tint of 1912. Most of this line is solid ivory, with no wash or accent colors to show off the heavy embossed ivory. Ivory was used mainly on planters, wall pockets, spittoons and jardinieres. It came in matt to shiny glaze and was seldom marked. Several planters have been found with paper stickers.

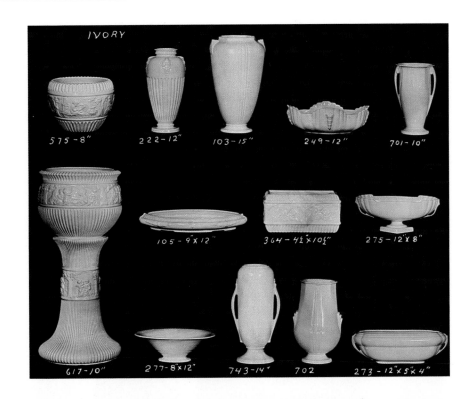

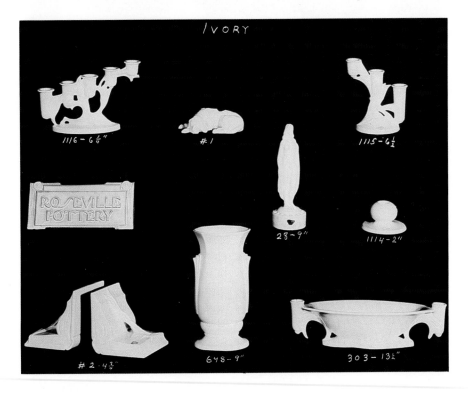

Compliments of the George Krause collection.

Ivory - Circa 1933

This pattern used many of the old molds from earlier designs, such as Donatello, Carnelian I, Savona, Topeo, Florentine, Foxglove, Orian, Russo and Luffa. Included in this design was a nude figurine and a small dog. Roseville continued its production into the late forties. Some styles were glazed with a matt finish, while others had a high gloss glaze. They were marked with stickers, or an impressed Roseville. The styles that were made from other lines will demand considerably less retail than the original pattern.

Compliments of the George Krause collection

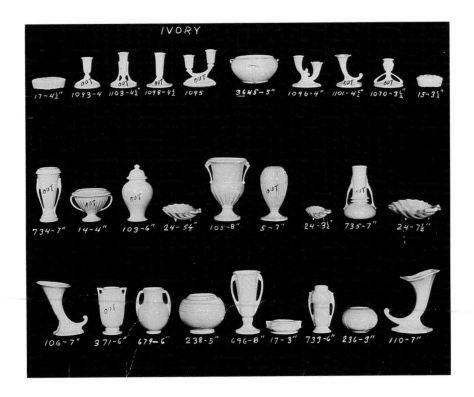

Compliments of the George Krause collection

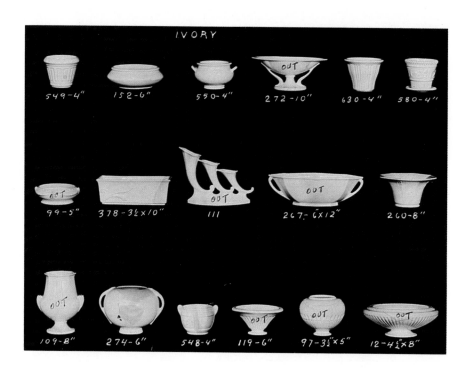

Compliments of the George Krause collection

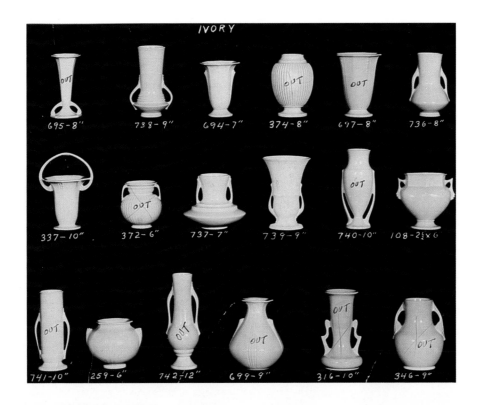

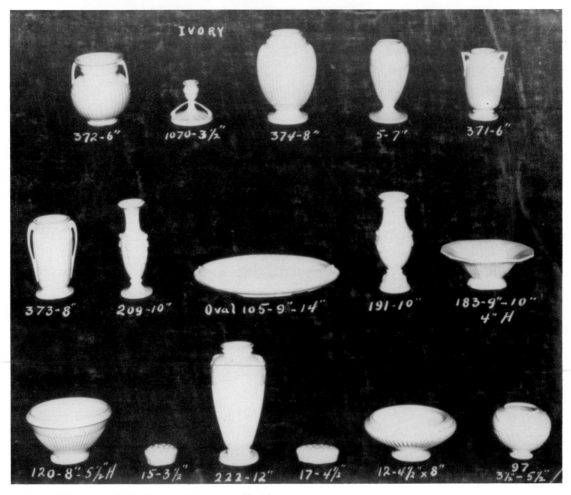

Compliments of the George Krause collection.

191

Tea Set No. 4.

228.

Compliments of the Ohio Historical Society

Ivory Tint - Circa 1912-1914

A creamware line with deep embossed designs on such items as wall pockets, planters, tankards, mugs, smoker sets, and jardinieres. The pieces had an ivory background with what looks like a wash of green, blue, yellow or pink. The colors accent the embossed design. Many of the old styles were used again. A matt glaze was applied to those items and like most of the old designs, there were no marks.

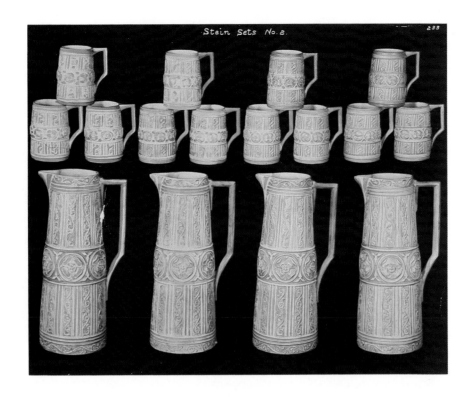

Compliments of the Ohio Historical Society

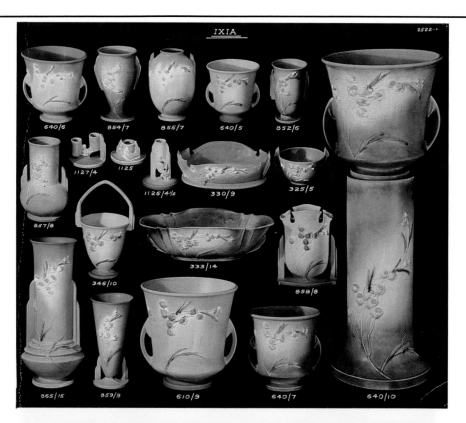

Compliments of the George Krause collection

Ixia - Circa July 1937

Ixia design boasts a tiny upright bell shaped Ixia flower embossed on a soft light color background. A white flower on a pale pink background shades to darker pink and blends at the base into an almost green; lavender flower on a white/green shade to a darker green and blends to a dark almost black base and a lavender flower on a pink/tan shade to a light tan and blends to a red/brown base. A matt glaze was used and the line was marked with an impressed "Roseville" and style number. The catalog shows 38 different styles.

Compliments of the Robert Bettinger collection

Jeanette - Circa 1915

A part of the creamware line with decals or overlays of a woman dressed in formal attire. A matt to high gloss glaze was applied over the decal. The few found were unmarked and were on blank Olympic shapes. A rare find.

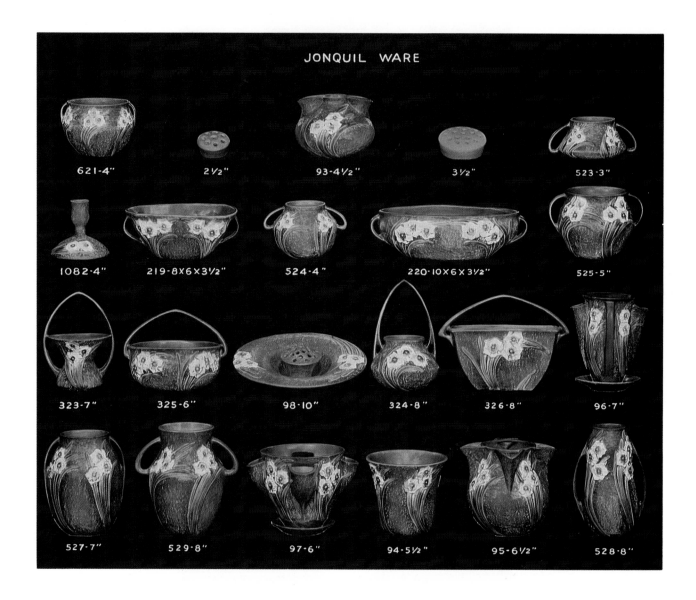

JONQUIL WARE

621-4" 2½" 93-4½" 3½" 523-3"

1082-4" 219-8X6X3½" 524-4" 220-10X6X3½" 525-5"

323-7" 325-6" 98-10" 324-8" 326-8" 96-7"

527-7" 529-8" 97-6" 94-5½" 95-6½" 528-8"

Compliments of the Ohio Historical Society

Jonquil - Circa 1931

    A bunch of three Jonquil flowers with yellow centers embossed above tall green leaves on a mottled light brown background, with darker brown shading around the flowers, rims and handles. The darker brown tends to fade into the lining. These pieces were glazed with a matt to satin finish. Free flowing handles and large pointed handles on all the baskets were common in this line. Either unmarked or when lucky enough to find, marked with a paper label. Forty-one different styles are shown on the catalog pages.

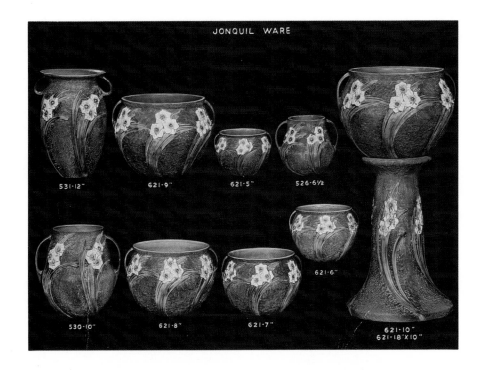

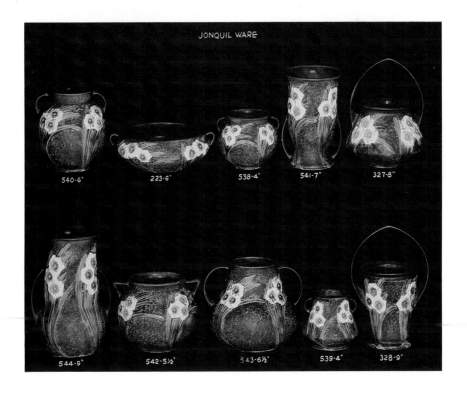

Compliments of the Ohio Historical Society

Compliments of the Ohio Historical Society

Juvenile Ware - Circa before 1916

Various decals decorated a light background with a colored band around every shape. Juvenile I was considered to have a matt glaze while Juvenile II had a shiny glaze. Most of the line was unmarked although several designs are marked with a small Rv stamp. Came in a wide variety of shapes and different size plates, cereal bowl, cup, egg cup, mug, sugar and creamer, milk pitcher, teapot, custard cup, pudding dish, and even a chamber pot. Also, it came in a variety of designs; chick, bunny, duck, pig, dancing cat, sitting dog, sunbonnet girl, bear, rooster, dancing bear, and considered to be the most sought after, a Santa Clause. The plates were in different shapes and sizes; flat and round edge, and were 6"-7" and 81/2" wide. The Roseville catalog pages show over 75 different designs, shapes and sets.

Compliments of the Ohio Historical Society

Compliments of the Ohio Historical Society

ROSEVILLE POTTERY 'NC.
ZANESVILLE, OHIO

No. 1 JUVENILE SET

Three Piece Set Contains:

No. 1 — 3" **Mug** — Blue band with Duck decoration

No. 2 — 6" **Bowl** — Pink band with Dog decoration

No. 3 — 7" **Plate** — Green band with Rabbit decoration

Packed in attractive gift box

WHOLESALE PRICE

$2.50 PER SET
(Box Included)

F.O.B. Zanesville

749

Kettle and Skillet Set - Circa late 1940's

One of the hardest to find and to identify products manufactured by Roseville. It originally came in a cardboard box marked "Roseville Pottery, Inc., Zanesville, Ohio" on one side and Kettle and Skillet Set packaged by "H. Bettes Co." This is believed to have been produced in the 40's but other wise unmarked except for numbers. The set consisted of a glazed 2" x 5" bowl, a skillet ashtray and an oven glazed bean pot. It came in a choice of white, blue or black. Both the bowl and bean pot were footed. Little else is known about this venture by Roseville.

GENUINE ROSEVILLE POTTERY TABLE LAMPS

Flexo PRODUCTS CORPORATION

7001

7009

7007

7003

Height Approx. 19" to 21"
Colors - Rust, Rose, Green & Blue
Note: Furnished with either hand
painted or fabric covered pleated
shades.

7005

7011

Compliments of the Ohio Historical Society

Lamps

Although the catalog pages display the same pattern lamps with different design shades, there were countless different designs and patterns produced. It seems that many special shapes and patterns were produced just for the lamps. They were made with both a matt and a shiny glaze. All color combinations were produced. Flexo Products Corporation was the main company that sold the Roseville lamp. Some were marked only with a number, some with a paper sticker, but most were unmarked.

Landscape - Early Teens

This was a limited line of creamware decorated with decals of a sailboat, windmill or a stream running through the forest on an ivory background. The decals were in light brown or blue. Available only in two sugar, creamer and teapot sets and in a large coffee and chocolate pots. Unmarked and decorated with a matt glaze. Around 1910, several other styles of planters were decorated with the Landscape decal. Both the earlier and later line used piping to emphasize the rim.

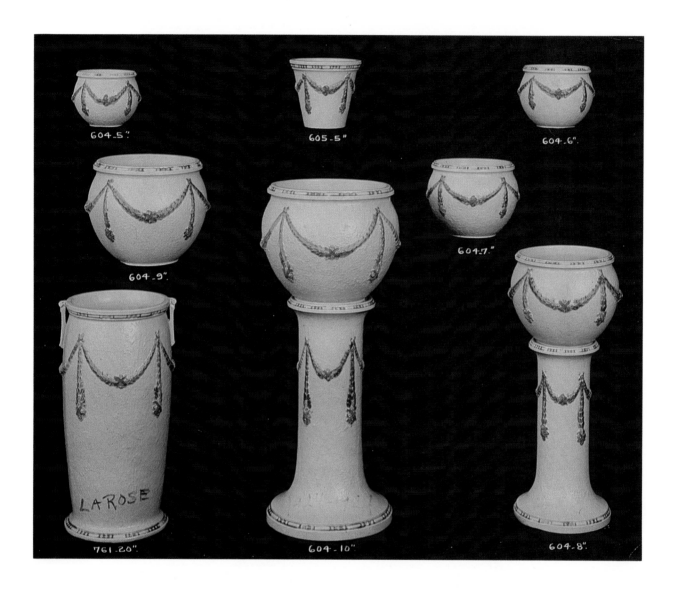

604-5"
605-5"
604-6"
604-9"
604-7"
761-20"   LAROSE
604-10"
604-8"

Compliments of the Ohio Historical Society

LaRose - Circa 1924

A cream colored line, with the rim evenly marked with groups of green dots separated by small blank spaces. The garland completely surrounds the shape. A ribbon drapes along the rim and is marked evenly with miniature green leaves and small clusters of tiny pink roses. Most of the line is ink stamped Rv but many are unmarked. Traditional shapes express the French influence and very small handles are common. There are over 35 known shapes, all are a matt finish.

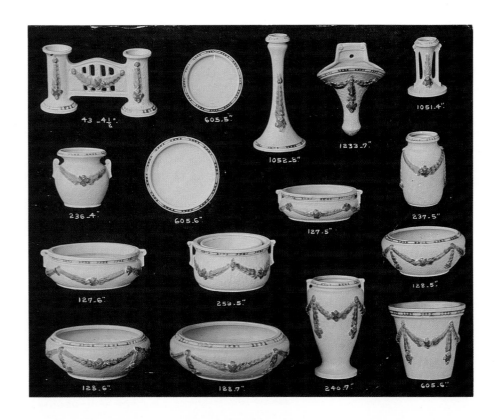

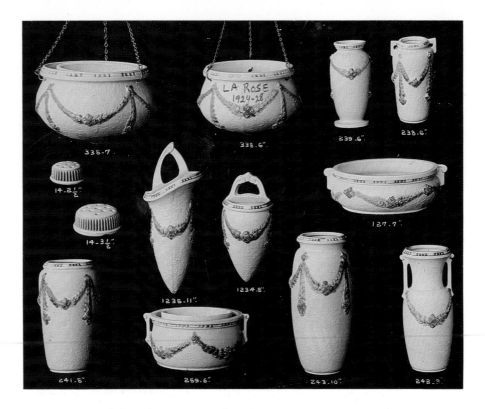

Compliments of the Ohio Historical Society

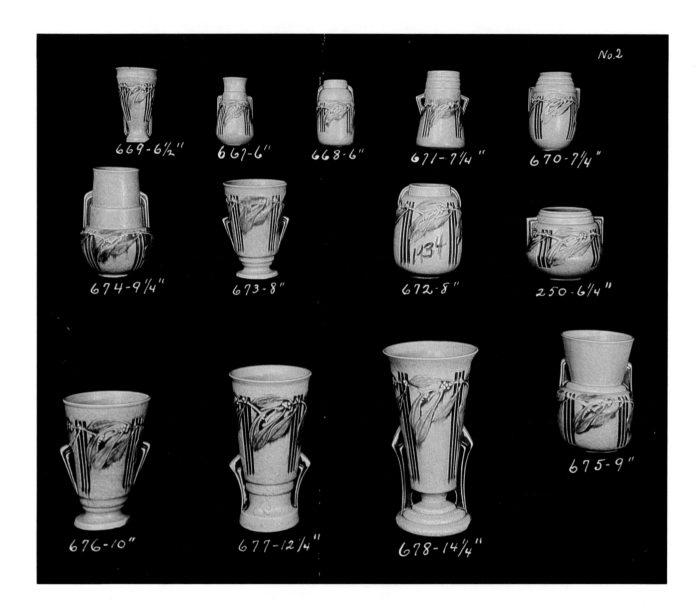

No.2

669-6½"   667-6"   668-6"   671-7¼"   670-7¼"

674-9¼"   673-8"   672-8"   250-6¼"

676-10"   677-12¼"   678-14¼"   675-9"

Compliments of the Ohio Historical Society

Laurel - Circa January 1934

Long laurel with berries embossed in a smooth textured background are featured on this design. The leaves seem to drape completely around the style. They are a darker shade of the major background color, while a lighter pale green/white is shown directly behind the leaves on the green background. The leaves are a slightly darker tone on the terra cotta and yellow/gold backgrounds. Evenly spaced panels of three vertical black or white ribs accent the display of laurel leaves. The handles are all closed and the line is marked with paper labels or a blue carbon "R" and came in a semi-matt glaze. Only 13 different styles are shown.

Compliments of the Ohio Historical Society

Lemonade Sets - Circa early 1900's

Listed in the Roseville catalog pages as "Conventional - Lemonade Sets". These sets consisted of a large pitcher and four to six mugs. It was a very simple creamware line which used decals and assorted light toned colors or ivory. Typical of the creamware lines, a darker color piping was used to accent the rim, spout and base. Only two different patterns are shown, but there are unlimited possibilities of other designs. A matt or high gloss glaze was used and all pieces were unmarked.

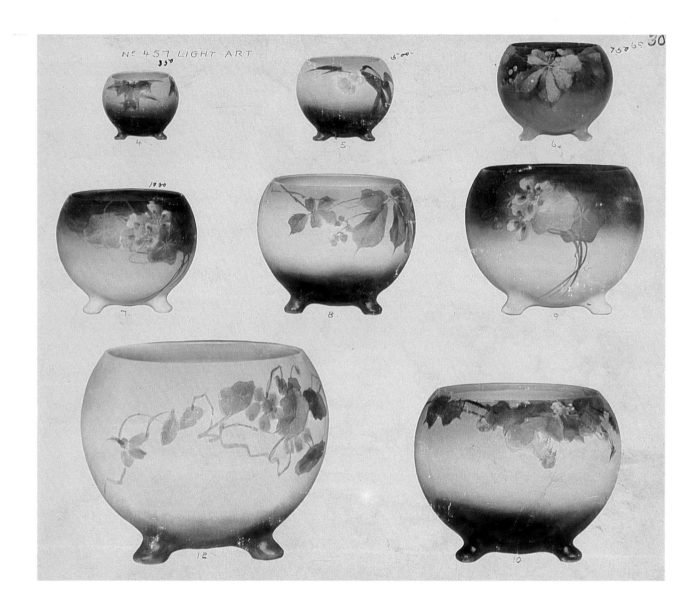

Compliments of the Ohio Historical Society

Light Art - Circa 1900

Produced around the turn of the century as a line of hand painted jardinieres. There are only nine different size footed jardinieres shown. The design was hand painted on a soft blended background - white, yellow, gray or blue. Many different combinations of florals and leaves were used. A soft matt or high gloss glaze was applied over the painted decorations.

Compliments of the Ohio Historical Society

Lodge Line - Circa Early Teens

Roseville never missed the opportunity to promote business. The utility creamware with piping around the rim was promoted for use by clubs and businesses. Mainly tankers, different style mugs, and ash trays were included in this line. They were decorated with brightly painted transfer patterns or decals, under a matt glaze. Some of these notable clubs or lodges were: Eagle . . . Moose . . . Osman Temple . . . Aladdin Patrols . . . Knights of the Pythias . . . etc. Like most of the creamware lines, they were unmarked.

Compliments of the Ohio Historical Society

Lombardy - Circa 1924

This line has its own characteristic, which consisted of rounded, convex, and fluted rim, three footed stand and a vertical ridge completely around the shape. The limited basic shapes are smoothly finished and came matt glazed. Thirteen styles are shown in this very small line. Solid colors of green, blue, and black have been found but any of the Roseville colors are possible.

L3 — 10" CYLINDRICAL VASE   L6 — 9" ROUND BOWL
L4 — 10"x8" SQUARE VASE   L7 — 10" OBLONG BOWL
L5 — 3" CANDLESTICK   L8 — 7" WALL POCKET
L9 — 4" SQUARE PLANTER

Compliments of the George Krause collection

Lotus - Circa October 1951

    Natural looking lotus flowers with folded petals preparing to open are featured in this line. This style is reproduced on several tall pieces giving them an elongated appearance. The details are accented by a contrasted color band around the rim and base. Believed to be the last flower line produced by Roseville. The high gloss glaze highlights the tight petal of the Lotus flower which came in a wide variety of colors; mulberry pink & red, powder blue & beige, forest green & chartreuse, and cocoa brown & yellow. Marked with its own trademark of a flowing capital L, which underlines the rest of the name Lotus in raised letters.

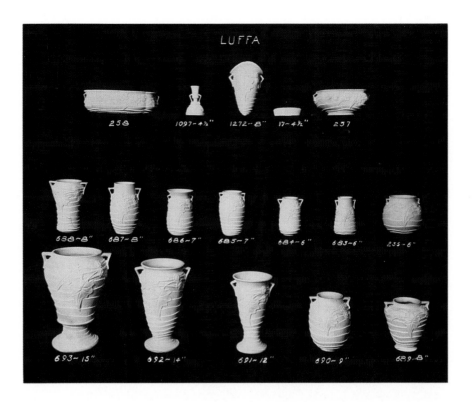

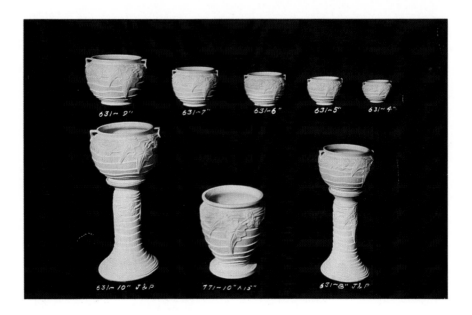

Compliments of the George Krause collection

Luffa - Circa July 1934

The best description of this pattern is a band of large pointed ivy-like leaves with a small ivory or yellow embossed flower encompassing a ridged background. It has a satin matt finish over a blending or shading of terra cotta, brown, blue and green. It came in a basic round style with small pointed handles. Several of the styles were borrowed from other earlier patterns.

Compliments of the Ohio Historical Society

Lustre - Circa 1921

A simple pattern of untrimmed shapes from an earlier line of Rosecraft which came in a shiny glaze of colors such as pale pink, blue, azure, yellow, and purple. This glaze gave the line a metallic luster appearance. All the baskets had thin pointed handles while the vases and bowls were basically round. Usually marked with a black paper label. There are approximately 60 different styles.

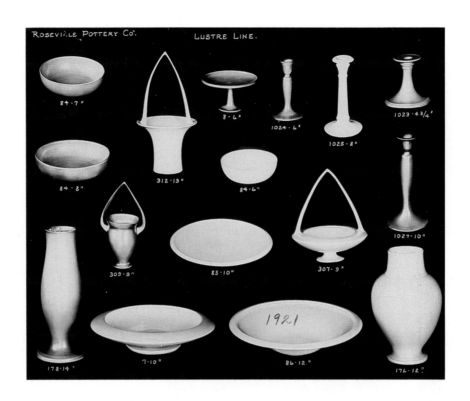

Compliments of the Ohio Historical Society

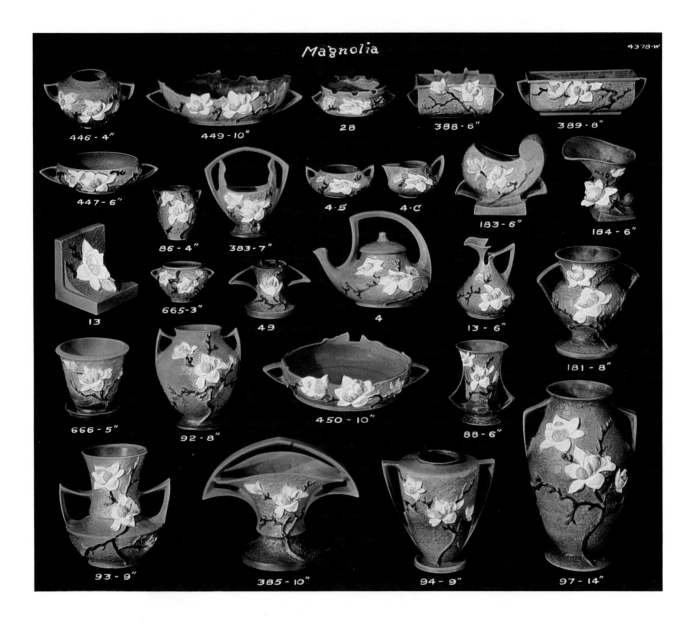

Compliments of the George Krause collection

Magnolia - Circa January 1943

Pattern shows an embossed massive white blossom on a rough background. The blossoms have rose centers. Some of the blossoms are not fully open. They are supported by wavy black twigs that wind throughout the pattern. The textured and soft background came in a blending of colors. The terra cotta is blended with green; the green is accented with terra cotta, and the blue is blended with a lighter blue. Each of the color combinations are highlighted by an almost black shaded section . . . usually around the base, handle or rim. Marked with a "Roseville" in relief and style number. The same molds were used before for other contemporary patterns. Over 60 different styles are shown on the catalog pages.

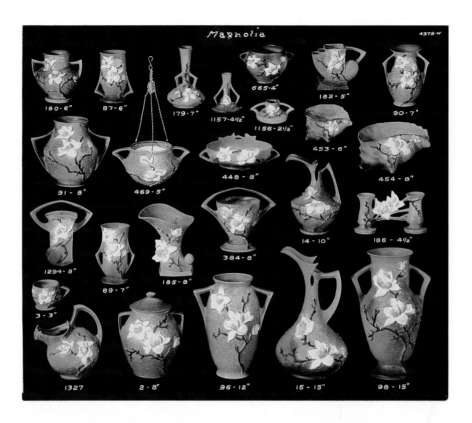

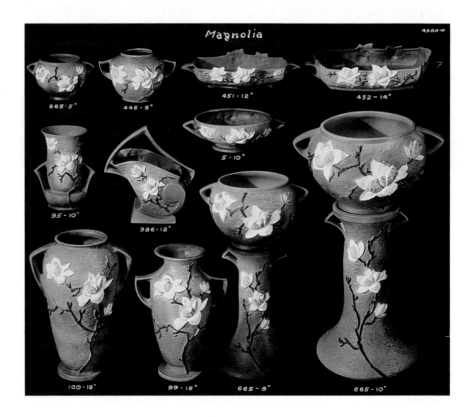

Compliments of the George Krause collection

609-6" 607-4" 236-3" 608-6"

548-4" 236-4" 624-4" 549-4"

625-5" 22 550-4" 364-5"

Compliments of the Ohio Historical Society

Matt Color - Circa 1920

A line of completely unrelated shapes and designs. Some have fluted sides, some are embossed, some have open handles while others were closed, some are trimmed, others are not. The one feature they all have in common is the solid color with a smooth satin matt finish. Usually marked with a black or silver paper label, if you find them marked at all. Catalog pages show 12 different styles.

Compliments of the Ohio Historical Society

Matt Green - Circa 1910

A line of heavy dark green matt glazed shapes which were often confused with the Egypto and Chloron. The Matt Green line has a darker green glaze than the other two patterns. Chloron has black pepper dots throughout its glaze. Egypto is more designed to resemble ancient pottery and Egyptian art. Still the easiest way to identify any of the three patterns is to refer to the Roseville catalog pages. There are over 100 styles pictured in these pages. Some pieces are heavily embossed, while others are untrimmed. If found marked, they should have a paper label or sticker.

Note: Pieces with liners add 25%

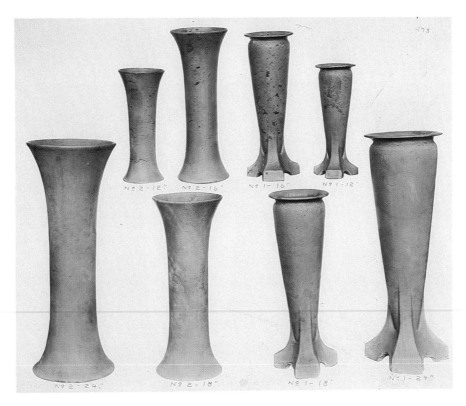

Compliments of the Ohio Historical Society

Compliments of the Ohio Historical Society

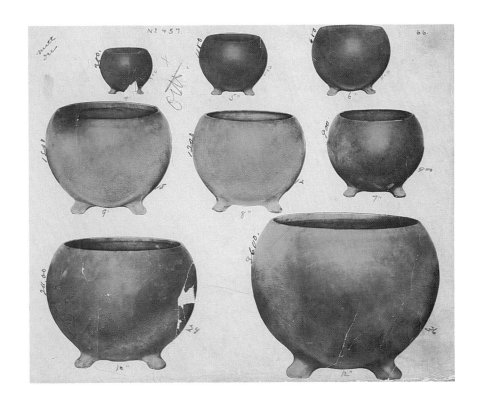

Compliments of the Ohio Historical Society

Compliments of the Ohio Historical Society

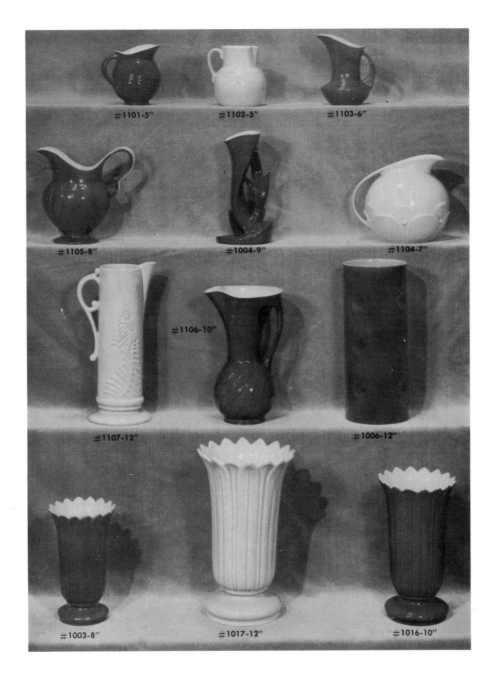

#1101-5"   #1102-5"   #1103-6"

#1105-8"   #1004-9"   #1104-7"

#1106-10"

#1107-12"   #1006-12"

#1003-8"   #1017-12"   #1016-10"

Compliments of the George Krause collection

Mayfair - Circa late 1940's

A totally unrelated line of shapes and designs which include tankers, planters, teapots, pitchers, bowls, candlesticks, and cornucopias. Some are impressed, some have swirls, and others are untrimmed. Several of the colors were bold and new, all were solid . . . forest green/chartreuse, cocoa brown/pink, and gray/beige. Marked with a raised "Roseville" and style number. They came in a high gloss glaze.

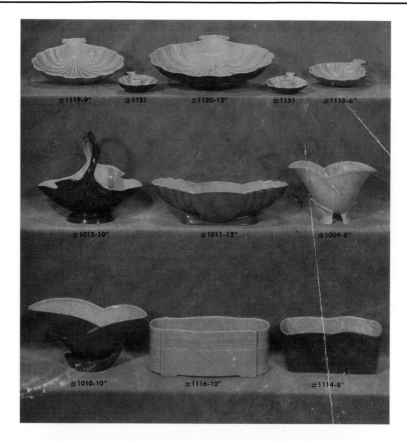

#1119-9"   #1151   #1120-12"   #1151   #1118-6"

#1012-10"   #1011-12"   #1009-8"

#1010-10"   #1116-10"   #1114-8"

#1111-5"   #1109-4"   #1110-4"   #90-4"

#1121   #71-4"   #1018-6"   #1122

#1112-8"   #72-5"   #1014-8"   #1113-8"

#1117-5"   #73-6"   #1115-10"

Compliments of the George Krause collection

Medallion - Circa before 1916

This design has an oval cameo decal of the Greek god "Mercury" hanging from a gold floral wreath on an ivory creamware. Most of the styles have gold piping around the edge and rim. They are unmarked and have a satin high gloss glaze. Designs consist of tea sets, dresser sets and other small related pieces of creamware.

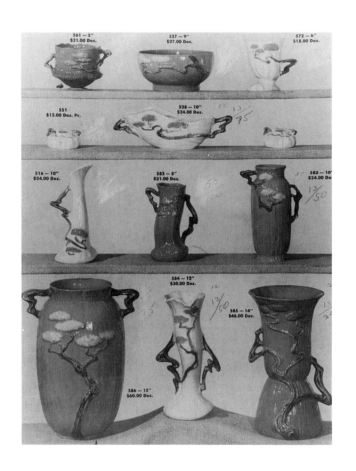

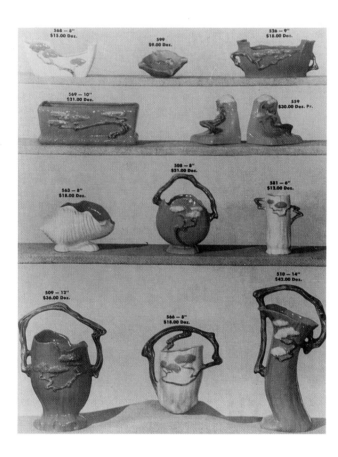

Compliments of the George Krause collection

Ming Tree - Circa July 1949

A twisted Bonsai tree climbs each shape with brown limbs protruding from the sides or the top to form handles. The brown branches are joined with white puffs of foliage. The smooth textured background is enhanced by the vertical ridges of the tree. Twenty-two shapes were produced in Jade Green, Celestial Blue or Temple White. The glaze was of such poor quality that we now find most of the line with heavy crazing. The real beauty is not deterred because of the poor quality. Marked with a raised "Roseville U.S.A." and style number. All are finished in a high gloss glaze.

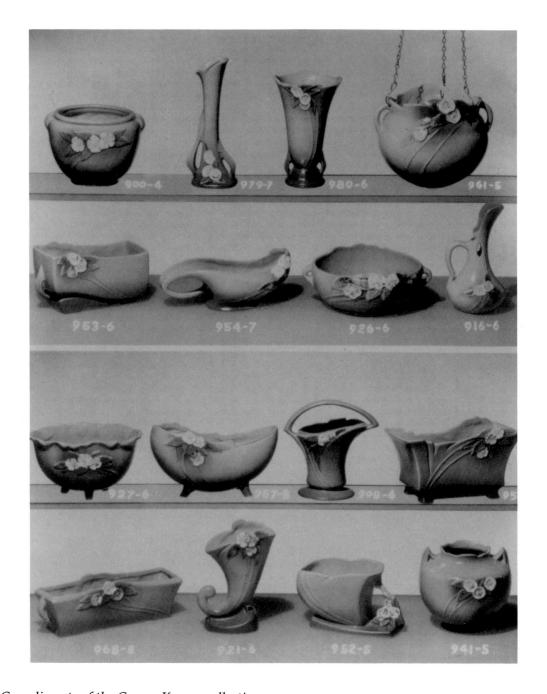

Compliments of the George Krause collection

Mock Orange - Circa 1950

A wavy wind blown design with two or more tiny white mock orange blossoms nestled in a cluster of green leaves. Long stems climb across and up the shapes while supporting the blossoms on a smooth satin finished background. Several shapes have three or more protruding feet while others have very uneven curves across the rims. Most of the line is marked with "Roseville U.S.A." and "Mock Orange" across the bottom or with a foil label. They come in rose, green, yellow, orange, and blue with darker tones of the same color to accent the base and the floral section.

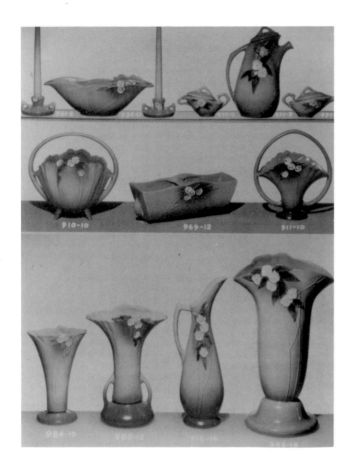

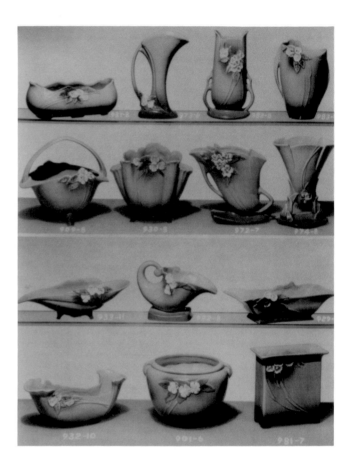

Compliments of the George Krause collection

Both photo's are compliments of the
Ohio Historical Society

Modern Art/Gold - Circa 1905

A line of jardiniere and pedestals designed to appeal to the Deco of the 1900's. The jardinieres had solid special handles completely enclosed and wide bands painted around the rim and base. The center displayed a variety of hand painted flowers, vines and trim on a smooth high gloss glaze. The pedestals were designed with the same style and came in either 11 x 26" or 10 1/2 x 26". To

give more of a rich look and offer a little extra, the same styles of jardiniere and pedestal were offered with gold trim. Six styles are known, three are trimmed in gold. This line is very hard to identify as they are unmarked and are very hard to authenticate.

Compliments of the Ohio Historical Society

Compliments of the George Krause collection

Moderne - Circa July 1936

A very modern design of the thirties with an Art Deco look of a small embossed flower or spiral extended or closed in a few vertical lines on a smooth matt background. Catalog pages show 30 of these classic shapes. The pattern came in soft colors of ivory, pink, brown, green and blue and were marked with an impressed "Roseville" and a style number.

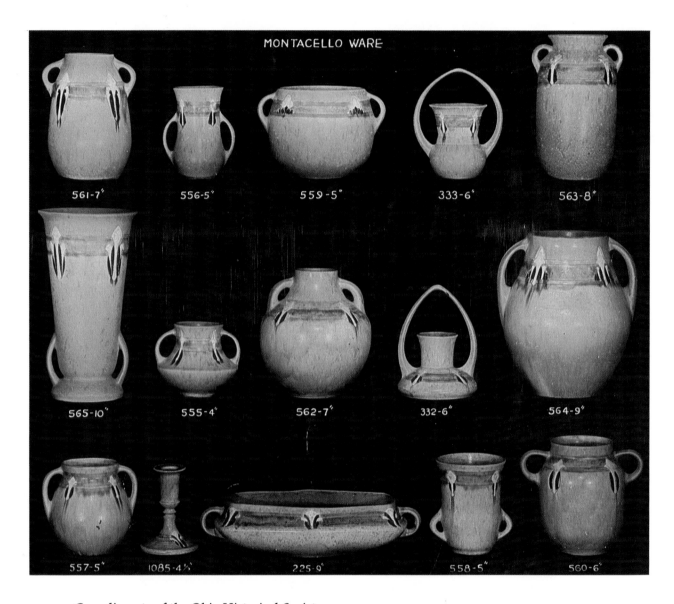

Compliments of the Ohio Historical Society

Monticello - Circa 1931

An Indian appearance line which came in a limited number of shapes, in fact, only 15 shapes are shown on catalog pages. Of course, several others have been found. These shapes are round and rough with handles or braces on every shape. Most of the artwork and shapes are crude in appearance. A wide impressed band going around the neck is enhanced by a white cross that seems to flow off the band and into a black circle. These crosses are evenly spaced around the band. Their coloring is either terra cotta or green with a satin matt glaze. The background colors range from light green and terra cotta to pale blue. The center sections seem to be blended to a soft white or terra cotta to enhance the white flowing crosses. They came marked with a black or silver paper label or a style number written with red ink.

MORNING GLORY

340/10"   268/4"   724/6"   723/5"   271/10"-5"-5"   727/8

269/6"   725/7"   270/8"-6"-4½"   1102/4½"   120/7"   1275/8"   726/8"

732/14"   730/10"   729/9"   728/9"   731/12"

Compliments of the George Krause collection

Morning Glory - Circa July 1935

Open faced white, yellow and lavender blossoms are embossed on a smooth surface. The blossoms are entangled with vines and green leaves on a satin matt glaze finish. The shapes are standard except the baskets which have high pointed handles and vases with squared off handles. The basic background colors were white or green. It was marked with silver paper labels and came in over 17 different shapes.

Compliments of the George Krause collection

Moss - Circa July 1936

This pattern depicts an embossed Spanish Moss hanging in clusters in vertical lines from brown branches with green leaves. Rounded traditional shapes and closed handles were common in this line. Background colors are blue, green, pink and terra cotta. The center of each background is shaded with light colors of soft pink, yellow and white. Marked with an impressed "Roseville" and a style number. These pieces were made in a semi gloss glaze with over thirty-five different styles.

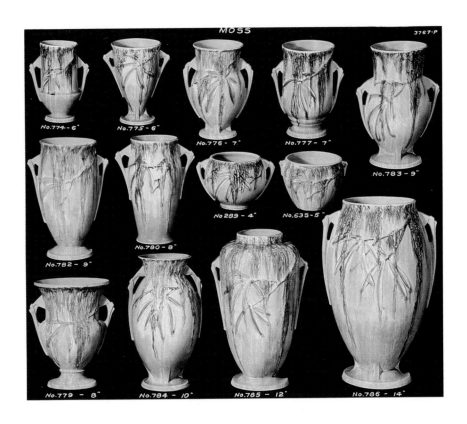

Compliments of the George Krause collection

Compliments of the Ohio Historical Society

Mostique - Circa 1915

Pieces were made in a light gray, tan, or brown background with a heavy and rough looking design and a matt finish. The lining is usually a dark green with a high gloss glaze. A variety of Indian designs were used; arrowheads, abstract Indian designs, ceremonial dancing Indians and forms of vegetation. This line was created to do real homage to the Native American Indian. There are over 80 different styles, with many of the designs unprofessionally decorated and others with more pride put into the workmanship. All are unmarked.

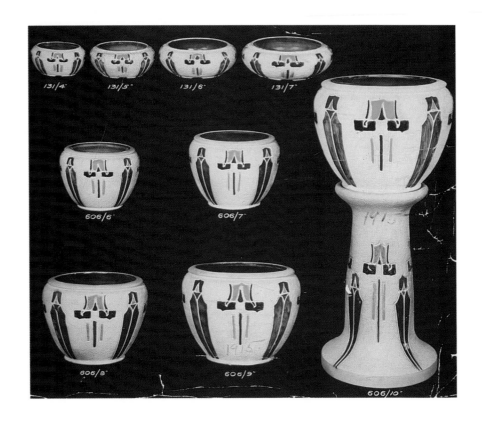

Compliments of the Ohio Historical Society

Compliments of the Ohio Historical Society

Compliments of the Ohio Historical Society

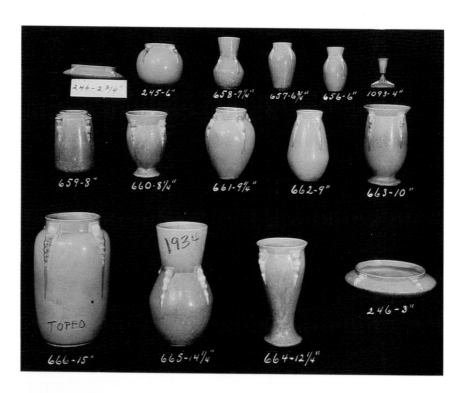

*Compliments of the Ohio
Historical Society*

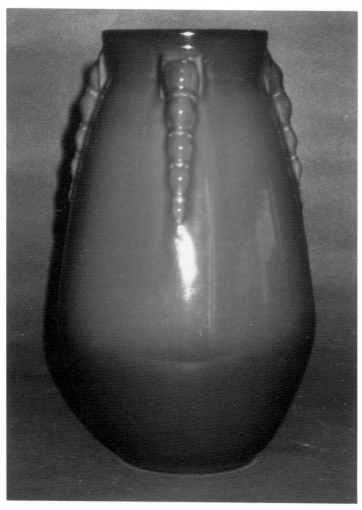

Mowa - Circa 1917 or 1934 (dates are not clear)

Referred to in several old Roseville records and again in "Roseville Art Pottery in Color" by N.F. Schneider and L. & E. Purviance but with no supporting information. Believed to be another name for the blood red Topeo line that was introduced around the mid 1930's. It was marked with a silver paper label. The shapes have a blending of red/brown to an almost complete brown at the base. Fifteen styles are displayed in the old Roseville catalog pages, but several other variations have been found.

Compliments of the Ohio Historical Society

Normandy - Circa 1924-1928

A take off of one of the most successful lines of Roseville, the Donatello pattern. It was manufactured with hopes of rejuvenating the company sales, however, it was short lived. The ivory vertical fluted lines on a green background were the opposite of the Donatello. A wide terra cotta band with embossed pink grapes and green leaves engulfed on ivory grape like vines surrounded the top of each shape. A satin matt glaze was used to set off this line. There are only ten different shapes listed. However, others have been found. Most of the line was unmarked or had a paper label.

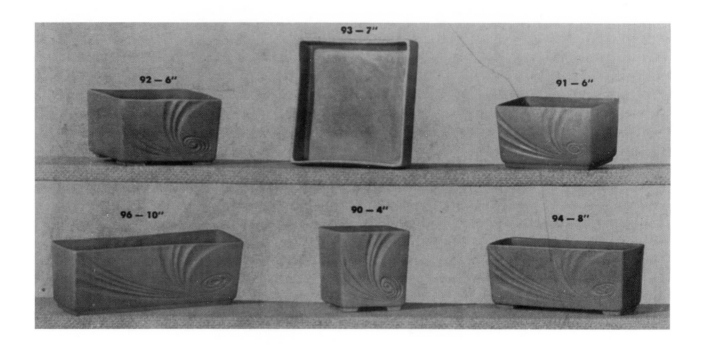

Compliments of the George Krause collection

Nova - Circa 1949-1950

The pattern had plain and simple shapes with an impressed swirl on a matt glaze finish. Three colors were used in this line; tan, blue or green and all came with a tan or apricot lining. The Nova and Etruscan pattern were part of the Florane II line. All the shapes were also used in the Mayfair line. Marked with a raised "R. U.S.A."

Compliments of the Ohio Historical Society

Novelty Steins - Circa before 1916

Novelty steins were a series of creamware mugs decorated with a comical decal and an appropriate printed message. Many of these mugs were created for special promotions or to relay a special message. Six different shapes of ivory creamware mugs with dark piping around the rims were utilized. They were used in all of the other creamware lines. There are approximately 12 different steins known to be in existence.

Compliments of the Charlotte Buchanan collection

Nursery - Early Teens

An early line of creamware baby plates with brightly colored nursery rhyme decals and a verse printed above the scene. The rim of the plate is turned over to create a wide lip on which the words "BABY'S PLATE" is engraved. Other similar plates have a brightly colored band around this wide lip. Several rows of dark colored piping accent the ivory creamware. Most of this line is unmarked but there have been a few plates with the colored band marked with a small Rv stamp.

(Believed to have been made in approximately 10-12 different nursery rhymes.)

Opac Enamels - Circa before 1900

A very smooth matt finished glaze on a blended, untrimmed, plain utility line. Possibly painted with plain enamel house paint. A Roseville catalog page shows 8 different sizes and shapes. The brightly colored line was offered in pink, yellow and green but other color combinations and shapes are possible. Few records are available. It is possible this may be one of the first lines produced by Roseville. All were unmarked.

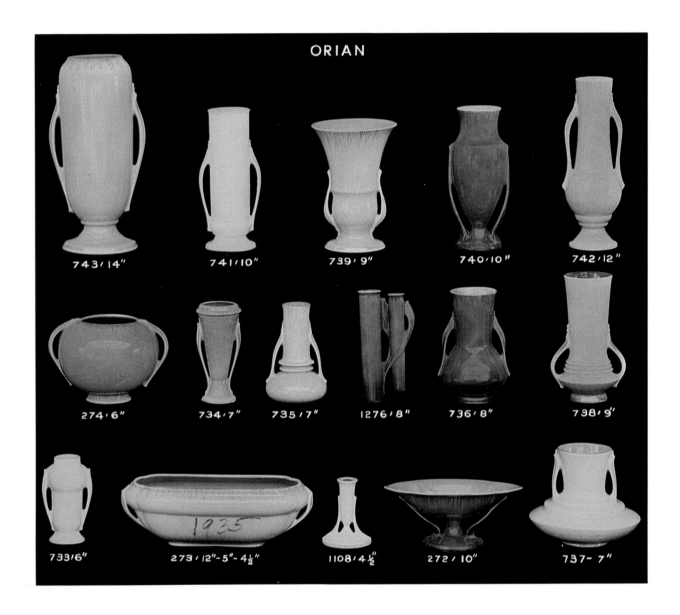

ORIAN

743/14"   741/10"   739/9"   740/10"   742/12"

274/6"   734/7"   735/7"   1276/8"   736/8"   738/9"

733/6"   273/12"-5"-4½"   1108/4½"   272/10"   737-7"

Compliments of the George Krause collection

Orian - Circa July 1935

A typical thirties Art Deco line. It was a two toned line which was made in a smooth high gloss glaze; yellow is lined with green, turquoise with orange or brown, bright rose with turquoise and brown with green. A trace of white or gray along the edge highlight the rim. A series of black vertical lines from the rim fade into the background. The handles are a blending of long leaves that form together and attach near the bottom of the blend and display a cluster of berries. Several colors seem to shade at the base into a much darker color; turquoise to blue, or rose to dark brown. A drip effect of the main color flows into the base color. Marked with a paper sticker or impressed with "Roseville" and the style number. There are approximately sixteen shapes.

Orisis - Circa 1914

    Mentioned in old pre World War I records, but no descriptions were mentioned. One line of early creamware pitchers could fit this name. Two shapes are shown on a catalog page with other creamware pitchers. They are described as an embossed wavy purple leaf like grass over-powering a brown like base and blending into a soft green matt glaze at the top of each pitcher. All were unmarked.

    These long leaf plants may be papyrus, a bulrush of the Nile. The flower of the papyrus plants were used to honor the Egyptian gods, including OSIRIS, who was an ancient Egyptian god of the lower world.

Compliments of the George Krause collection

Pasadena Planters - Circa 1952

The Pasadena line is best known for smooth plain shapes with translucent or frosted colors over another base color. It resembles an oil slick, as if several colors were floating on top of the first color; white on pink, white or gray on black, and pastel green on dark green. The frosted color carries over into the lining. The base color is usually a matt finish while the top color is a high gloss glaze. Much of this line came on wire stands or wire supports. Some of the line was marked "Roseville Pasadena Planter", the style number, "U.S.A.", while others are marked "Roseville", a style number and "U.S.A."

*Compliments of the
Robert Bettinger collection*

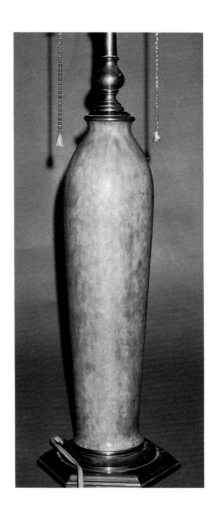

*Compliments of the
Hardy Hudson collection*

Pauleo - Circa 1914

This line was developed by the art director, Harry W. Rhead. The name was derived from the name Leota, George Young's daughter and his daughter-in-law, Pauline. It was produced to be a quality line and priced as such and came in unlimited color combinations with either a red metallic luster glaze or a marblized finish. Oriental shapes were widely used. Marked with an Rv (v inside R) or a gold sticker "Paulo Pottery" seal.

Note: This is a line in which every piece is different. Each piece must be rated or valued on its own artwork depending on the success of the firing, glaze application and in the painted pieces of the artist's work.

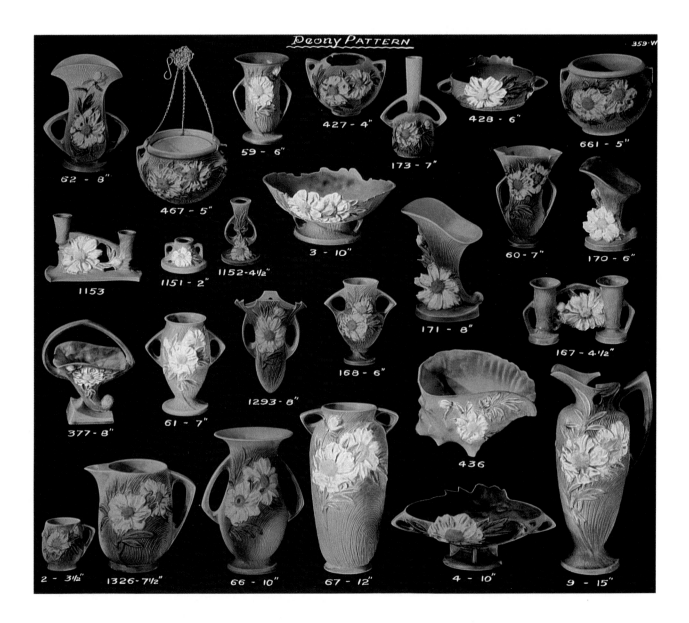

Compliments of the George Krause collection

Peony - Circa July 1942

The peony has a tightly filled background of leaves and stems swirling upward from the base to the top of each shape. A large blossom in full bloom with a dark center is featured with partially open blooms surrounded by pointed leaves used for an accent. The leaves and stems are a dark green and blend into the background color. These colors feature coral fading into green, Nile green fading to an almost black and a Sienna brown fading to a green. Over 65 shapes are known to be in existence. All are marked with a raised "Roseville U.S.A." and style number.

Compliments of the George Krause collection

Persian - Circa 1908

An early line of creamware decorated with decals on such items as tea sets, jardinieres, pedestals, wall pockets, planters and bowls. The decals were in bright colors often with an Eastern appearing design of birds and flowers with a matt or high gloss finish. A single ring or two of the dark colored piping is used to highlight the rim on each style. Unfortunately, as most creamware lines, they are unmarked. Only six different jardinieres and two jardinieres and pedestals were shown in the Roseville catalog pages.

Compliments of the Ohio Historical Society

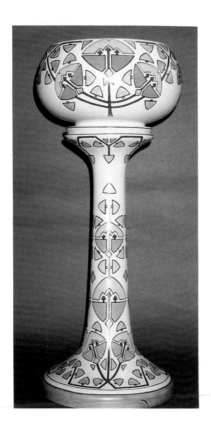

Courtesy of the
Hardy Hudson collection

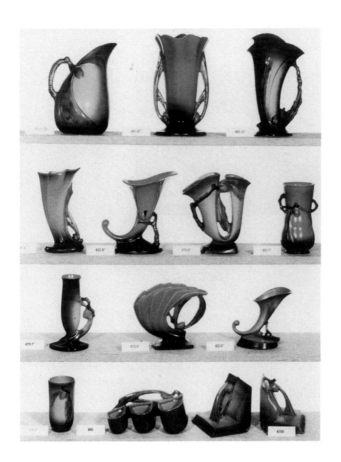

Compliments of the George Krause collection

Pinecone - Circa January 1935

Originally designed by Ferrel before 1910 for the Weller Company, but was rejected because of it being a poor risk. Again, he tried and designed a Moss Aztec line of the Pinecone for Peters and Reed while he was employed there. Ferrel then made a sample Pinecone vase for Roseville which was rejected and the sample ended up in a museum. In 1931, a salesman for Roseville, Charles Snyder saw the piece and was sure he could sell it.

This pattern is believed to be the savior of the company in the thirties. Without it, Roseville would have closed its doors then.

Its design was very realistic with handles in the form of branches joined to a pinecone with green pine needles protruding from the cone. Backgrounds were either blue, green or orange and are covered with a matt to satin glaze. Mostly marked with an impressed Roseville and the style number. More than 150 styles were designed and sold over the next fifteen years. Each pinecone was embossed and decorated by hand and then dipped in a matt glaze.

The wide range on pricing is not only due to the quality but the color plays a very important part. Prices vary from green (lowest) to brown and up to blue. A very limited variety were made in pink. This color is the rarest and hardest to find.

Compliments of the George Krause collection

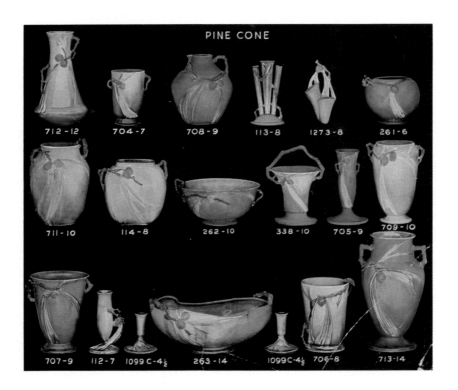

Compliments of the George Krause collection

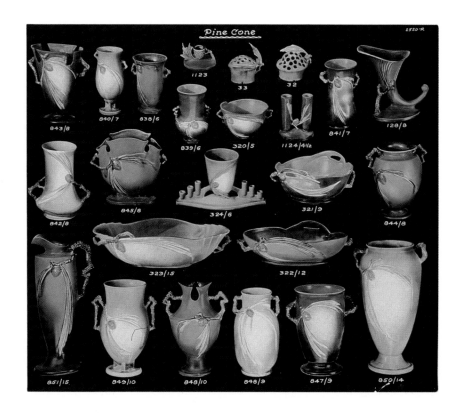

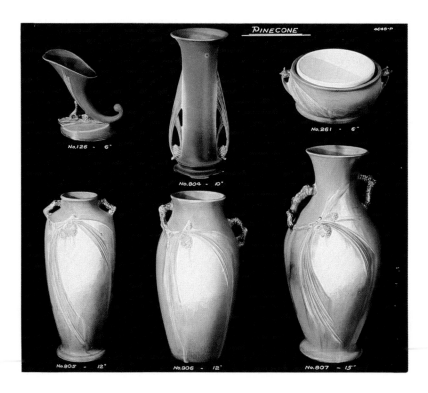

Compliments of the George Krause collection

Courtesy of the George Krause collection

PINE CONE, in the modern and functional shapes shown in this folder, is ROSEVILLE'S new interpretation of a very popular decoration. Soft, mat finishes in underglaze colors of Brown, Blue and Green, harmonize completely with nature's own colors, which have been captured in the PINE CONE motif.

Double serving tray, hostess set, water pitcher and tumblers, with novelty flower holders, book ends, planters, bowls and vases, give you a complete line of functional items for the modern and traditional home.

The complete line is in popular price ranges for quick retail sales.

Enclosed Order Price List is for your convenience to be mailed to the address below.

GEORGE LUMMER
1110 Washington Ave.
IOWA FALLS.   IOWA

ROSEVILLE POTTERY INC.
2505 Linden Ave., Zanesville, Ohio

PINE CONE
by
Roseville

ROSEVILLE POTTERY INC.
Zanesville, Ohio

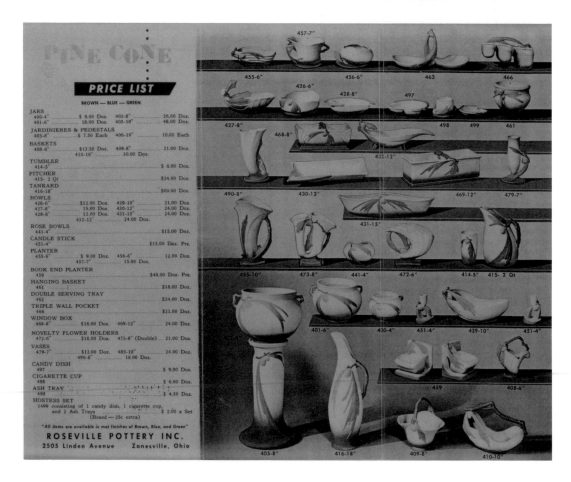

PINE CONE

PRICE LIST

BROWN — BLUE — GREEN

JARS
400-4" $ 9.00 Doz.   402-8"   36.00 Doz.
401-6"   18.00 Doz.   403-10"   48.00 Doz.
JARDINIERES & PEDESTALS
405-8" $ 7.50 Each   406-10"   10.00 Each
BASKETS
408-6" $13.50 Doz.   409-8"   21.00 Doz.
                                 410-10"   30.00 Doz.
TUMBLER
414-5" $ 6.00 Doz.
PITCHER
415- 2 Qt $24.00 Doz.
TANKARD
416-18" $60.00 Doz.
BOWLS
426-6" $12.00 Doz.   429-10"   21.00 Doz.
427-8"   15.00 Doz.   430-12"   24.00 Doz.
428-8"   12.00 Doz.   431-15"   24.00 Doz.
432-12"   24.00 Doz.
ROSE BOWLS
441-4" $15.00 Doz.
CANDLE STICK
451-4" $15.00 Doz. Prs.
PLANTER
455-6" $ 9.00 Doz.   456-6"   12.00 Doz.
457-7"   15.00 Doz.
BOOK END PLANTER
459 $48.00 Doz. Prs.
HANGING BASKET
461 $18.00 Doz.
DOUBLE SERVING TRAY
462 $24.00 Doz.
TRIPLE WALL POCKET
466 $21.00 Doz.
WINDOW BOX
468-8" $18.00 Doz.   469-12"   24.00 Doz.
NOVELTY FLOWER HOLDERS
472-6" $18.00 Doz.   473-8" (Double)   21.00 Doz.
VASES
479-7" $12.00 Doz.   485-10"   24.00 Doz.
490-8"   18.00 Doz.
CANDY DISH
497 $ 9.00 Doz.
CIGARETTE CUP
498 $ 6.00 Doz.
ASH TRAY
499 $ 4.50 Doz.
HOSTESS SET
1499 consisting of 1 candy dish, 1 cigarette cup,
and 2 Ash Trays $ 2.00 a Set
(Boxed — 25c extra)

"All items are available in mat finishes of Brown, Blue, and Green"

ROSEVILLE POTTERY INC.
2505 Linden Avenue   Zanesville, Ohio

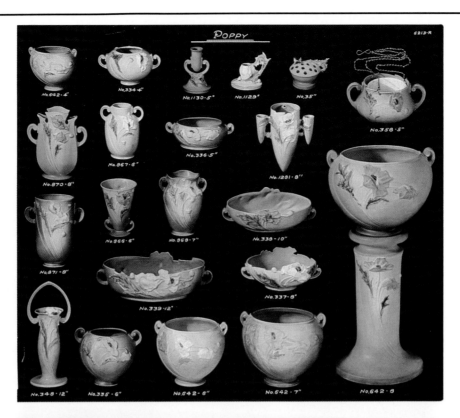

Compliments of the George Krause collection

Poppy - Circa January 1938

A large blossom of the poppy is raised on a smooth matt glaze. The blossom appears on both sides of the shapes and boasts a green pod-like center with green leaves. The stems and leaves tend to blend into the background. They are long, thin and usually stretch the length of the shape. A shading occurs on each background color of either yellow, pink, blue, or green. Most of the shapes are re-used from other lines. The handles are small and round. There are over 50 pieces marked with an impressed "Roseville" and style number.

Compliments of the George Krause collection

Primrose - Circa January 1936

A cluster of small ivory blossoms extend to the top of each shape with a long thin stem that hides beneath small heart shaped green leaves. Many of these blossoms extend completely to the edge. The backgrounds come in blue, orange/tan and rose/pink. Many of the older molds were reused for this line. Almost every shape has flat pointed handles. There are reports of 45 different shapes, but only 37 are shown in the Roseville catalog pages. This line is marked with an impressed "Roseville" and a style number.

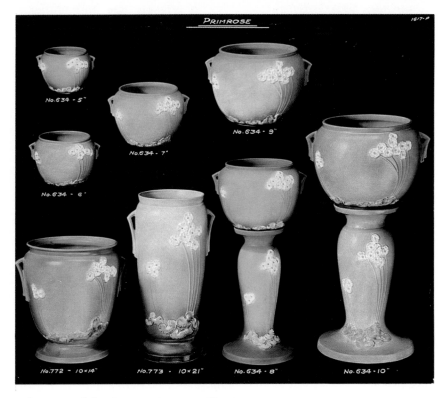

Compliments of the George Krause collection

Compliments of the Robert Bettinger collection

Quaker - Circa Early Teens

An early line of creamware produced on shapes that were used for other creamware lines. They feature a solid wide band of red/brown trimmed with black piping. It has a decal of two Quaker men in pointed black hats, and long white hair wigs. They are smoking long handled bowl pipes. The Quaker appear on several creamware lines; smoker set, mug, tanker, tea set, and even on dresser sets. They are unmarked and came in a matt to shiny glaze. This pattern is fairly rare but there have been several found of a similar design with three children on the decal instead of the two men. Referred to as Quaker children because of the similarity in color and design. These appeared in the same shapes and with the same glaze.

Compliments of the Ohio Historical Society

Ramekin - Circa 1905

A serving line of bowls and casseroles offered in its own nickel plated racks. They came in a red brown color with a pure white interior. The bottoms of each piece show red clay with various ridges. This line is in addition to the Romafin line and was used to accent as serving pieces. Both were made in the same plant in Zanesville. The nickel plated rack is a true treasure and almost impossible to find.

Raymor - Circa July 1953

A line of every day dishware designed by Ben Siebel, with the hopes of saving a dying company. Roseville needed a savior to push them back into the lime light as a leader among American potters. This pattern was designed to be an oven to table dinnerware with the mix or match color combinations of white, green, terra cotta, gray, black, ice blue, or brown. To produce this line, a new machine had to be purchased and old employees had to be retrained.

The line had a very contemporary shape, bold colors, and a full variety of serving pieces. Many of the shapes were considered to be far ahead of their time and had very little acceptance by the public. The Roseville Company failed on perhaps one of its biggest gambles. (Note: The company closed its doors two years later.) The line was marked "Raymor", the style number and had a high gloss glaze.

(Price depends a lot on color. Starting at the bottom price color and working upward to the top price . . . ice blue being the rarest.)

Photo of the Raymor display

No. 12 — 10" Mixing Bowl
$1.00 each

No. 11 — 8" Mixing Bowl
80c each

No. 10 — 6" Mixing Bowl
70c each

No. 15 — 5½" Pitcher
Capacity 2 pints
85c each

No. 16 — 6½" Pitcher
Capacity 3½ pints $1.00 each

No. 17 — 7½" Pitcher
Capacity 6 pints
$1.25 each

**3 Piece
Tea Set
$2.50 each**

No. 14C — Creamer
62½c each

No. 14P — Tea Pot
Capacity 6 cups $1.25 each

No. 14S — Sugar Bowl
62½c each

No. 13 — 11" Fruit Bowl
$1.25 each

Compliments of the George Krause collection

Raymor Modern Artware - Circa mid 1954

Was created as a support line for the Raymor dinnerware. When the decision was made to proceed with the Raymor line, it was also decided to go all the way with a modern looking and bright supporting design and color. The line consisted of ashtrays, bowls, vases, wall pockets, candy dishes, and other pieces in a high gloss glaze. They were marked "Raymor Modern Artware" by Roseville U.S.A. and a style number . They came in tan, blue and green.

Compliments of the George Krause collection

Raymor Gourmet - Circa January 1954

A very extensive line of cookware manufactured as an addition for the Gourmet chefs of the world which was added to the Raymor line. It came in at least two colors, gray and terra cotta with white speckles. These speckles appear round the top half of each shape and appear as if they were the result of a sloppy painter dripping paint as he works. The line consisted of several utility bowls. The larger pieces were marked on the bottom "Raymor Gourmet Service for the Gourmet", Roseville, U.S.A. and a style number. The smaller pieces were marked "Service for the Gourmet Roseville, U.S.A." and a style number. Lids were often not the same color. The handles were often extended from the sides to properly carry them hot from the oven.

Romafin - Circa 1902

This company is believed to be a distributor for the Roseville Pottery Co., perhaps even a sub-division of it. These pieces were produced by Roseville from 1902 to approximately 1906 as part of their German Cooking Ware Line. A special set of twenty one pieces were offered by the Romafin Pottery Company of Chicago for $3.50 which included shipping and handling. They were produced in green or brown on a red/brown clay and were advertised as Fire Proof and the Perfection of Art Pottery. Additional pieces could be purchased for $5.00 to $10.00 each. A person could send $.10 + $.08 shipping and handling and receive a custard cup or a corcotte for inspection before purchasing the complete set. Believed to be mostly unmarked, but several pieces with red clay bottoms have been found marked Romafin on a very uneven base.

(A complete set of 21 pieces still in the original box would be impossible to price in todays market.)

Any find with the Romafin mark is extremely rare and the price is what you are willing to pay.

Rosalie - Circa 1909

A line of umbrella stands, spittoons, jardinieres and pedestals which were produced before 1910. They were made with an ivory background trimmed with a band of pale green or blue around the rim. A cluster of four roses are displayed in the center of a green or blue medallions trimmed with a band of gold. Large vines of green and gold extended from the medallion outward and upward. The extensions are joined by a ribbon of green or blue and gold decoration moving to a smaller design of bows under the medallion. The smaller bows were used more freely on the larger pedestals and umbrella stands. Dark piping was used around the base and rim. A soft high gloss glaze was used, and all were unmarked.

Rosecraft-Black - Circa 1916-1919

A sister line of Rosecraft, but with less success. One of only two totally black lines produced. Black shared the same basic shapes with the Carnelian II line and the high gloss glaze as the Rosecraft line. Pieces were untrimmed, had no embossing, but several styles of vases had unique shaped handles. The catalog page shows only 23 shapes but other pages of Rosecraft displayed an additional 20 different shapes. This line is a hard one to identify because it is unmarked. A silver paper label was used.

Compliments of the Ohio Historical Society

Rosecraft-Blended - Circa 1917

A line of plain and simple shapes produced with a blending of more than one color. Many unrestricted color combinations were used; blue with green, red with white, gray with white, or green/pink with white or yellow. Many of the same Rosecraft molds were used for Blended. Most of the line is unmarked, however, there are a few marked with an Rv and a style number and came in a bright matt glaze.

Compliments of the Ohio Historical Society

Rosecraft-Color - Circa 1916

A lusterware line of simple basic shapes with no decoration or embossing. Over 66 shapes are reported to have been made in a variety of solid colors; yellow, blue, green, and red/orange. They were made with a high gloss glaze and marked with Rv.

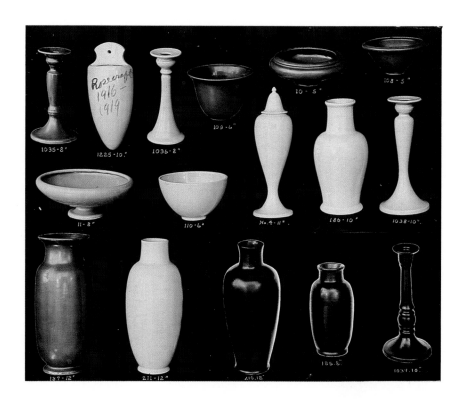

Compliments of the Ohio Historical Society

Compliments of the Ohio Historical Society

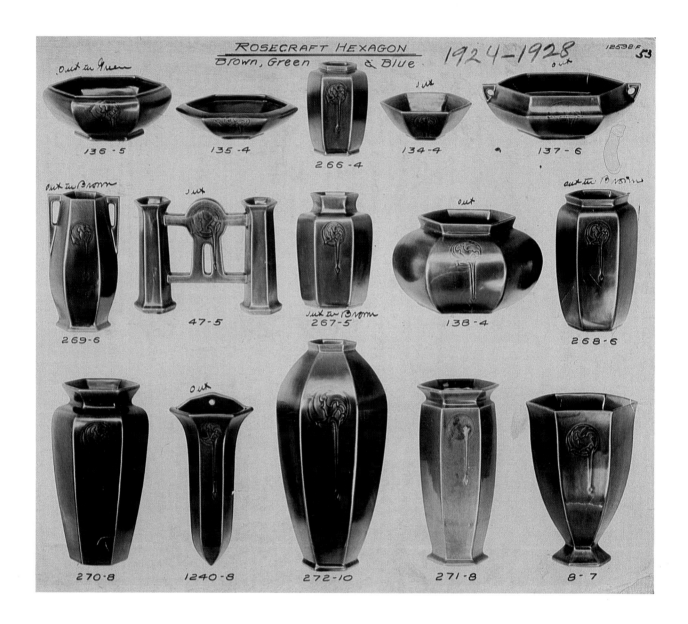

ROSECRAFT HEXAGON
Brown, Green & Blue
1924-1928

Compliments of the Ohio Historical Society

Rosecraft-Hexagon - Circa 1924

A six sided smooth traditional shape with a high gloss glaze. Every shape was specifically created for this line. The most popular color combination was a dark brown with orange lining, but there is also a forest green with a light green or yellow lining and a rare black and still rarer, blue. A small impressed circle with a slender stylized leaf extending downward in orange or gray appears on two of the six sides. Always marked with a blue ink Rv.

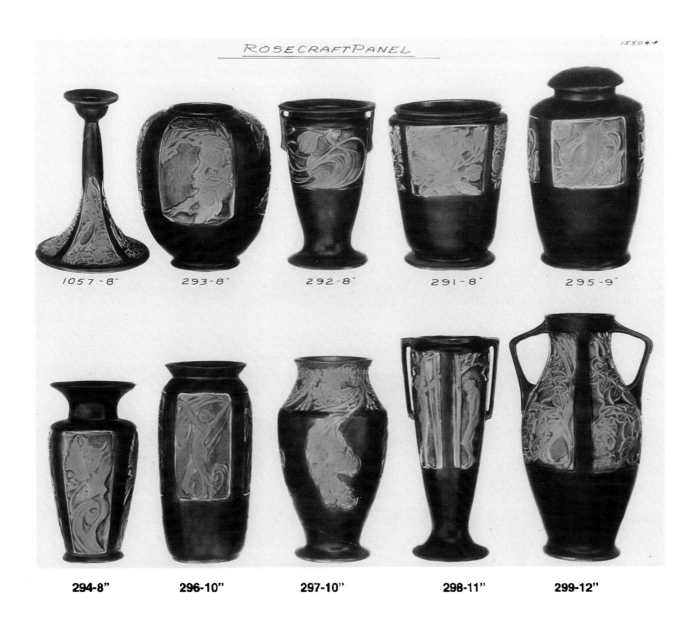

ROSECRAFTPANEL

1057-8" 293-8" 292-8" 291-8" 295-9"

294-8" **296-10"** **297-10"** **298-11"** **299-12"**

Compliments of the George Krause collection

Rosecraft-Panel - Circa 1920

A line of common shapes with identical panels of decoration encompassing the shape. The panels are full of nudes, florals, fruit, and vines with a matt finish. The background colors of dark green or brown flow into the lining. Several of the shapes come with lids and are marked with a blue ink stamp or paper label. Depending on the shape and size, there could be one or more panels on each piece. The display inside the panels are often orange, green, ivory, pink, or lavender.

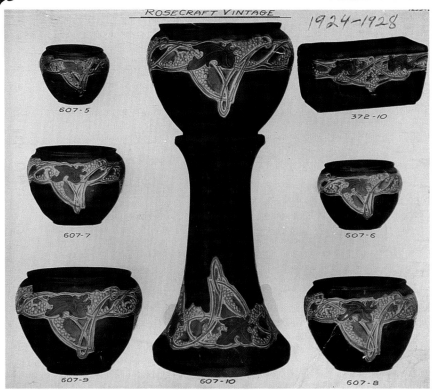

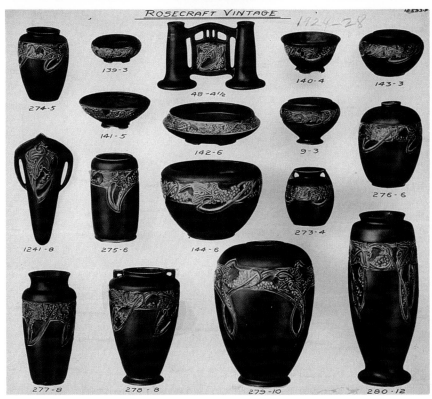

Compliments of the Ohio Historical Society

Rosecraft-Vintage - Circa 1924

An almost black or brown design on simple classic shapes with a satin matt glaze finish. Wandering lines and a cluster of grapes provide the embossed bands. A small section of the vines appear to have a hint of pink. The vines are more confined on the small pieces while on the larger shapes they seem to wander downward. There are over 24 known shapes. A true ART DECO line.

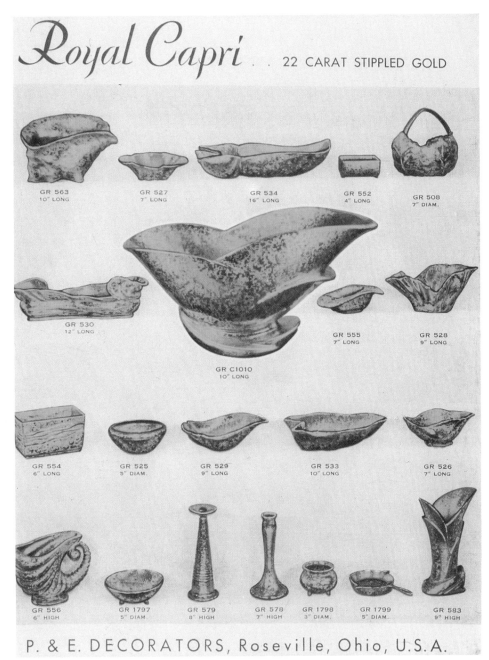

Royal Capri . . . 22 CARAT STIPPLED GOLD

GR 563 10" LONG	GR 527 7" LONG	GR 534 16" LONG	GR 552 4" LONG	GR 508 7" DIAM.

GR 530 12" LONG

GR C1010 10" LONG

GR 555 7" LONG

GR 528 9" LONG

| GR 554 6" LONG | GR 525 5" DIAM. | GR 529 9" LONG | GR 533 10" LONG | GR 526 7" LONG |

GR 556 6" HIGH · GR 1797 5" DIAM. · GR 579 8" HIGH · GR 578 7" HIGH · GR 1798 3" DIAM. · GR 1799 5" DIAM. · GR 583 9" HIGH

P. & E. DECORATORS, Roseville, Ohio, U.S.A.

Compliments of the George Krause collection

Royal Capri - Circa 1952-1954

Over the years, Roseville experimented with a lot of new colors, glazes, and designs or patterns.

George Krause was obsessed with gold and in 1952 he designed a line of gold. He took the Capri line and added gold in hopes that the rich would bring these beautiful pieces into their homes. The line was unlimited with endless molds available. Unfortunately, the line was not a success and fell on hard times along with the rest of the patterns. George Krauses' obsession with gold and Roseville ended in 1954 along with the close of the company. The high gloss gold glaze wore and developed glaze spots on many patterns. Gold Capri is in short supply and has a high demand when found in mint condition.

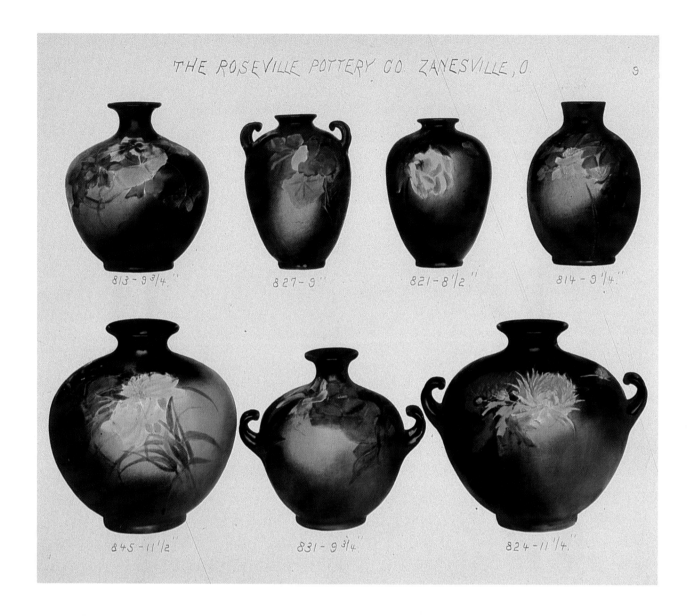

THE ROSEVILLE POTTERY CO. ZANESVILLE, O.

813 - 9 3/4"   827 - 9"   821 - 8 1/2"   814 - 9 1/4"

845 - 11 1/2"   831 - 9 3/4"   824 - 11 1/4"

Compliments of the Ohio Historical Society

Rozane - Circa 1900's

Rozane was Roseville's first experience at true art pottery. They were mostly dark brown backgrounds with true handpainted designs of flowers, portraits, and scenes with a high gloss glaze. Designed and painted by many of the best artists of the times, they were signed or marked by such artists as; Ferrell, John J. Herold, Myers, Pillsbury, Steele and Timberlake, just to name a few. Many of the artists were allowed to create what ever they desired, thus such a wide variety of creations. No two pieces were 100% alike. Many of the first pieces were unmarked but later they were stamped "RPCo." or "Rozane RPCo." All shapes and sizes were used, depending on what design the artist wanted to create. For instance, if an artist wanted to do a portrait, he would need a much larger area to work with, thus he may use a pillow vase or a large base vase; or if he were to do a floral design he may use a long neck vase. An unlimited amount of shapes were available for the artist to use for their masterpiece.

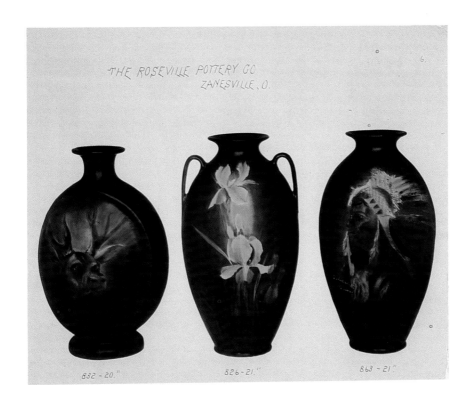

Compliments of the Ohio Historical Society

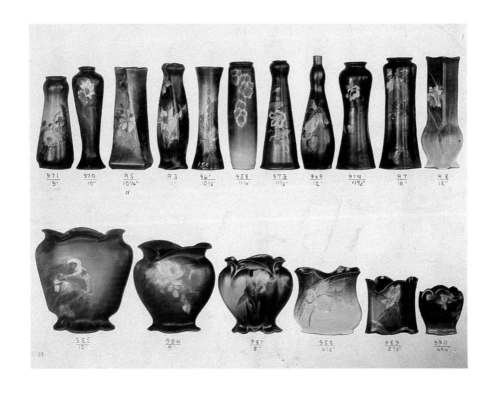

Compliments of the Ohio Historical Society

THE ROSEVILLE POTTERY CO. ZANESVILLE, O.

903-9 1/4." 871-8." 901-9." 876-8 1/2." 896-8 1/4."

888-4." 817-4 860-4 3/4." 846-4."

864-8 1/2." 886-5." 856-4 1/2." 897-5 1/2." 900-6."

ASSORTMENT Nº 50

Compliments of the Ohio Historical Society

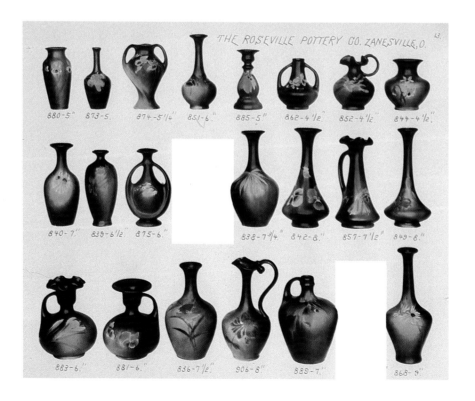

Compliments of the Ohio Historical Society

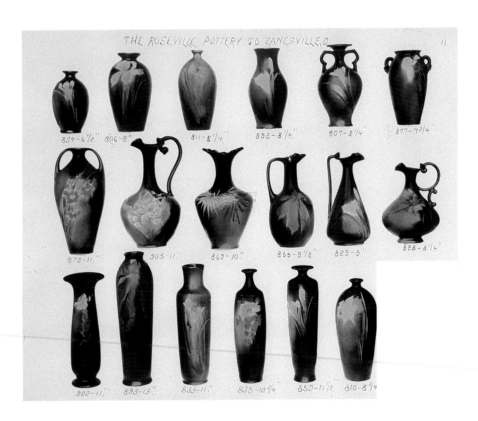

Compliments of the Ohio Historical Society

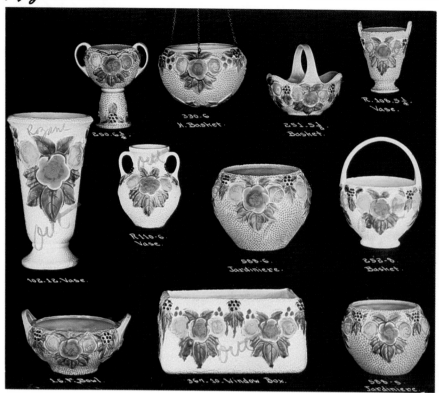

*Compliments of the Ohio
Historical Society*

Rozane Line - Circa 1917

A re-use of the name Rozane,
this line bears no resemblance to the
original. It depicts a heavy embossed
roselike flower with green leaves in pastel colors on a cream honeycomb background. It came in several colors: blue,
yellow, green, or pink which were used to highlight the floral designs.

Most of the line had simple and traditional shapes with only a few displaying handles. As many as thirty differ-
ent shapes have been found but only 14 were displayed in the old catalog pages. Most of the line is marked with a black ink
stamp "Rozane". However, many are found unmarked. The entire line used a matt glaze finish.

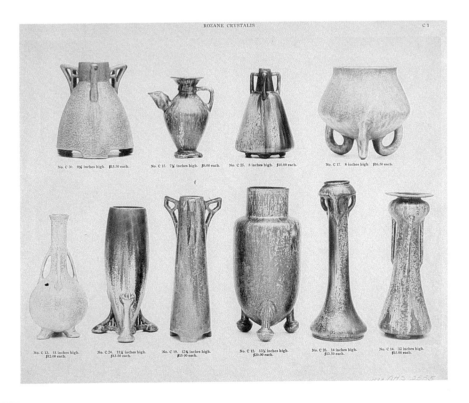

Compliments of the Ohio Historical Society

Rozane-Crystalis - Circa 1905

A delicate use of a glazing process that left a crystallized matt finish flowing over thickly applied layers of dripping glazes, both a matt and high gloss glaze. Many of the shapes were created for this line, which came in a wide range of handles and footed bases. The shapes looked similar to the Egypto but had its own identity. The old Roseville catalog pages only touch on the possible shapes with 14 different styles shown. Many more have been found. Over time, most of the line has become unmarked since the original marking was a paper Rozane Ware label.

DELLA ROBBIA.

Compliments of the Ohio
Historical Society

DELLA ROBBIA TEA POTS

Rozane-Della Robbia - Circa 1906

This was possibly the best line designed by Frederick H. Rhead and probably the most individualized style ever produced by Roseville. The artist was turned loose to create his master-piece. As many as 75 different styles are recorded in numerous colors and glazes. The designs were decorated and applied by the sgraffito process (decoration by cutting away part of the surface layer of clay to expose a different level) and stenciled on with a special round darning needle. The unwanted clay was removed. The lower level was then painted a different color. Unlimited designs, mostly unmarked, but several have been found with a Rozane Ware wafer.

Compliments of the Ohio Historical Society

Compliments of the Ohio Historical Society

Compliments of the Ohio Historical Society

Compliments of the Ohio Historical Society

Compliments of the Ohio Historical Society

Compliments of the Ohio Historical Society

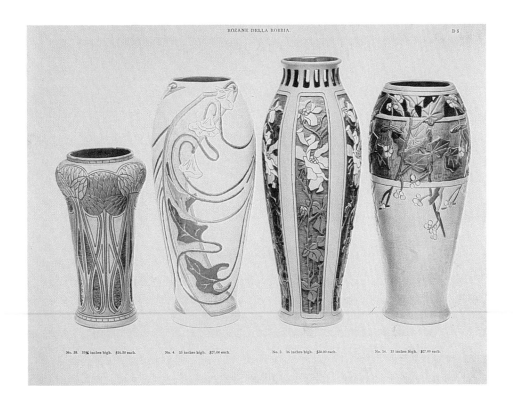

Compliments of the Ohio Historical Society

ROZANE EGYPTO.

E 3

No. E 19. 5½ in. high.
$7.00 each.

No. E 44. 6 in. high.
$6.00 each.

No. E 30. 4½ in. high.
$4.00 each.

No. E 31. 7 in. high.
$4.50 each.

No. E 21. 6½ in. high.
$5.00 each.

No. E 17. 6 in. high.
$9.00 each.

No. E 11. 9½ in. high.
$13.50 each.

No. E 36. 10½ in. high.
$10.00 each.

No. E 12. 10½ in. high.
$10.00 each.

No. E 50. 12 in. high.
$12.00 each.

No. E 46. 12½ in. high.
$13.50 each.

No. E 37. 10 in. high.
$15.00 each.

Compliments of the Ohio Historical Society

Rozane-Egypto - Circa 1905

Often referred to as Egyptian Art, this design is embossed on a soft matt green glaze. Many shapes were copies of original Egyptian designs, while several had a touch of medieval times. There were some variations in the glaze, as many were thicker than others. Several were not marked. To be sure you have an Egypto look for the styles marked with a Rozane Ware Wafter with "Egypto" in the wing.

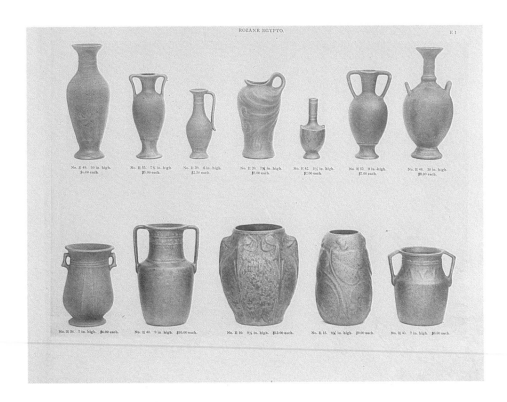

Compliments of the Ohio Historical Society

Rozane Egypto
Thought Made Permanent in Pottery

ALL Rozanes being the creations of individual artists, who bring their own wonderful talent and skill into the expression of their ideas of form, color and design, it is only natural that some very unusual products should be the result.

¶ Rozane Egypto may be classed as one of the oddest styles of Rozane, although its soft finish and coloring, in varying shades of old greens, suggest a very beautiful color found in some of the rarest and most ancient potteries of old Egypt. The shapes and decorations, too, are reproductions of Egyptian art antiques.

¶ Each piece of Rozane Egypto expresses a complete thought of its artist, savoring of the restfulness and freedom of nature. Through the shades of old green are seen glintings of those rich violets and blues which often entered into the colorings of rarest old Egyptian pieces. The prevailing color of these latter was a green which came to be almost as famous as the old red of the Chinese.

¶ Rozane Egypto is indispensable in a collection of Rozanes—or of any pottery. Not only is the color in itself peculiarly attractive and restful, but the forms of this variety, like all Rozanes, are graceful and well proportioned. The low modelings of mat decoration, too, retaining the prevailing hues, contribute effectively to its beauty.

¶ A touch of green in a room is never amiss—such greens, soft and harmonious, as Egypto presents. As a container for flowers, a piece of this ware is most charming. The fascination of an Egypto bowl or jar containing a mass of nasturtiums, their flaming blossoms seen against the perfect green background of the vase, can hardly be described.

¶ Egypto is well suited, as a background, for almost any flower, and is therefore as useful and practical as it is beautiful. It is ideal in rooms where colonial and other old-style decorative schemes are carried out.

¶ In many ways, Rozane Egypto may be regarded as an ideal pottery.

¶ "The entire vitality of art depends upon its being either full of truth or full of use," says Ruskin. "It must state a true thing or adorn a useful one." Rozane Egypto does both.

¶ The ceramic is the union of two branches of art, the architectural and the graphic. It combines form and proportion with drawing and color. In the architectural, is demanded skill, beauty and use; in the graphic, skill, beauty and likeness. Essentials of the best in ceramic art are, therefore, skill, beauty, use and similitude (statement of truth), according to best authority.

¶ Rozane Egypto meets every one of these requirements to the complete satisfaction of good ceramic judges, placing it at once among the very best potteries of the age.

25

27

Original Rozane-Egypto Catalog Pages

E-50

24   ROZANE
            EGYPTO

E-21

E-51

E-12

26   ROZANE
            EGYPTO

Original Rozane-Egypto Catalog Pages

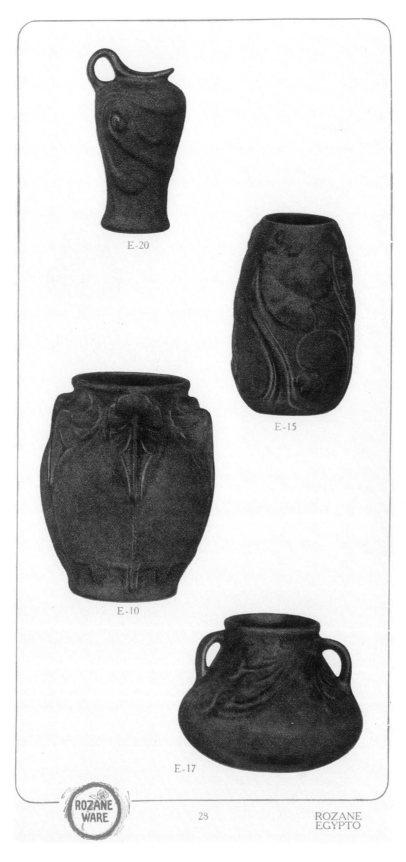

E-20

E-15

E-10

E-17

ROZANE
WARE

28

ROZANE
EGYPTO

Original Rozane-Egypto Catalog Pages

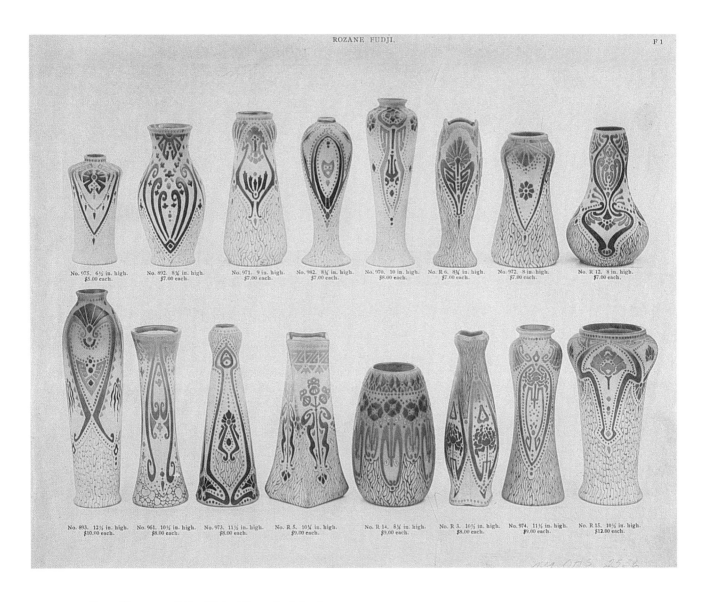

ROZANE FUDJI.   F 1

No. 975. 6½ in. high. $5.00 each. No. 892. 8¼ in. high. $7.00 each. No. 971. 9 in. high. $7.00 each. No. 982. 8¼ in. high. $7.00 each. No. 970. 10 in. high. $8.00 each. No. R 6. 8¼ in. high. $7.00 each. No. 972. 8 in. high. $7.00 each. No. R 12. 8 in. high. $7.00 each.

No. 893. 12½ in. high. $10.00 each. No. 961. 10½ in. high. $8.00 each. No. 973. 11½ in. high. $8.00 each. No. R 5. 10¼ in. high. $9.00 each. No. R 14. 8½ in. high. $9.00 each. No. R 3. 10½ in. high. $8.00 each. No. 974. 11½ in. high. $9.00 each. No. R 15. 10½ in. high. $12.00 each.

Compliments of the Ohio Historical Society

Rozane-Fujiyama/Fudgi - Circa 1906

Designed by Fujiyama, a famous Japanese artist, to compete against Wellers line of Dickens Ware. It was produced in a Sgraffito style design covered with high gloss glaze. A strong use of "dots" and "studs" were used to highlight the decorative calligraphic lines that formed a web like design over the bisque shape. Many of these patterns tell a story. The interior of the vessel is usually bright and followed through with the predominant color of the overall design. Marked with a Rozane Ware wafer, if marked at all. Sometimes marked with a green ink stamp Fujiyama.

Compliments of the Ohio Historical Society

Rozane-Hand Decorated - Circa 1905-1910

Old books have referred to this pattern as Blue Porcelain or Decorated Mongol, while others have referred to them as a hand decorated Rozane manufactured in Zanesville between 1905 and 1910.

Several backgrounds have been found: black, dark blue and even a dark mongol red. All pieces have a rough hand painted feel to the touch. A bright light colored display of flowers with branches and a small leaf spray enhance these beautiful jardinieres and vases. Gold was used to highlight the floral design and rim, while the interior of each piece was accented in a high gloss white. The appearance is truly porcelain but is, of course, pottery. Mostly found with a Rozane wafer, but several have been found with no mark. All pieces are very valuable and extremely rare.

Compliments of the Ohio Historical Society

Rozane-Hollywood Ware - Circa 1905

A line of Rozane molds were used to produce a package deal of special wares with a round starburst label. Many of these molds were used before as Rozane, but with a slightly different floral design. The label displayed "Hollywood Ware's" instead of a Rozane label. Style #R22-3 1/2 was a letter box with a beautiful design of four open flowers but was previously displayed as a hand of playing cards as Light Royal Rozane and again used as a regular Rozane. The catalog pages show 24 styles, all floral with a satin glaze. They range from a 2 3/4" high vase to an 11" tanker. This line is believed to be a salesman special promotional line, with the hope of capitalizing on the Hollywood scene.

Compliments of the Hardy Hudson collection

Rozane-Mara - Circa 1904

It derives its name from the Sea and came in red with pale rose tints to the deepest magenta. The softness of gray and opal remind us of shells. It also came in varied colors of red, purple, and pearl white with a metallic luster glaze. Many of the old Victorian style molds were re-used. Many of the larger styles were decorated with a damask type design which repeated itself within the glaze. It was often mistaken for Weller's Sicardo, and was manufactured to compete against this pattern but unfortunately it never succeeded. Most are unmarked but a few have been found with a Rozane Ware wafer with MARA on a wing.

Original Rozane-Mara Catalog Page

Rozane Mara

Where the Rainbow Comes From

As changing as the sea, from which it derives its name, and from which, like an opalesque and dainty shell, it seems to have caught every morning hue of irridescence when the sunbeam kissed the spray, Rozane Mara is one of the most decorative as well as one of the most pleasing results yet obtained at the Roseville Potteries.

¶ Studying to obtain the exquisite rainbow tints seen in rarest pieces of old Italian glass, our artist chemist evolved this oddity. The surface, in texture much resembling the lining of the ocean's rarest shells, is somewhat irregular, presenting surfaces most favorable for catching every ray of light, throwing it back in all lustrous shades imaginable. With all this play of colors, Rozane Mara is subdued and in good taste, the prevailing tones running under and through the irridescense being odd reds, varying from pale rose tints to the deepest magentas, the soft tones of gray and opal suggesting the pearly surface of a shell, being always present.

¶ As an oddity, Rozane Mara is not only rare and admirable, but possesses qualities of real artistic merit. It will be found especially useful in rooms where elaborate decorations are desired, as it is highly ornamental, while in rooms of more simple style it often adds just the finish needed to give the room a touch of elegance.

33

ROZANE WARE

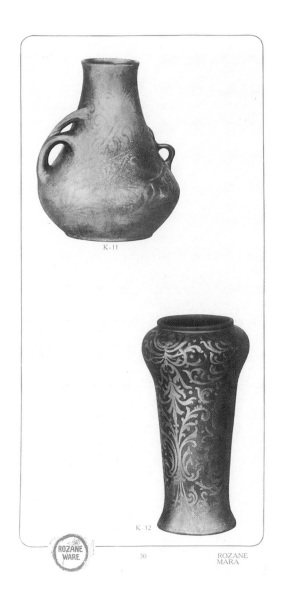

K-11

K-12

ROZANE
WARE

30

ROZANE
MARA

K-21

K-22

K-24

K-15

K-14

ROZANE
WARE

32

ROZANE
MARA

Original Rozane-Mara Catalog Pages

Compliments of the Marvin Stofft collection

Rozane-Mongol - Circa late 1903

Roseville art director, John J. Herold, was responsible for their re-creation of a lost ancient Blood Red Chinese line called Mongol. This line was known as "Sang de Boeuf" for the Chinese but was named after the Mongolian potter who first produced this glaze for pottery. Roseville received international acclaim when, at the 1904 St. Louis Centennial Exposition, they won first prize for the Mongol line. Ornamental shapes with a shiny red high gloss glaze with no decorations, created a rich looking pattern. However, it was not received well by the public. For years, boxes of returned Mongol sat under the steps at the Roseville plant. It has been learned over the years, that Roseville potters and artists were encouraged to experiment with this line. It was said that if they refired the red Mongol, it would change to blue or green depending on how many times it was refired. The artists would often decorate with overlays of gold and silver. Several styles were hand painted with ancient floral and bird designs in bright colors. The line was marked with either a paper label or with a Rozane Ware wafer with Mongol in the wing.

Rozane Mongol
The Vase of Single Color

ROZANE MONGOL is the name found upon all pieces of Rozane decorated in the rich, beautiful red, known as "Sang de Boeuf" and which, until very lately, was produced only by the ancient Chinese. For centuries, potters have endeavored to reproduce it, and only in the present generation has this been done. In honor of the famous Mongolian potters who first produced, in pottery, this color of wonderful richness and permanence, the name Mongol was given to this variety of Rozane.

¶ It is a peculiar fact that any one shape reproduced in a number of styles is more admired in this beautiful Mongol red than in any better known color of the day. While ornamentation and design are attractive, especially when viewed by themselves, as single elements of a perfect whole, nothing is better, in the furnishing of a harmonious room, than art objects in a simple color, wisely placed to lend just the right, pleasing effect to the eye.

¶ A late writer, comparing vases of plain color and those decorated, gives a vivid figure by comparing those of one color to the single musical notes which, combined, produce a harmony. Were each a complete tune, simultaneously sounded, the result would be a jangling discord.

¶ Thus, while elaborate decoration is desirable for certain places (against a plain wall, a drapery of plain material or in a niche by itself), as a unit in the decoration of an entire room, the vase of single color, or in varying hues of the same color, is often most pleasing—most harmonious.

¶ To this harmony is added still another result upon a room by the addition of a piece of Rozane Mongol—its effect of richness.

¶ It is the famous, long-sought red of the Chinese, revealing many harmonious hues made brilliant by any reflections, in its glaze, from window or artificial light, and wherever placed the Mongol vase imparts a rich, luxurious touch of warmth, needed in every room where a a feeling of comfort is desired.

21

ROZANE WARE

Original Rozane-Mongol Catalog Pages

M-957

ROZANE WARE

18

ROZANE MONGOL

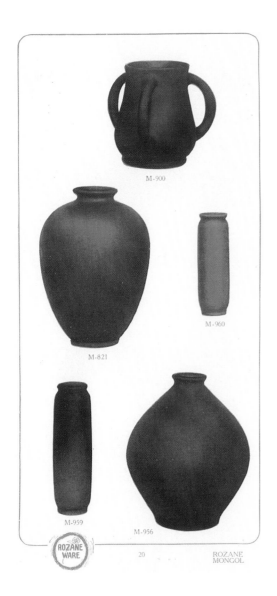

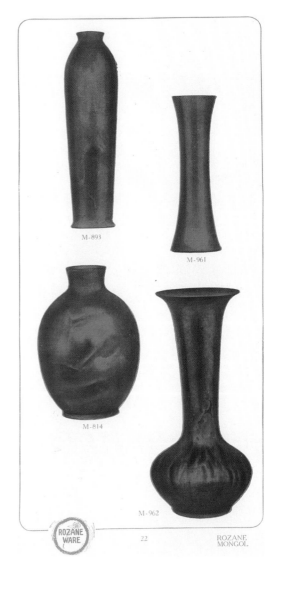

Original Rozane-Mongol Catalog Pages

Compliments of the Robert Bettinger collection

Rozane-Olympic - Circa 1905

A cousin to the creamware line, it was one of the first lines that used the transfer printing style. A Greek God or Goddess printed on paper in clay color was transferred onto the pottery. Often the figures were outlined in black on red background. Marked Rozane "Olympic", it came in a variety of shapes and sizes with a matt finish.

Compliments of the Ohio Historical Society

Rozane-Pattern - Circa 1941

 This Rozane line is free of embossing, decoration, and came in bright colors and unusual shapes. It had simple contemporary shapes with a soft blending of mottled background colors of: blue, brown, green, or white with a lighter softening as the color approaches the top of the shape. A very soft matt to a soft satin glaze was used. There are believed to be only 26 different styles which were all shown in the catalog pages.

ROZANE ROYAL—LIGHT.
Made also in Dark.

No. 954. 21 inches high. $30.00 each. No. R 27. 19½ inches high. $25.00 each. No. 932. 17 inches high. $30.00 each. No. 865. 19 inches high. $20.00 each. No. 815. 20 inches high. $25.00 each.

*Both photo's are compliments of
the Ohio Historical Society*

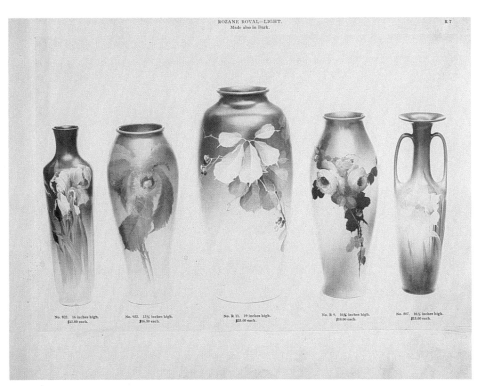

ROZANE ROYAL—LIGHT.
Made also in Dark.

No. 822. 16 inches high. $15.00 each. No. 933. 13½ inches high. $16.50 each. No. R 11. 19 inches high. $25.00 each. No. R 9. 16½ inches high. $19.00 each. No. 887. 16½ inches high. $15.00 each.

Rozane-Royal - Circa 1904

A second coming in the Rozane saga, this was a prestige line which was produced and sold with both light and dark blended backgrounds. The light Rozane was referred to as Rozane Royal. The first Rozanes of the 1900's were all made with a dark background. This hand decorated line of portraits, flowers and animals were similar to the Weller Louwelsa and the Owens Utopian line. ROZANE WARE (a new mark created) was embossed across the figure of a rose. Often the word "Royal" appeared in a wing-like addition at the bottom of the seal. A high gloss glaze brought out the soft light colors. Most of the styles either start out with a light color on the bottom and blend into a dark shade at the top or just the reverse on others. The hand painted designs would flow through the light and into the dark sections. The same molds were used for both the original and new Royal Rozane. Most pieces can be found with an artist signature. There are over 100 styles in the light Rozane.

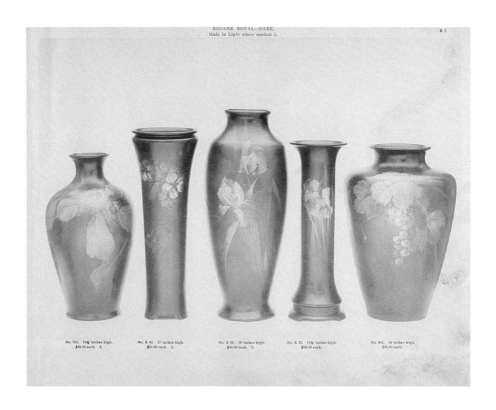

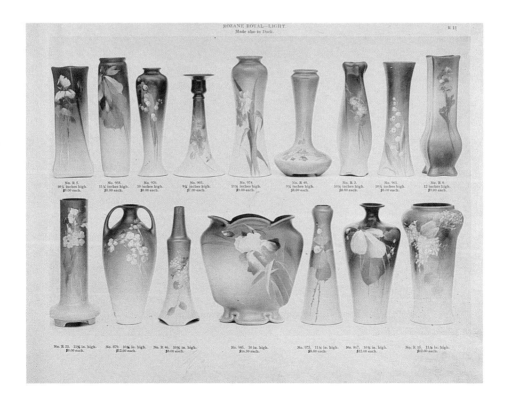

Compliments of the Ohio Historical Society

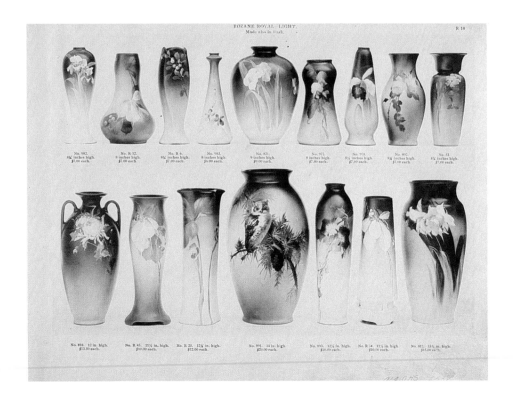

Compliments of the Ohio Historical Society

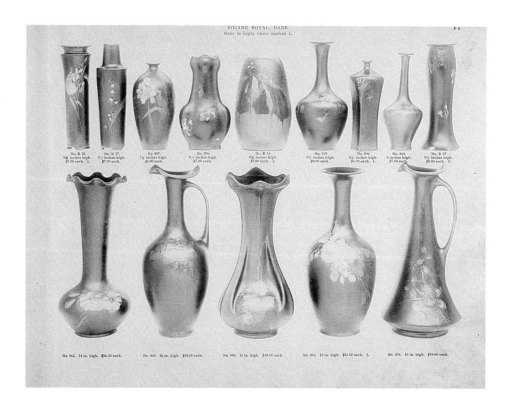

Compliments of the Ohio Historical Society

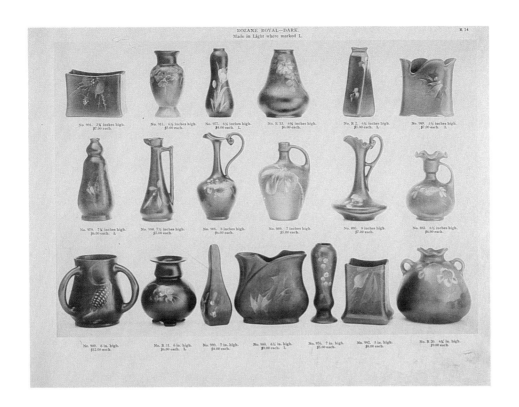

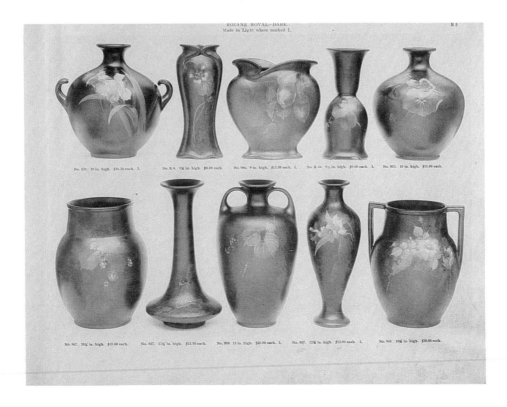

Compliments of the Ohio Historical Society

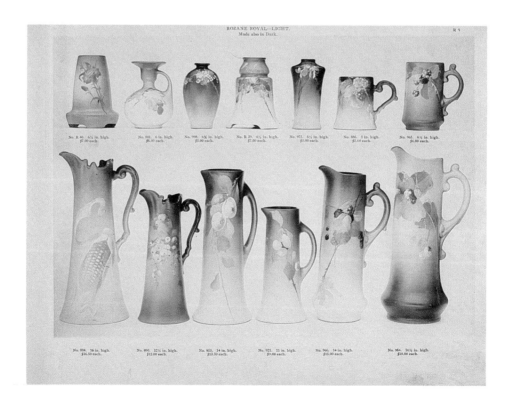

Compliments of the Ohio Historical Society

Compliments of the Ohio Historical Society

How Rozane Originated

MANY collectors have asked how we came to make Rozane.

¶ It was like this:

¶ A certain well-known artist whose special delight was the painting of flowers, sat one evening before a half-finished canvas, intently poring, by the last fading rays of daylight, over a book. At last, sighing, he looked up at his canvas across which reflections of the sunset were cast, mingled with deep shadows.

¶ "Too bad, too bad," he said, slowly shaking his head and, in his earnestness, speaking half aloud.

¶ "What's too bad, my friend," said the voice of a stranger, who had been drinking in the charm of the scene.

¶ "You startled me," said the artist, turning, "but listen to this," and he lighted a candle while he read, never thinking to ask who the stranger might be. "It is Ruskin I was reading. Mentioning the permanency of ceramic works as compared with those of other branches of art, he says:

¶ 'It is surely a severe lesson to us that the best works of Turner could not be shown for six months without being destroyed. I have hope of one day interesting you greatly in the study of the arts of moulding and painting porcelain; and of turning the attention of the workmen of Italy from the vulgar perishable mosaic to the exquisite subtleties of form and color possible in the perfectly ductile and afterward imperishable clay. And one of the ultimate results of such craftsmanship might be the production of pictures as brilliant as painted glass—as delicate as the most subtle water colors, and more permanent than the Pyramids.'

¶ "I was only thinking, when you spoke, what a shame it is that these efforts of mine have to go the way of Turner's. I'd like to try my hand at the clay."

¶ It reads like a romance, but just here began the Rozane idea of reproducing in art pottery fine productions in oils. The stranger, it chanced, was a skilled potter, then engaged in making models for our less expensive potteries. He set aside a laboratory for experiments and so successful was he that, with the aid of his new-found

7

collaborator, the artist, the soft and natural tints of nature were not only transmitted to the clay but preserved, practically unaltered, even through the intense firing to which the ware is subjected.

¶ The natural tendencies of the Ohio clays run to golden browns and yellows, and these tones, artistically blended, formed the body and background of the first Rozane and are retained in all designs of this first style, now called Rozane Royal, to distinguish it from the new varieties constantly being designed in our studios.

¶ With permanence in art as the prime motive, the first attempts in Rozane have resulted in the organization of a company of artists attracted by the worthy object which prompted the first experiments. These artists are all earnest students in ceramics and all have ideas of their own which they are anxious to work out. The spirit of experiment always prevails in our studios and laboratories. Moreover, each artist has his or her own style and no design is ever duplicated. This accounts for the wide variety of subjects and the strong individuality found in Rozane.

¶ Holding up an ideal for the perfect pottery, a well-known authority on ceramics says:

¶ "Let us suppose that a piece of pottery has been painted, and that the action of the fire has made the coloring perennial, so that we find in it a design as everlasting as the ware itself. Let us suppose, further, that the tints are natural, that, in short, the design is all that it should be, and that in the painting nature is displayed as on the canvas—then we would have a specimen of the perfect union of the potter's and of the painter's art."

¶ This is ROZANE ROYAL.

11

Original Rozane-Royal Catalog Pages

R-858

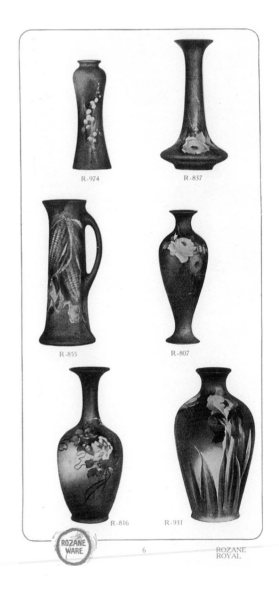

R-974   R-837

R-855   R-807

R-816   R-931

Original Rozane-Royal Catalog Pages

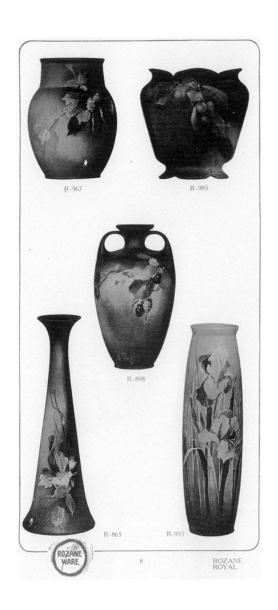

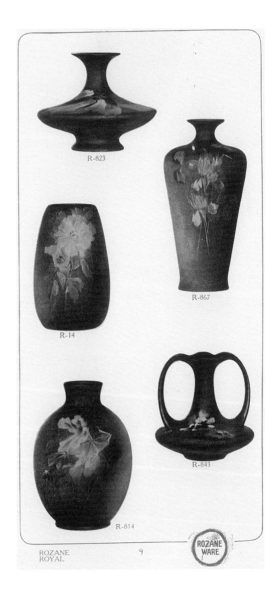

Original Rozane-Royal Catalog Pages

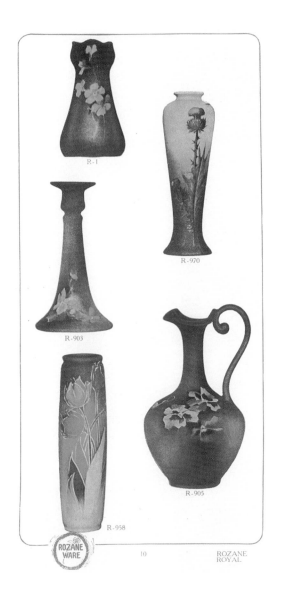

Original Rozane-Royal Catalog Pages

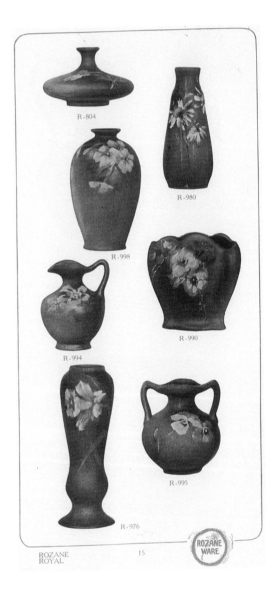

Original Rozane-Royal Catalog Pages

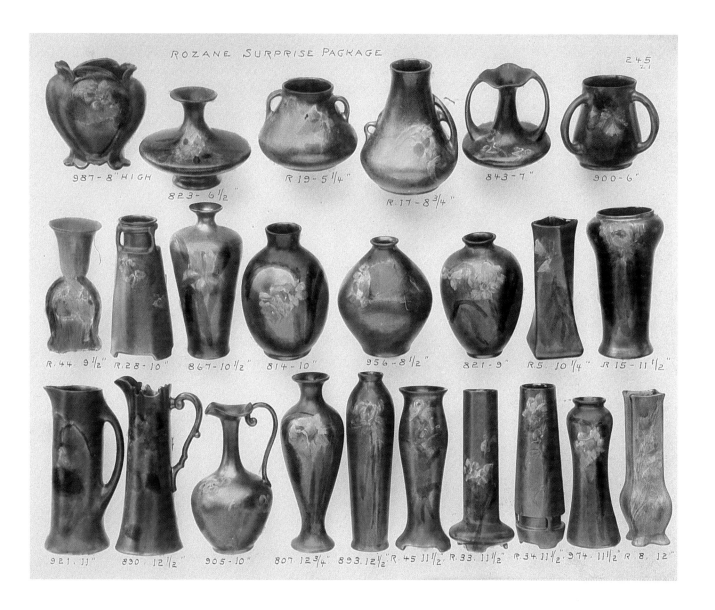

Compliments of the Ohio Historical Society

Rozane-Surprise Package - Circa 1905

This package was a salesman line of about 25 different shapes and colors. It was offered by a salesman to potential buyers at a special discount rate in hopes of enticing them to carry the Rozane Line. A variety of these shapes would be packaged and shipped at Roseville's discretion. No selected quantity or amount of each shape could be ordered by the purchaser, thus the Surprise Package.

Compliments of the Ohio Historical Society

Rozane-Untrimmed - Circa 1900

This pattern was part of the original line, trimmed or untrimmed, with the same Victorian shapes in dark brown with green or orange shading and a high gloss glaze. No hand painting of designs, portraits, or trim were used. There are approximately 24 different shapes which are marked, mainly, with a die stamp "Rozane RPCo" or "RPCo."

Compliments of the Mike Nickel and Cynthia Horath collection

Rozane Woodland
Ancient Spirit in Modern Art

WE do not deny that the resemblance of Rozane Woodland to one of the oldest and rarest of Chinese potteries is no accident. While Woodland is not an attempt at imitation of the old Chinese Celadon, familiarity with the latter, and with its exquisite qualities, was inspiration to the artist who created the idea of Rozane Woodland. Old Celadon, like Woodland, was decorated by incising either floral or conventional designs in the moist clay, or "biscuit," after moulding, and was further ornamented by studs or dots.

¶ The old Celadon was very hard, opaque, closely akin to stoneware, and covered with a partially translucent enamel. There were vases of gray earth, shading into browns and yellows and scattered with little laminae of mica, or sometimes picked with tiny points, almost imperceptible. The value of old pieces in this style is almost inestimable.

¶ The description of Rozane Woodland is almost identical with this of the old Chinese ware, except that Woodland has not the mica. The laminae mentioned, however, are daintily picked into the surface of the softly shaded mat background, lending just an agreeable relief from its plainness, which is further broken by the dots or "studs," while the enameled designs stand out in pleasant contrast. The latter are usually in foliage hues, the browns resembling late autumn woodlands, when the dun, frost-exposed oak leaves — brown; mellow and glossy — still cling, rustling, in final glory, to the trees.

¶ Rozane Woodland is exceptionally beautiful in every point that contributes to the excellence of an art pottery. It is a pleasure to present this as our final argument for the true worth of Rozane.

37

Original Rozane-Woodland Catalog Page

Rozane-Woodland - Circa 1905

Mainly floral designs incised on clay and then colored on a bisque-like background. This line was decorated by the sqraffiti method and then covered with a high gloss glaze and usually done in autumn colors. Sometimes, stripling was used to accent or decorate the rim. The flowers and leaves were bright colored while the background was soft colored and often referred to as dull. Many Rozane shapes were used, but there were a few original shapes produced. Marked "Woodland" in a wing on a Rozane Ware Wafer.

Note: This is a line in which every piece is different depending on the success of the firing, glaze application, and in the painted pieces of artist work. Each piece must be rated on the artwork.

W-893

34

ROZANE
WOODLAND

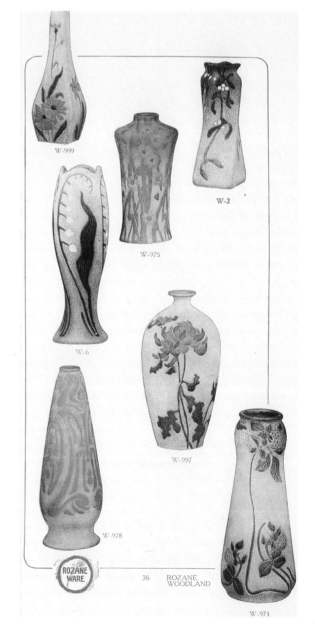

W-999

W-2

W-976

W-6

W-997

W-978

W-971

ROZANE
WARE

36

ROZANE
WOODLAND

Original Rozane-Woodland Catalog Pages

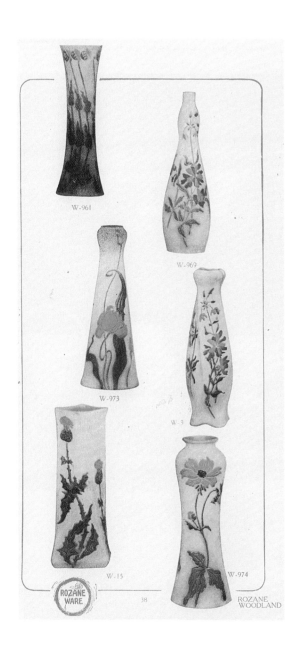

Original Rozane-Woodland Catalog Pages

Compliments of the Ohio Historical Society

Russo - Circa July 1934

A modern appearing line of solid color glaze with a few sprayings of crystallized glaze or metallic gold. It came in matt or semi gloss glaze and in such colors as blue, gold, green, pink or cream. A blending of green with cream, green with yellow, and brown with cream are a few of the blends in this line. A simple trim of embossed lines travel from top to bottom on most shapes.

Pedestal like bases are common. White Russo are found but they are part of the Ivory line. They are either unmarked or came with a silver paper label.

Compliments of the Ohio Historical Society

Savona - Circa 1924-1928

A fluted and embossed design on a variety of shapes with a narrow border of a classic looking design which embraces the rim and occasionally travels around the border. Hook shaped handles and wide bases are common. Solid colors of salmon, blue, yellow or lime green were used with a high gloss glaze. When found marked, they would have a paper sticker. Molds were utilized from the Volpato line of 1918.

Compliments of the Hardy Hudson collection

Compliments of the Clark & Vicki McLean collection

Signs

Produced mainly as an advertising material, signs were used by vendors to identify the pottery ware they were displaying for sale. Usually one sign would be placed in front of a large variety of Roseville pottery. These signs came in a large variety of sizes, colors, and lettering. The most common one was a thirties simple block letter sign that was about 6" long. Later in the forties, the signs got more creative and bolder. At that time, a five inch high by seven inch long script, "Signature" sign was produced. It followed the advent of this trademark. Smaller ones from two inch by six inch appeared around the twenties and possibly before. All were free standing, and came in all standard color blends and glazes. Any size, color, and form was possible.

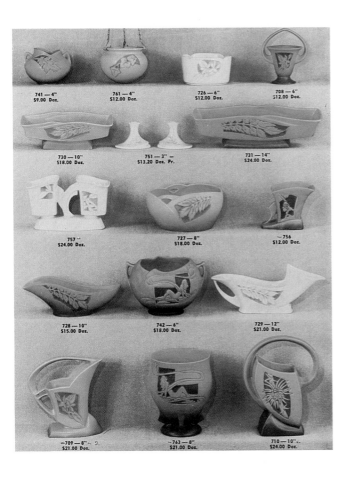

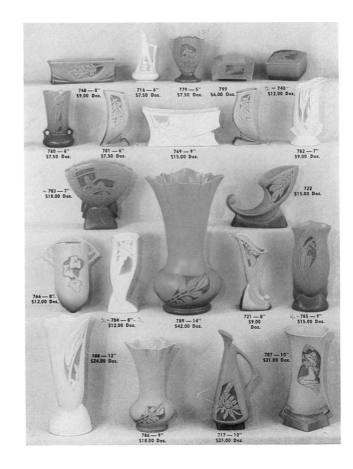

Compliments of the George Krause collection

Silhouette - Circa July 1950

A modern-shaped design with panels of nudes or floral designs on a high gloss glaze. The panel background was red, blue, orange, green, or tan. The white background had a pale blue backing in the panels. Marked with a "Roseville" in relief and a style number. The basic modern shapes were designed to blend in with any modern Decor.

Compliments of the Ohio Historical Society

Smoker Sets - Circa before 1916

Smoker Sets were of the creamware line which was introduced around 1914. The sets included a wide variety of decal designs with a dark piping trim. The decals included; Dutch, Holland, Ivory Tints, Indians, Coat of Arms, and humorous carton characters with humorous sayings. They included tobacco jars, ashtrays, and match holders on trays and came in a matt to high gloss glaze.

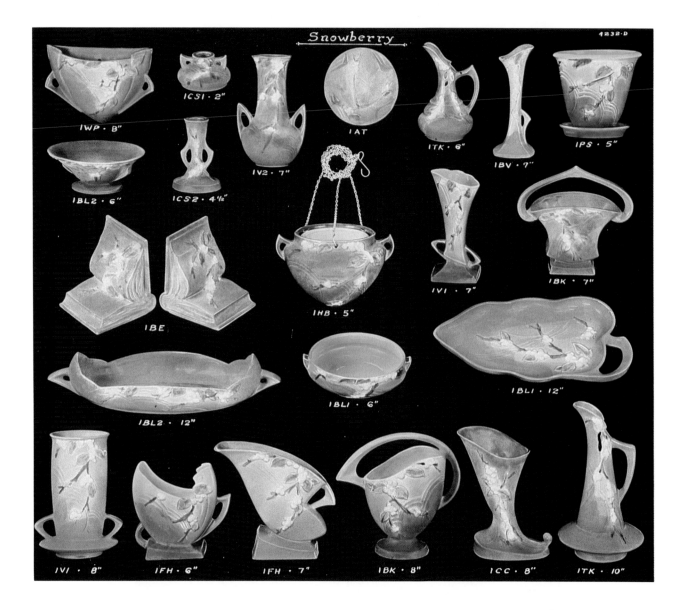

Compliments of the George Krause collection

Snowberry - Circa July 1947

This pattern has several clusters of white berries with sparse green leaves on brown winding branches in a variety of designs. It came on a smooth satin finish with an assortment of background colors; blue, green or soft rose. Each shape has a blending or shading to highlight handles, bases, and edges, plus a blending of a lighter color to show off the cluster of snowberries. Few of the 62 available shapes were exclusive of this line. Most of the molds were borrowed from other lines. Some of the changes made were the addition of pointed handles. They were marked with a raised "Roseville, U.S.A." and used a special letter code in the style number to identify the type of shape; V-vase, BL-bowl and CS-candle stick.

Compliments of the George Krause collection

An original photograph of the Snowberry Line
Compliments of the George Krause collection

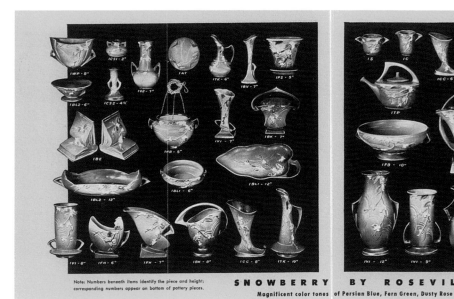

Note: Numbers beneath items identify the piece and height; corresponding numbers appear on bottom of pottery pieces.

SNOWBERRY BY ROSEVILLE

Magnificent color tones of Persian Blue, Fern Green, Dusty Rose

Look for the registered trade-mark "ROSEVILLE" embossed on the bottom of each piece when you buy art pottery. It is your guide to quality and good value.

☆ ☆ ☆

ROSEVILLE is America's most popular art pottery. It is nationally advertised in leading women's and home service magazines and is sold everywhere.

☆ ☆ ☆

All ROSEVILLE colors are handpainted under glaze. This means permanency of color beauty — no fading, rubbing or wearing off and guaranteed waterproof.

ROSEVILLE POTTERY, INC., ZANESVILLE, OHIO

"A THING OF BEAUTY IS A JOY FOREVER"

Snowberry
decorative art pottery

from the famous kilns of

ROSEVILLE

. . . enchanting loveliness fused in the form and color of truly beautiful pottery

Roseville is refreshingly different from ordinary art pottery. The distinctive designs are inspired by lovely garden flowers. Then master potters faithfully sculpture the floral motif on original art forms of the most graceful contour. Each dainty blossom and leaf . . . each dominant color tone . . . bespeaks the natural beauty of the flower itself. Little wonder that Roseville creations are frequently known as "living art pottery."

ROSEVILLE'S *Snowberry*

. . . tastefully lends itself to many charming decorative effects

Snowberry is strikingly beautiful singly or in groupings . . . with or without flowers. Its rich, hand-painted colors of Persian Blue, Fern Green and Dusty Rose are unrivalled for harmonious or contrasting effects in either traditional or modern interiors. Choose Snowberry for yourself . . . and for gifts to others, 52 intriguing pieces — vases, bowls, jardinieres, baskets, cornucopias and novelty pieces . . . at better gift and department stores.

Snowberry is sold only in retail gift and department stores. Please do not send orders to the factory, for it will be impossible to fill them.

See inside for interesting selection of SNOWBERRY items

Original mailed brochure for Snowberry

*Both photo's are compliments of
the Ohio Historical Society*

Special - Circa early 1900

    A line of umbrella stands and jardinieres in the Art Nouveau and Victorian style. The umbrella stands were embossed with flowers and ribbon divided by large solid hand painted areas that tapered from the top to a smaller area at the bottom. The flowers and ribbons were hand painted in bright colors of red, yellow, and orange on an ivory background with high gloss glaze.

    The jardiniere and pedestal were also hand painted floral designs in bright colors with blended colors encompassing each piece. The jardiniere had enclosed handles while the pedestal had a large crest design evenly spaced around the base. They range upward to 26 1/2" in height with a high gloss glaze and a high sprinkling of gold. Mugs and tankers have also been found in this line. All are unmarked.

Compliments of the Ohio Historical Society

Stork - Circa 1900

The stork was a heavily embossed jardiniere, pedestal and umbrella stand line with a large stork standing in a marsh-like area with large blades of marsh grass surrounding it. The jardiniere had a wide rim and concaved side and came in basic colors. The umbrella stand was very Victorian with heavy embossed designs from top to bottom. The background colors were; brown, red, orange, green, or blue. They came in several sizes ranging to 18" tall, and all were unmarked.

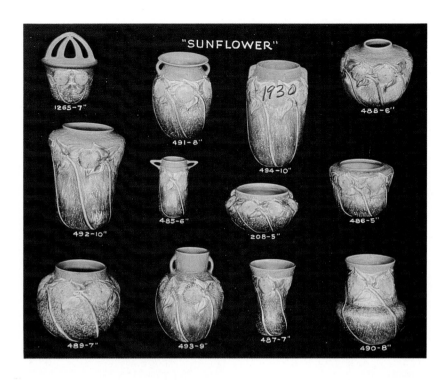

Compliments of the Ohio Historical Society

Sunflower - Circa 1930

This pattern depicts a large blossom of sunflower extending from long green stems which are encircling the shape. The backgrounds are mottled earth tones in terra cotta across the top and a mottled dark green grass encompassing at least two thirds of the shape. Usually marked with a black paper label, but as time has gone on, the labels have worn off, thus many are unmarked. The old Roseville catalog pages show only 15 shapes, but there have been many more shapes reported all with a satin matt finish.

Compliments of the Ohio Historical Society

Sylvan - Circa 1918

Referred to as Frank Ferrel's 90 day wonder line because in 1918 Ferrel replaced Harry Rhead as Art Director of Roseville and within 90 days he had Sylvan on the market. It was designed to give the appearance of tree bark, with leaves and branches throughout. Additional designs of fox, quail, pointer hunting dogs, owls, rabbits, and other wild life are molded into scenes surrounding each piece. Usually came in light brown and gray with a light matt finish on the outside and a high gloss inside. The line was originally marked with paper labels, but now are found unmarked.

Compliments of the Ohio Historical Society

Compliments of the Ohio Historical Society

Tea Sets - Circa 1910

A term used by Roseville to group a combination of tea sets. The set included teapot, sugar and creamer. Such lines as Dutch, Gibson Girl, Seascape, Landscape, Forget-Me-Not, Persian and a host of ceramic sets were included in this pattern. Most of the line were either of the transfer pattern design or the decal style. A few handpainted sets did exist. Many teapots were made from 3" to 6" in height, some even came with fancy handles and lids. All are unmarked.

Compliments of the Ohio Historical Society

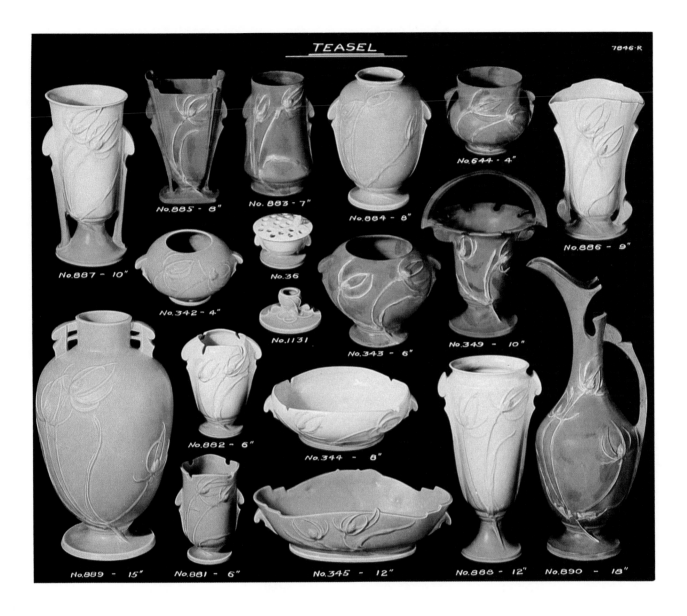

Compliments of the George Krause collection

Teasel - Circa April 1938

A raised pointed weed looking teasel on long stems highlight this line. The points continue into the rim and on occasion over the rim. The plain shape was borrowed from other patterns with the one addition of small block handles on the entire line. Many of the basic background colors of gray, blue, beige, gold, pink or green are complimented with a soft shading of a lighter color. The line has "Roseville" impressed and the style number. It came in approximately 18 shapes and were made in a smooth matt finish.

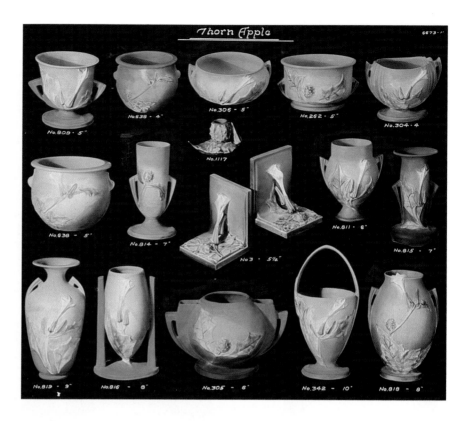

Both photo's are compliments of the George Krause collection

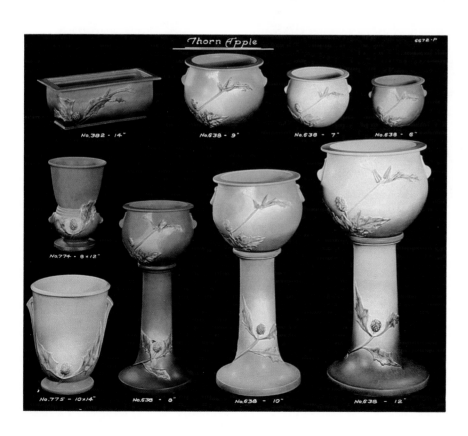

Thornapple - Circa January 1937

A line of two sided embossed designs with one side having a trumpet-like blossom surrounded by pointed green leaves and the other a thorny pod on a long stem with pointed leaves. The matt background blends terra cotta into a soft orange, blue into turquoise and rose into green. Several shapes were exclusive to this line, small pods became candlesticks, several frogs had large leaves and blooms extending upward. The large leaves and trumpet-like flowers extend out of the shapes to create handles or braces to support other parts of the shape. Marked with an impressed "Roseville" and a style number and came in approximately 50 different styles.

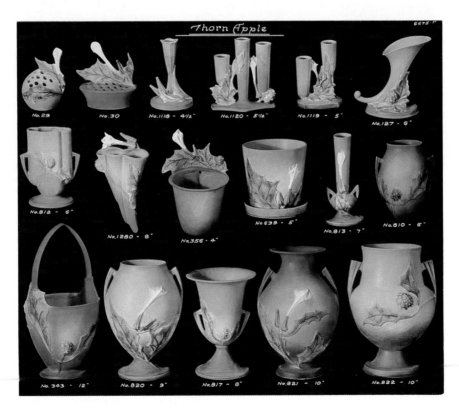

Compliments of the George Krause collection

246-2¾"   245-6"   658-7¼"   657-6¾"   656-6"   1093-4"

659-8"   660-8¼"   661-9¼"   662-9"   663-10"

666-15"   665-14¼"   664-12¼"   246-3"

TOPEO   1934

Compliments of the Ohio Historical Society

Topeo - Circa January 1934

A rich looking design with four evenly spaced cascades of leaves protruding downward for a short distance. The simple basic shapes came in pink, red, yellow, blue and green with either a matt or high gloss glaze. The background colors tend to darken near the base or rim; in some cases, they turn almost black. The red high gloss glaze Topeo may actually be the lost line of MOWA. The catalog pages show only 15 different shapes but several additional consoles have been found. The Topeo design holds a lot of mystery. The dark red glaze is also another possible lost line called ART CRAFT. As we now stand, Topeo, Art Craft, and Mowa are one and the same line.

Compliments of the John J. Zolomij collection

Tourist - Circa 1910

A creamware line with scenes of an early touring car on a high gloss glaze. The design has a handpainted transfer pattern that is applied to the shape. The touring car is shown on a country scene with wide dark bands used as a accent. An unknown amount of shapes give us something to think about. Prizes are the window box, jardiniere and pedestal. All pieces are unmarked. Pricing varies depending on mold, color, and availability. About 55 different shapes have surfaced.

TOURMALINE

616-10" A-429-9" A-332-8" A-65-6" 614-8" 615-9" A-435-10"

238-5" A-308-7" A-152-7" 152-6" 241-12" 1089-4½"

612-7" A-517-6" 613-8" A-444-12" 611-6" A-200-4" A-425-8"

Compliments of the George Krause collection

Tourmaline - Circa 1933

A variety of simple shapes with a variety of glazes. Several styles have both a matt and a satin high gloss glaze. A blending of colors are common as well as the blending of glazes. Many of the shapes were borrowed from other lines; Velmoss, Futura, Matt Color, and Cornelian I. A strong use of blending and glazes provide the trim with each piece having very little embossing. On several styles, a ribbon affect with blending of assorted colors is common; blue/green over pink, white over blue and gold over terra cotta plus salmon and gold have also been found in a high gloss glaze. Over 20 styles have been found. This pattern was marked with a silver paper label but of course are now unmarked. Pricing increases from pink, green, brown, and the highest value of blue.

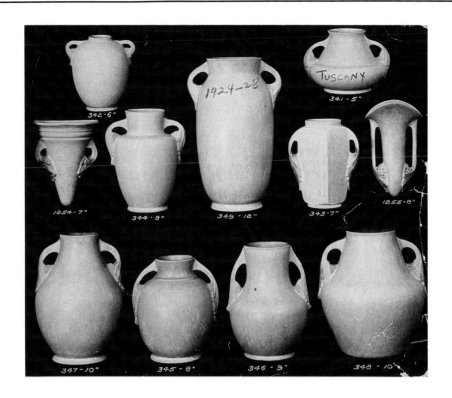

Compliments of the George Krause collection

Tuscany - Circa 1924

A very plain designed line with a hint of blue grapes and green leaves used to form rounded handles. A very low key and classic style in colors of pink or gray high gloss and a dull turquoise with a matt glaze. There are over 20 different styles which were marked with a black paper label, as with most of the older lines, they are now unmarked.

Compliments of the Ohio Historical Society

Unique - Early Teens

Pictured in the old Roseville catalog pages as a dark blue lily pod floating in a greenish water pond. It was produced in a high gloss glaze. This line included coffee pots, teapots and chocolate pots with the possibility of a sugar and creamer. The shapes were similar to others from that era, all are unmarked.

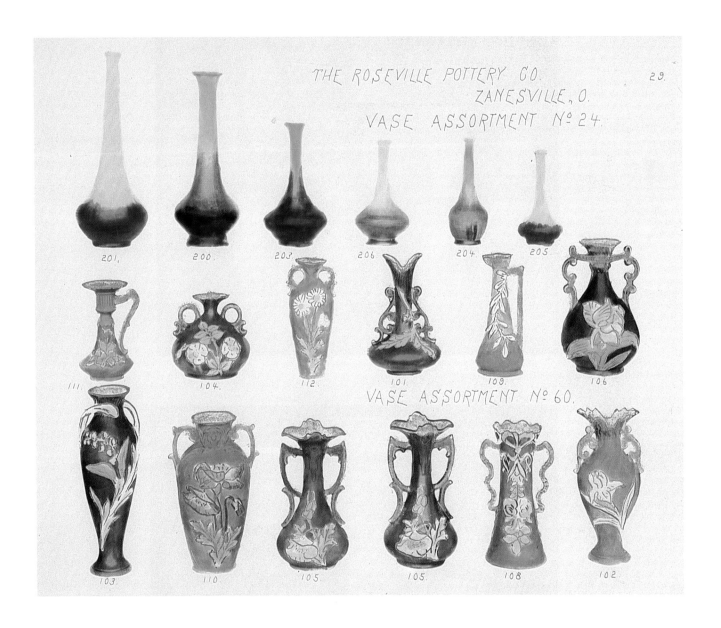

Compliments of the Ohio Historical Society

Vase Assortment - Circa 1903

A line of Rozane look-a-like vases pictured in the Roseville catalog pages as Vase Assortment No. 24. They were plain, tall and slender necked developing into a wide base with no embossing or art work. A strong melting of color flowing from a dark color into a bright light color was created in a variety of shapes and colors. They came in a matt glaze to enhance the design. Also displayed on this page is a line referred to as Vase Assortment No. 60. A Majolica type line with heavy embossed designs of large flowers and leaves on a solid handpainted background. The decorations were usually white or pastel colors with a dark background of brown, green, blue, tan, orange or yellow. A variety of floral designs created a much sought after decorative vase assortment. The styles had creative shaped handles and wide fancy lips. A high gloss glaze was used and each style was marked with a raised mold number.

Compliments of the George Krause collection

Velmoss I - Circa 1916-1919

Most commonly known as Velmoss Scroll. A solid cream matt glaze background with little red roses and small green leaves impressed on a brown/red branch like design. The roses encompass the basic shape. This pattern was offered for a short time in 35 different shapes and with no variation of color combination. They came with no handles on plain rounded shape and had no baskets with large handles. They were all unmarked.

Compliments of the George Krause collection

Velmoss II - Circa January 1935

An embossed pattern of long pointy leaves in a cluster hanging downward across three wavy horizontal lines. Every so often a small white berry pops out between the leaves. A smooth satin matt glaze was used over the traditional shapes of this line.

There are approximately 20 different styles displaying pointed handles. They came in turquoise, green, blue or rose. Several colors came with a lining of orange, while others were the same solid color as the design.

Note: *Rarity - A wide range due to color variations. Pricing from low end green, strawberry, blue to very rare cream. All are unmarked.*

Both photo's are compliments of the
Ohio Historical Society

Venetian - Circa before 1900

One of the original utility cooking ware lines. There is a major difference in this line compared to the others of this time. This pattern is almost always marked. It was possibly a second thought but none the less, the mark looked to be hand impressed and sometimes the first N was inverted.

Often the spaces and lines are uneven. The rim of each mixing bowl, casserole, custard cup, and baking dish are embossed with a scalloped design and the bottom is of a cross hatched design. They are mostly made in soft blue, yellow, or white outside with a dark brown or white high gloss glaze interior. It is believed these pieces were reproduced several times in the later years.

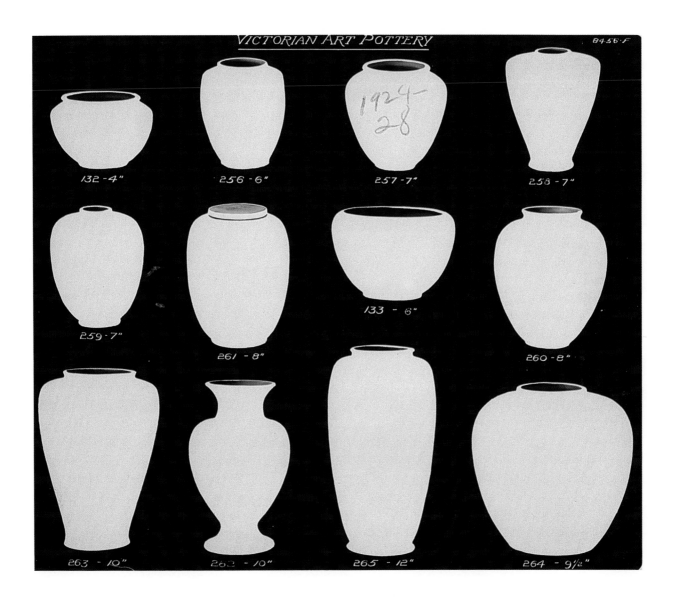

Compliments of the Ohio Historical Society

Victorian Art Pottery - Circa 1924-1928

This art pottery is displayed only in a black and white silhouette picture in the old Roseville catalog pages. There are twelve different shapes embossed in Egyptian or floral designs around a band of soft blended colors on a smooth matt glaze. The most common background colors were brown, gray, blue, green or a dark red/black. The background bands were usually a lighter color white, orange, gray or yellow. Mostly unmarked but a few have been found with an Rv ink stamp.

Compliments of the George Krause collection

Volpato - Circa 1918-1921

    A line of solid ivory glazed shapes with a fluted "Donatello" like appearance and a row of hanging garland encircling it. Several shapes have no fluting or garland but are still members of the Volpato line. There are 33 known shapes and if found marked they would have a black paper label. The molds were used in a later line called "Savona", but unlike the Volpato, they came in other colors.

Compliments of the Ohio Historical Society

Compliments of the George Krause collection

Water Lily - Circa January 1943

  This design consists of a large embossed open water lily on a watery background of horizontal wavy ridges. The large blossom is surrounded by large green leaves and branches. The flowers vary in color from white, pink or yellow depending on the background which starts out at the bottom with a dark shade (brown, green or blue) and blends into a lighter color (pink, blue or terra cotta). There are more than 50 shapes known to be in existence.

  This pattern had many larger than normal shapes, all marked with Roseville in relief and a shape number. It came in a satin matt finish. Extremely good molds are common in this line.

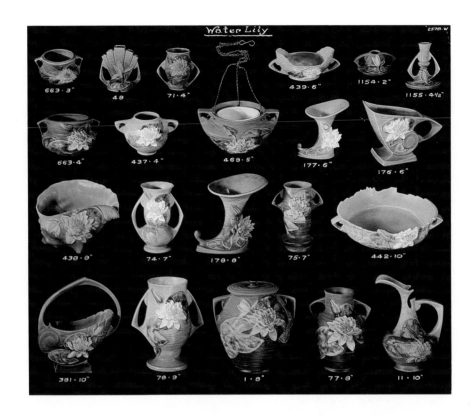

Compliments of the George Krause collection

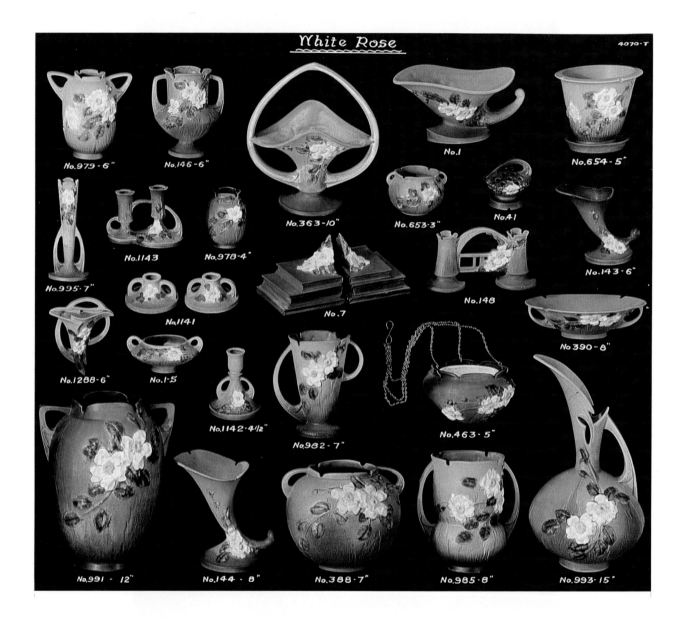

Compliments of the George Krause collection

White Rose - Circa July 1940

This design boasts a cluster of one or as many as four small white roses with yellow pistils enhanced by small green leaves and branches with a satin matt glaze. Vertical grooving accent the area around the design of flowers and leaves with a blending of background colors of green with terra cotta, blue with azure, pink with green and brown with green. A very unusual shaped rim and large handles are common. Over 70 shapes are pictured in the catalog pages, making it one of the more extensive lines. They are all marked with Roseville in relief and a shape number.

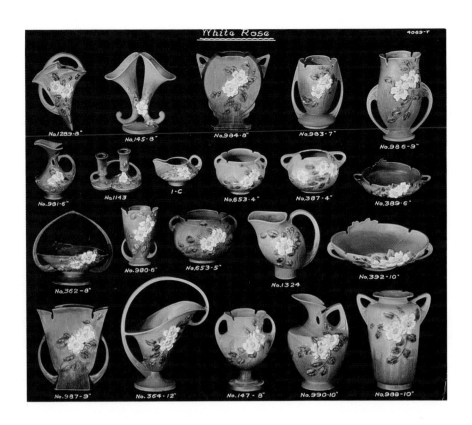

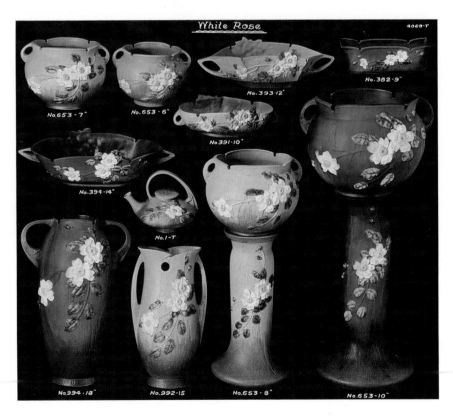

Compliments of the George Krause collection

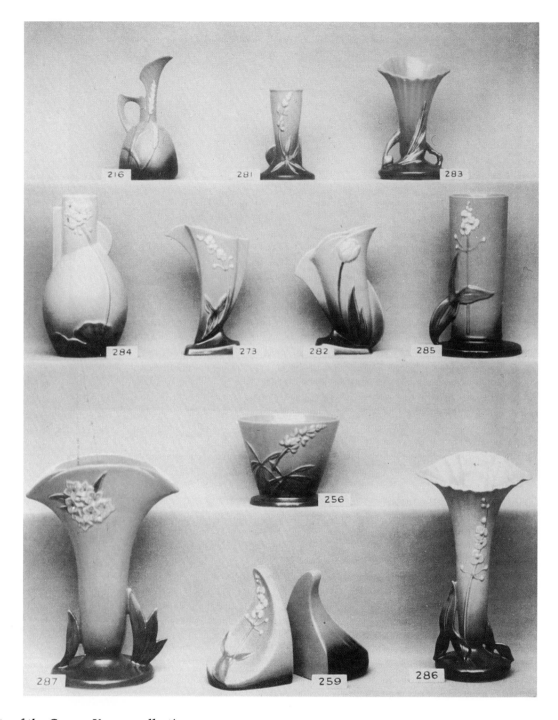

Compliments of the George Krause collection

Wincraft - Circa January 1948

In the waning years of the company, Roseville turned to a glossy glaze. In hope to stimulate sagging sales, the company introduced this line. Even though it was artistic, it had no success with the public. Other successful lines, like the Pinecone, were included with the addition of a high gloss glaze.

This line was credited to the company president of that era, Robert Windisch. In fact, he suggested and even inspired some of the design. Free flowing Art Deco shapes were embossed with flowers or animals on bright high gloss colors of azure blue, chartreuse, and apricot with a darker shade around the bottom. Many of the shapes were borrowed from earlier lines with a little update. Few shapes were originally made for this line. Marked with a Roseville in relief and a shape number. Over 50 styles are pictured in a brochure made to promote the Wincraft line.

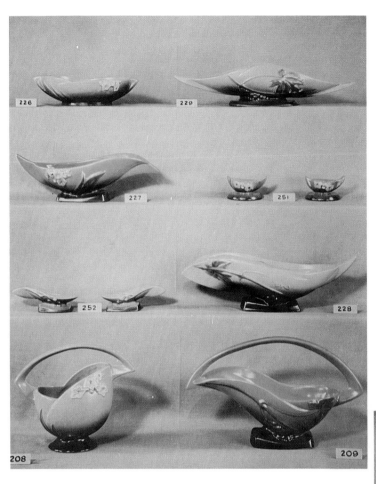

*Both photo's are compliments of the
George Krause collection*

*Both photo's are compliments of the
George Krause collection*

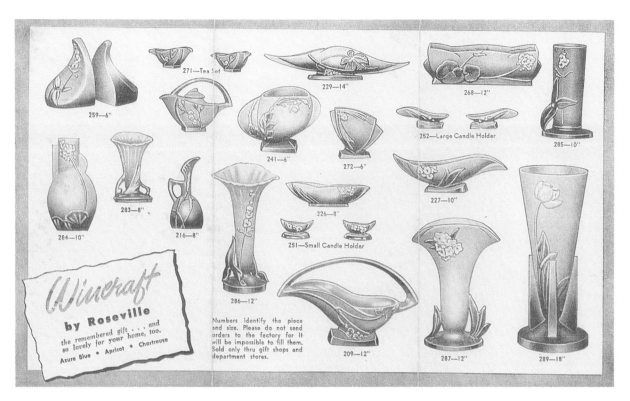

Compliments of the George Krause collection

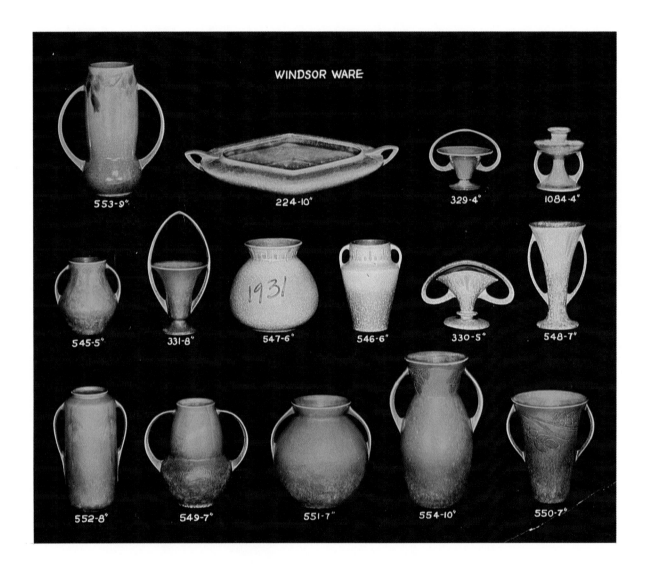

Compliments of the Ohio Historical Society

Windsor - Circa 1931

A line of smooth shadowy motif of vines, ferns, leaves or geometric designs on a tinted blend of blue or brown. A blue blending into green or terra cotta blending into dark brown were satin matt glazed. Most of the baskets and vases have thin handles and rounded bottom and came in approximately 15 shapes. Additional bowls and consoles have been reported. Most of the line is rounded and marked with either a black or silver paper sticker.

632-5"   242-4   630-6"   631-6"   629-4"   1091-4"

634-7"   636-8"   637-6½"   635-8"   243-5"x9"

640-12"   638-9"   633-8"   639-10"   641-15"

Compliments of the George Krause collection

Wisteria - Circa 1937

This design contains heavily embossed lavender wisteria blossoms hanging from green vines and a large mass of green leaves. A brown textured background blends into a dark green or almost a black/blue at the base. Most of this lines round shapes were repeated from earlier lines. A typical satin matt glaze was used and like most of the lines from this period, most of the shapes are unmarked. They were originally marked with a silver paper label. Roseville pages show only 16 different shapes but there are at least 10 more known at this time.

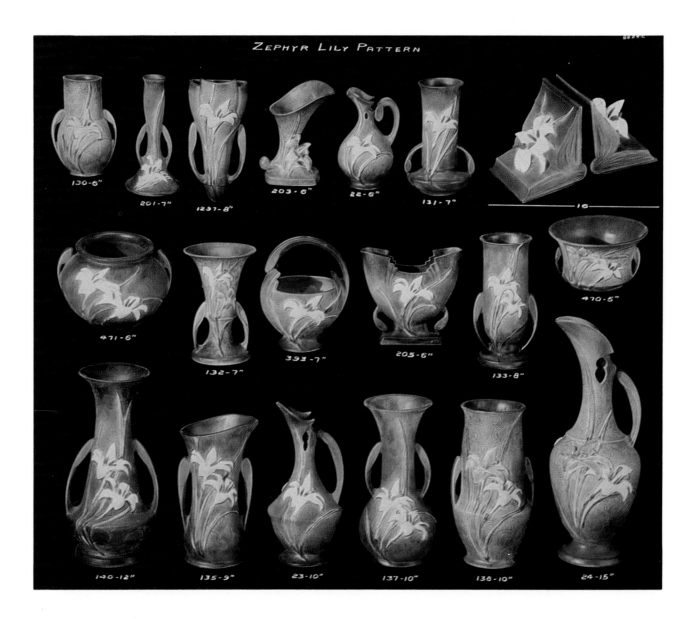

ZEPHYR LILY PATTERN

130-6"   201-7"   1297-8"   203-6"   22-6"   131-7"   16

471-6"   132-7"   393-7"   205-6"   133-8"   470-5"

140-12"   135-9"   23-10"   137-10"   138-10"   24-15"

Compliments of the Ohio Historical Society

Zephyr Lily - Circa July 1946

    A line of tall lilies and slender stems among long thin leaves. The designs have different colored lilies; yellow on an evergreen background, white or yellow lilies on bermuda blue and a soft rose colored lily on a sienna or yellow background. The background colors blend; dark green into sienna, dark blue into bermuda blue and dark green or blue into evergreen. All are marked with Roseville in relief and a style number and were made in a satin matt glaze. Many large styles are featured: 12", 15" and 18" vases, and 10" and 15" ewers to name some. There are over 50 shapes.

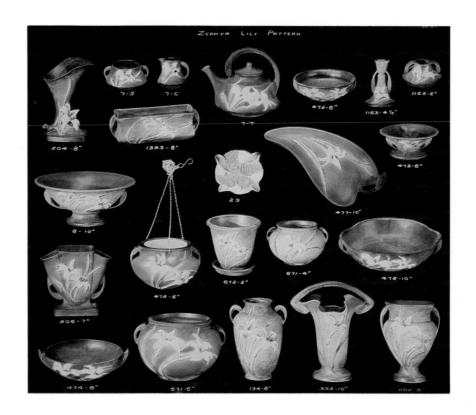

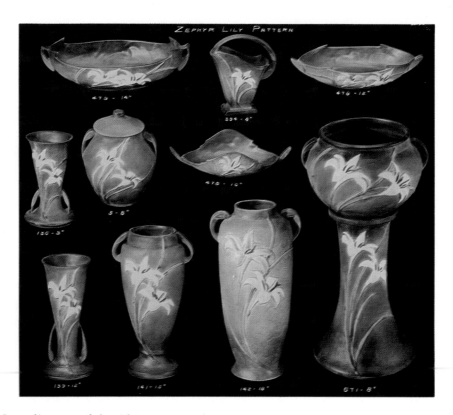

Compliments of the Ohio Historical Society

Around the turn of the century, almost every home had a large umbrella stand in their entrance way. They were all marked with a paper label or a number and came in every possible design, size, color combination and glaze.

Sand jars were used mainly for business to hold large plants at entrances for theaters and such. They could also be used in the home. These pieces came in all patterns and ranged from 15" to 24" in height.

A sign of prosperity was a fancy jardiniere and pedestal. They came in a large variety of sizes and shapes to fit the needs of each household. As times and decor changed, so did the jardiniere and pedestal. Every design had at least one or more sizes.

(The mold numbers on these jardinieres and pedestals, jardinieres, umbrella stands and sand jars were almost impossible to put in some sort of order. We have tried to list them by plate instead of numerical.)

Both photo's are compliments of the Ohio Historical Society

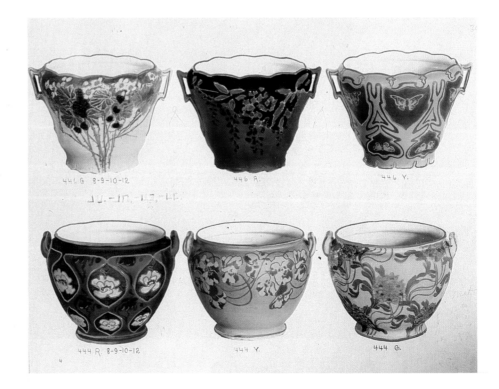

372

Compliments of the Ohio Historical Society

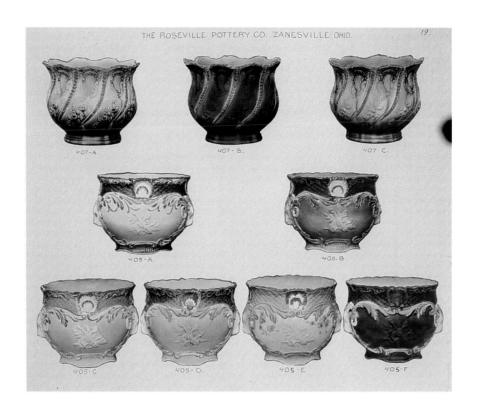

Compliments of the Ohio Historical Society

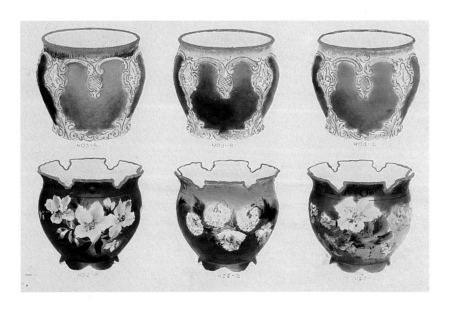

Compliments of the Ohio Historical Society

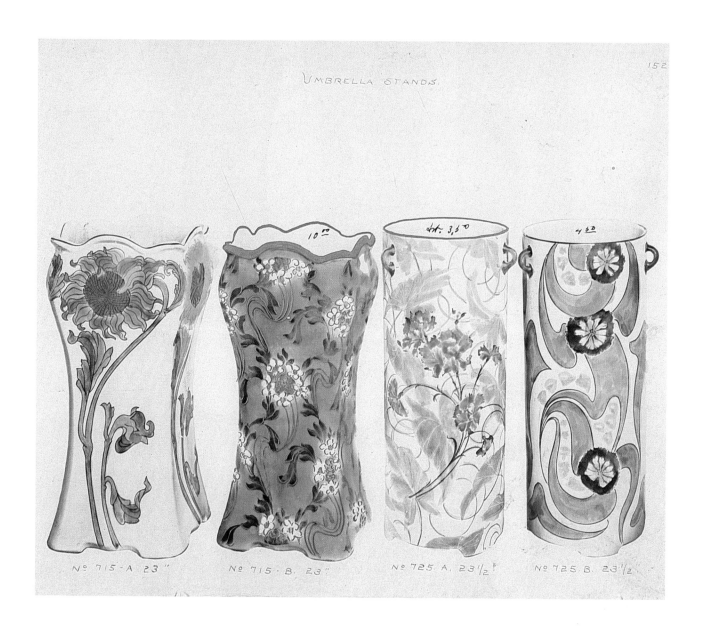

Compliments of the Ohio Historical Society

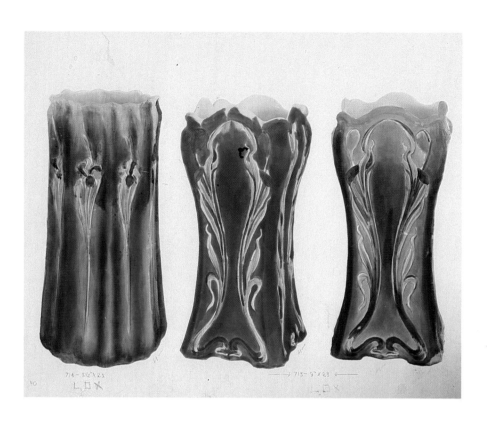

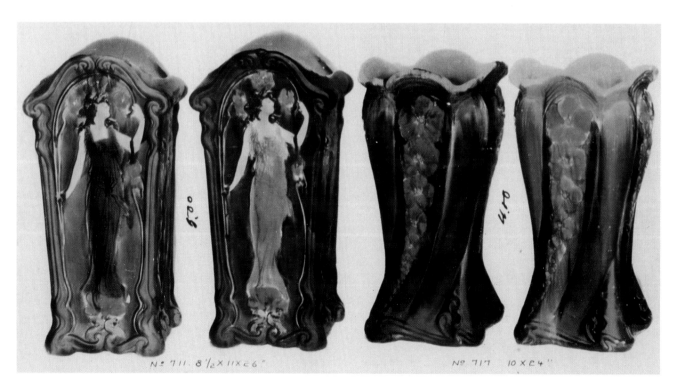

Both photo's are compliments of the Ohio Historical Society

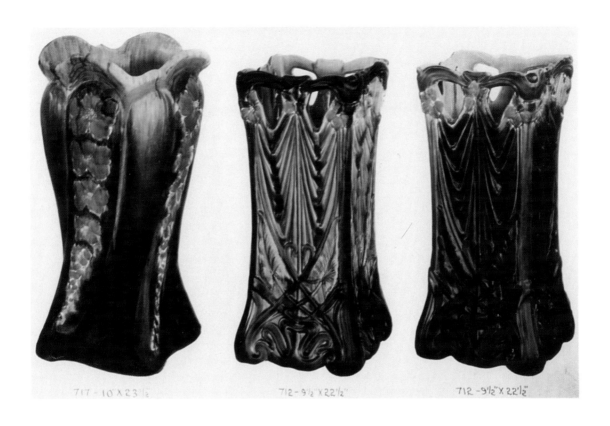

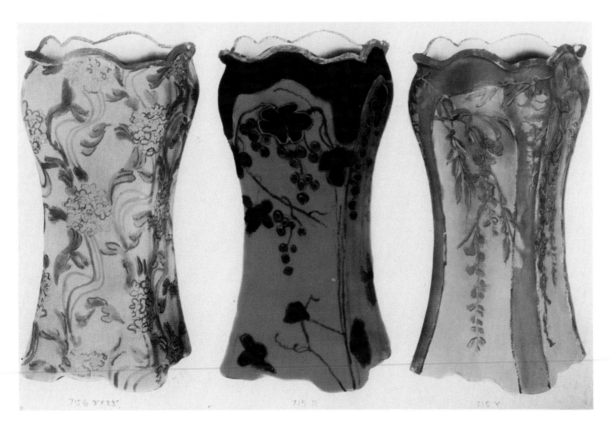

Both photo's are compliments of the Ohio Historical Society

Compliments of the Ohio Historical Society

705 - 8" X 18"   708 A - 8" X 19½"   708 B - 8" X 19½"

718 - 9" X 21½"   703 - 9" X 22"   721 - 8" X 21½"

Compliments of the Ohio Historical Society

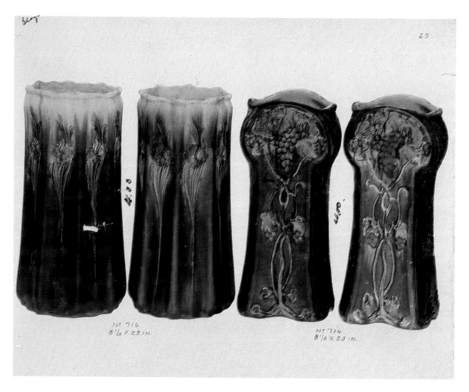

Compliments of the Ohio Historical Society

Compliments of the Ohio Historical Society

383

Plate 1

Plate 2

Compliments of the Ohio Historical Society

Plate 3

Plate 4

Compliments of the Ohio Historical Society

Plate 5

Plate 6

Compliments of the Ohio Historical Society

Plate 7

Plate 8

Compliments of the Ohio Historical Society

Plate 9

Plate 10

Compliments of the Ohio Historical Society

Plate 11

Plate 12

Compliments of the Ohio Historical Society

389

Plate 13

Plate 14

Compliments of the Ohio Historical Society

Plate 15

Plate 16

Compliments of the Ohio Historical Society

Plate 17

Plate 18

Compliments of the Ohio Historical Society

Plate 19

Plate 20

Compliments of the Ohio Historical Society

Plate 21

Plate 22

Plate 23

Plate 24

Compliments of the Ohio Historical Society

Plate 25

Compliments of the Ohio Historical Society

The patterns listed on these pages are known patterns of the Roseville Pottery Company. We have no further information at this time. Hopefully, as we do further research, we will be able to supply more information on these lost patterns.

Acanthus

No more than a piece of the Mayfair line with a larger than normal spout, a lighter colored inside than outside, but still no more than a Mayfair.

Birds

At this time there is no evidence of "Roseville" Ducks, but we have found mention regarding "Birds". In a price list of July, 1916, we found a list of bowls in white, black, and yellow (4"-6"-8" and 10") with birds on them. There also is a mention of separate birds which came in yellow, black, hand decorated red, blue and matt white. There is no mention of the size of these birds. It is believed that they must be unmarked or certainly someone would have mentioned them by now. Here is a mystery for us all to try to unravel.

Blue/Green Band - Circa 1910-1920

Part of the creamware pattern. Pieces have blue, green, and gold bands painted by hand and came in a matt glaze. Beige and white were used for backgrounds with black or darker figurines. Black piping used to edge the bands. Toilet sets, pitchers, and cuspidors were decorated in this style. Many styles of Dutch ware were used in this line, and marked with Rv or a paper label.

Brown - Circa Early 1900's

Produced around the turn of the century as another style of cuspidors. A combination of dark browns and a green blending with an embossed rim and covered with a high gloss glaze. Believed to have been marked with a paper label but in most cases unmarked now.

Canvasser's Outfit - Circa 1896

Back in the time when door to door salesmen were traveling across the country side selling their ware, Roseville ran this ad in hope to recruit salesmen.
Entire outfit $1.00
Included: #90 miniature umbrella stand, 3" x 4" . . . . $.50
      #91 was shown, the same as #90, different motif).
      Miniature cuspidor - 3" wide . . . . $.20
      (#219, #221, and #201 was the same cuspidor, different decoration).
      #315 miniature cooking crook . . . . $.10 (Ad says "Too well known to need comment).
      #21 apple bank and #120 orange bank . . . . $.10 each, finished to represent real fruit.
            Oranges and apples are unmarked.
ANY CANVASSER WITH THIS OUTFIT CAN MAKE $4 to $6 PER DAY.

Dog Dishes - Late Teens

Several styles of dog dishes have been found. The most common fact is that they are labeled on the front with the words "Dog Dish" and are stamped on the bottom with an Rv. One style is a plain pottery looking dish with little or no glaze while another was produced with a darker outside coloring and white or cream looking interior liner. This style had a matt to shiny glaze. The lips are rounded and emphasized more on this style.

Fern Trail - Circa Early 1900's

A popular design of cuspidor in a variety of colors. Mostly ivory background with trails running horizontally in basic black. Trapped between these trails are the prominent colors of blue, gray, green, brown or gold. A matt finish was used. Found unmarked, the same molds were used in other solid color combinations and glazes.

Figurals

There are no records of any such designs throughout the Roseville records. A single artist sketch of a Roman or Greek head shaped pitcher is the only evidence of such an item.

Gibson Girl - Circa 1910-1915

A popular line of ivory creamware in a matt glaze finish displaying decals of a gathering of women conversing. Such styles as teapots, sugar and creamer, and mugs have been found. Lids for the teapot and sugar have sharp angles coming to a point. Piping was used to highlight the rim and base. As all creamware, they were unmarked.

Green Band - Teens

There was specific mention of this line several times in the records, but no pictures are available. We are assuming this line to be similar to the Blue band line of creamware. It had a wide band around the middle and lid. Black piping was used to accent the band and all pieces were covered with a matt glaze. Of course, they were unmarked.

Holly - Circa Early 1900's

This creamware line was made around Christmas to create a holiday atmosphere. Holly leaves and red berries were used as a highlight for this pattern. A touch of green piping was used on the handles and rims in the early line, which was done in a matt finish. Later lines were done in a high gloss glaze. This pattern was made in a wide range of coffee pots, sugar and creamers, candle holders, mugs and tankers. No marks were used.

Ivy - Circa 1910-1915

A line of creamware embellished with a trellis, climbing vines and ivy leaves surrounding the shapes. The trellis was in white with a gray, brown, pale green or yellow background. The leaves were in a pale green, the pieces were finished in a matt glaze. The basic simple shapes of the ivory tint and ceramic lines were utilized for the ivy design. Most of the line is unmarked but there were reports of a few pieces found with a Roseville paper sticker. There are no pictures of this line in the Roseville papers.

Loerber

This is listed on an inventory sheet from around 1916 but no further information or pictures can be found. Lets all try to figure this one out.

Mahogany - Circa Early 1900's

An early line of cuspidors embossed on a Victorian style, believed to be referred to because of the mahogany color of the cuspidors. This pattern had wide flared rim with deeply embossed designs of ribbons or vine encompassing the shape below the rim. Solid in color with the embossing showing through the shiny glaze, all are unmarked.

Merican - Circa Early 1900's

Marked: THE ROSEVILLE POTTERY CO. - MERICAN

A newly discovered lost line of the early period with an extensive use of the creamware line. Several pieces came with a soft overtone of orange, light pink, green and blue with a wide variety of poppy-like flowers or poinsettias covered with a variety of green leaves. On several pieces, the leaves are part of the flowers while on others the five pointed leaves extend up from the base and encircle the flowers. The entire line is highlighted with a dark edge around the top and a lighter edge encompassing the base. A checkerboard band is used as an accent on several pieces while on others there were no bands. A wide variety of color combinations and designs were used. It is believed the mold number is 545 and came in a size of either 6", 7", 8", 10", or 12".

New Hampshire Vintage - Circa 1924-1928

Often referred to as Victorian Art Pottery. The same twelve shapes displayed on the Roseville catalog pages as Victorian Art Pottery were used for this line. These pieces had a soft almost pastel yellow, blue, green, or gray background with a high gloss glaze. Each piece had a blended band of large leaves with vines and a cluster of grape like berries draping from a white puff which surrounded the shape. Most of the shapes look as if they were covered jars and should have a lid but lids were not displayed on the catalog pages. When marked, the Rv ink stamp was used.

Pinecone 2 - Circa July 1953

This high gloss glaze pinecone line was an attempt to give a shot at stimulating the sales of the Wincraft line of the 50's. The bright colors of terra cotta, yellow and blue were used with a high gloss finish. Many of the old Pinecone line molds were used, even as far as the same numbers were used. The cones were brown with long green needle like leaves. Marked with a raised "Roseville U.S.A." and style number.

Rozane-Gold - Circa 1904

Metallic gold was very popular in this era. It was used in glazes, to border and to outline many designs. Gold added richness to the product, therefore, it was natural that a line of gold was introduced at this period of time. The basic shapes of many Rozanes were used, but the line was not very successful. Perhaps the cost of each piece was more than was expected. These pieces were unmarked and very hard to identify as Roseville.

Vernco

A company which distributed ashtrays made by Roseville during the time that they produced for several other companies. The ashtrays came in a wide variety of colors, any color or combination that would blend with the decor of the era; bright yellow, red, blue, black, green or pink. The designs were simple with a single cigarette holder in the middle versus the holders indented on the side of each piece. A high gloss glaze was used. They were marked "Vernco" and a style number. Unlike "The Hyde Park Co." that also sold ashtrays, these are a rare find.

Bibliography

1. *ZANESVILLE ART POTTERY IN COLOR*
    by Louise & Evan Purviance and Norris F. Schneider

2. *ZANESVILLE ART POTTERY*
    by Norris F. Schneider

3. *ROSEVILLE ART POTTERY IN COLOR*
    by Louise & Evan Purviance and Norris F. Schneider

4. *THE TIMES REPORTER - ZANESVILLE*
    Article by Norris F. Schneider, November 4, 1979

5. *ZANES TIME SIGNAL*
    Article by Norris F. Schneider, March 1959

6. *ROSEVILLE - FOR LOVE OR MONEY*
    by Virginia Hillary Buxton

7. *FREDRICK HURTEN RHEAD . . . AN ENGLISH POTTER IN AMERICA*
    by Sharon Dale

8. *THE TIMES REPORTER*
    Article by Norris F. Schneider, September 2, 1979

9. *SPINNING WHEEL VOL. 25 #10*
    Roseville Pottery 1892-1954
    by Lucille Henzke , November & December 1969

10. *ART POTTERY OF AMERICA*
    By Lucille Henzke

11. *THE KOVEL'S COLLECTORS GUIDE TO AMERICAN ART POTTERY*
    By Ralph & Terry Kovel, 1974

12. *MILLION & CHERUB*
    by Deb & Gini Johnson, February 1975

13. *THE COLLECTORS ENCYCLOPEDIA OF ROSEVILLE POTTERY SERIES I & II*
    by Sharon & Bob Huxford

14. *THE SPLENDOR OF AMERICAN CERAMIC ART 1882-1952*
    by Donald Karshan

History of the Pottery Club
Rosevilles of the Past - 1990 to Present

Since this is our first book, we would like to give you a bit of information about ourselves and our club.

I was born in Williamsport, Pennsylvania in 1941 and Nancy was born in McKeesport, Pennsylvania in 1942. I moved to McKeesport in 1956, where I attended school. Nancy and I met in high school, dated through that time and married June 1960. We have two boys, both married and have two beautiful grandchildren.

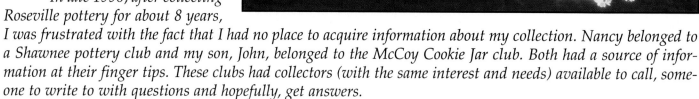

Most of our lives have been spent in the northeast, where I was a general store manager for a grocery chain. I worked there for 25 years. Within that time, we lived in New York, Pennsylvania and New Jersey.

As we got older, the weather in the north became too hard to handle and we decided to make the move to Florida where we had family. I am now retired and Nancy is a secretary for Lew Hudson Sales.

In late 1990, after collecting Roseville pottery for about 8 years, I was frustrated with the fact that I had no place to acquire information about my collection. Nancy belonged to a Shawnee pottery club and my son, John, belonged to the McCoy Cookie Jar club. Both had a source of information at their finger tips. These clubs had collectors (with the same interest and needs) available to call, someone to write to with questions and hopefully, get answers.

After lengthy research, I discovered there was no pottery club for Roseville in existence. We called Sharon Huxford, who publishes well known books on Roseville, and found there was no such club.

With a strong desire to learn more about Roseville and a need to meet fellow collectors, we decided to form our own club. We had both run a stock car racing club in New Jersey with over 200 members. How different could it be to run a pottery club?

With my business background, I knew it took advertising to get something like this started. Thus the start of ROSEVILLES OF THE PAST POTTERY CLUB. In January 1991, the first newsletter was published. It consisted of only one page. Several local collectors and dealers joined the club and with the help of selected advertising in the antique papers the club grew to over 100 members in the first year.

As advertising expanded, more and more inquiries about the club continued to pour in, the club and newsletter continued to grow.

We always keep in mind the main reason the club was formed . . . to meet fellow collectors and learn as much about our collection as possible.

In January 1998, the club held its fourth annual pottery show and auction in Orlando, Florida. With the passing of each year, we hope our show will continue to grow and perhaps someday be as large as the one in Zanesville, Ohio.

Since conception of the club, it has grown to over 500 club members in 48 states and 5 providences of Canada. My dream has come true. The club has grown far above my expectations.

This book is for all dreamers with hopes that your dream will also come true.

PRICE GUIDE / INDEX

ANTIQUE MATT GREEN . . . . Page 47
JARDINIERES

4"	$150-200	10"	$ 700- 900
6"	200-250	12"	1000-1500
7"	275-325	JARDINIERE & PEDESTAL	
8"	375-475	10" X 26¼"	$1400-1600
9"	500-600	12" X 33½"	2000-2400

APPLE BLOSSOM . . . . Page 48-49

35	$ 100- 175	330-10	$150- 225	373-7	$125- 200
129-7	100- 175	331-6	175- 200	379-7	100- 175
300-4	120- 190	331-12	150- 275	379-9	100- 175
301-6	150- 250	333-14	190- 300	381-6	100- 175
302-8	350- 500	337-4	125- 175	382-7	125- 190
303-10	500- 800	337-10	100- 175	385-8	125- 190
305-8	400- 600	342-6	150- 275	385-10	135- 225
306-10	1300- 1600	351-2	100- 150	386-6	100- 175
309-8	275- 400	351-10	175- 275	387-7	100- 175
310-10	300- 475	352-4	200- 375	387-9	150- 275
311-12	350- 500	356-5	150- 250	388-10	175- 300
316-8	200- 300	359-2	150- 205	389-10	175- 300
317-7	150- 250	363-18	800-1600	390-12	225- 350
318-15	600-1200	366-8	275- 400	391-12	300- 400
319-7	75- 100	368-8	100- 200	392-15	400- 650
321-6	100- 160	369-10	135- 175	393-18	650-1000
323-8	130- 240	369-12	200- 300	J&P-8	1000-2200
326-6	125- 200	371-P	250- 350	J&P-10	1300-2600
328-8	175- 250	371-C	75- 150	HP361-5	250- 400
329-10	150- 250	371-S	75- 150		
		373-6	130- 200		

ARTWOOD . . . . Page 50-51

1050-2	$ 30- 60	1054-8½	$100-150	1059-10	$150-200
1051-6	75-125	1055-9	100-125	1060-12	300-350
1052-8	125-150	1056-10	150-200	1061-10	150-200
1053-8	150-200	1057-8	100-150	1062-5	150-200
1058-8	150-200				

AUTUMN . . . . Page 52
MOLD NUMBERS:

Toothbrush Holder		Jardinieres:	
	$150-200	480-7	$250-300
Chamber Pot	400-500	480-8	300-400
Pitcher	275-350	480-9	400-450
Lg. Pitcher	400-500	480-10	450-500
Basin	300-350	498-7	250-300
Combinett	600-800	498-8	300-400
Powder Jar	175-225	498-9	400-450
Mug	150-200	498-10	450-500

AZTEC ART 53
MOLD NUMBERS:

1	$400-500	10	$350-450	19	$350-450
2	400-500	11	400-500	20	350-400
3	400-500	12	350-450	21	350-450
4	350-450	13	300-400	22	300-400
5	350-400	14	300-400	23	300-400
6	400-500	15	300-400	24	300-400
7	400-500	16	350-450	PITCHERS:	
8	400-500	17	300-400	1	300-400
9	400-500	18	300-400	2	475-525
				3	300-400

AZUREAN . . . . Page 54
MOLD NUMBERS:

812-12	$3000-3500	865-18	$ 4000-5000	933-15	$4000-5000
813-7¾	1600-2000	882-9	4000-5000	935-6	1500-2000
814-9¼	900-1000	888-9	275- 325	936-8	2000-2500
814-9¼	1800-2200	891-14	4500-5500	937-8	1500-1800
821-8½	800-1000	892-8½	1200-1500	955-17	2500-3000
832-15½	3000-3500	893-13	1200-1500	955-17	5000-6000
835-10¾	500- 600	900-6	400- 500	956-8	800-1000
845-11½	3500-4500	921-11	700- 800	957-16	1500-1800
855-14	1200-1500	931-15	3000-3500	958-11	1300-1600
856-4	250- 300	933-15	2000-2500	959-7	300- 350

AZURINE-ORCHID-TURQUOISE . . . . Page 55
MOLD NUMBERS:

66-4	$ 50- 70	182-12	$250-300	598-5	$175-200
93-8	60- 80	183-14	325-375	598-6	200-250
93-10	75-100	313-11	350-400	1029-3	60- 80
93-12	150-175	314-11	350-400	1030-4	75-100
94-5	125-150	315-11	350-400	1031-6	175-225
95-7	60- 80	316-9	325-375	1032-8	175-225
96-6	60- 80	317-13	400-500	1033-12	300-350
180-10	200-250	318-13	400-500	1034-15	400-500
181-12	250-300				

BANEDA . . . . Page 56-57
MOLD NUMBERS:

232-6	$275-500	594-9	$ 700- 1200	606-7	$ 550- 700
233-8	325-500	595-8	900- 1400	610-7	550- 700
234-10	375-550	596-9	900- 1500	626-4	275- 375
235-5	500-800	597-10	900- 1500	626-5	400- 500
237-12	450-550	598-12	1000-1900	626-6	500- 600
587-4	375-500	599-12	1200-2100	626-7	1000-1200
588-6	350-500	600-15	1800-3200	626-9	1700-2000
589-6	400-600	601-5	300- 350	626-8	3000-3500
590-7	450-650	602-6	325- 600	626-10	4000-5000
591-6	350-600	603-4	325- 500	1087-5	300- 350
592-7	450-650	604-7	450- 600	1088-4	300- 400
593-8	400-650	605-6	400- 500	1269-8	1600-1900

BANKS AND NOVELTIES . . . . Page 58

Bee Hive Sm.	$150-200	Laying Pig Lg.	$175-200
Bee Hive Lg.	200-250	Lion Head	150-200
Buffalo	150-200	Monkey Bottle 5"	100-150
Cat Head	225-275	Monkey Bottle	150-200
Dog Head	250-300	Standing Pig	150-200
Eagle Head Sm.	150-200	Uncle Sam	200-250
Eagle Head Lg.	200-250	Monkey Bank	200-275
Laying Pig Sm.	150-175	Ye Old Time Jug Sm.	100-150
		Ye Old Time Jug Lg.	150-200

BITTERSWEET . . . . Page 59-60

457	$ 125- 150	829-12	$125-200	871-S	$ 60- 75
672-5	150- 175	830-14	175-250	872-5	65- 75
800-4	100- 150	832-7	125-175	873-6	90- 110
801-6	150- 250	841-5	125-175	874-7	100- 125
802-8	150- 225	842-7	150-225	879-7	75- 100
805-8	1200- 1600	851-3	100-150	881-6	65- 85
807-8	150- 200	856-7	125-150	882-6	65- 85
808-6	150- 200	857-4	100-150	882-8	90- 110
809-8	250- 300	858-4	125-200	883-8	125- 150
810-10	200- 300	859	300-400	884-8	100- 125
811-10	225- 325	861-5	100-150	885-10	150- 175
816-8	150- 250	863-4	75-125	886-12	150- 250
822-8	125- 175	866-7	250-350	887-14	250- 300
825-6	125- 175	868-8	100-150	888-16	350- 400
826-6	100- 150	869-12	125-150	972-5	45- 55
827-8	125- 175	871-P	250-300	BK	225- 275
827-12	150- 200	871-C	50- 65		
828-10	100- 150				

BLACKBERRY . . . . Page 61

226-6	$ 450- 550	570-5	$ 425- 550	623-6	$ 475- 600
227-8	400- 475	571-6	500- 600	623-7	600- 900
228-10	950- 1100	572-6	550- 650	623-8	700-1000
334-6	700- 900	573-6	550- 650	623-9	1200-1600
335-7	800- 900	574-6	500- 650	JP623-10	3000- 3500
336-8	700- 850	575-8	700- 800	623-12	2000- 2500
348-5	900- 1200	576-8	600- 800	624-12	1300- 1400
378-12	1300- 1800	577-10	1000- 1200	1086-4	500- 650
567-4	400- 500	623-4	350- 450	1267-8	1000- 1500
568-4	450- 500	623-5	400- 500		
569-5	450- 550				

BLEEDING HEART . . . . Page 62-63

40	$100-175	381-10	$ 175- 200	965-7	$ 150- 250
124-8	200-250	382-10	150- 250	966-7	175- 250
138-4	100-150	382-12	250- 375	967-7	175- 225

Bleeding Heart continued

138-7	100-150	383-12	250- 350	968-8	200- 275
139-8	200-250	384-14	275- 400	969-8	225- 325
140-4	150-200	651-3	75- 100	970-9	275- 375
141-6	150-175	651-4	150- 175	971-9	250- 350
142-8	175-200	651-5	175- 225	972-10	275- 325
148-4	120-150	651-6	225- 275	973-10	300- 350
359-8	250-375	651-7	275- 350	974-12	400- 450
360-10	325-400	JP651-8	1500-3000	975-15	600- 800
361-12	350-475	JP651-10	1800-3800	976-15	600- 800
362-5	350-400	652-5	125- 225	977-18	1100-1800
377-4	175-300	961-4	125- 175	1139-4	175- 250
378-6	200-250	962-5	150- 200	1140-2	100- 150
379-6	200-250	963-6	175- 250	1287-8	425- 600
380-8	200-275	964-6	150- 200	1323	375- 500
#6BE	350-450				

BLENDED . . . . Page 64-72
MOLD NUMBERS:
UMBRELLA STANDS:

		407-10	$275-325	6"	$ 125- 150
701 10x21	$400-500	409-9	275-325	7"	150- 200
705 8x18	450-550	411-10	300-350	8"	250- 275
706 8x21	500-600	413-10	300-350	9"	300- 350
708 8x19	550-650	417-5	150-175	10"	375- 425
719 8½x21	500-600	418-4	125-150		

PAGE J-4

		419-7	200-225	JARDINIERE & PEDESTAL	
454-4	50- 60	419-9	250-300	404 12x27	800-1000
454-5	60- 80	419-10	275-325	405-35	1200-1500
454-6	80-100	420-7	300-350	406-30	700- 900
464 10x25	500-700	420-9	200-225	407-30	700- 900
458 10x25	600-800	420-10	275-325	410-37	1000-1200
460 10x25	800-950	421-8	300-350	414-33	1000-1200
459 10x25	800-900	421-9	250-300	422 10x24	600- 700

JARDINIERE

422-458-419		421-10	275-325	422 10x29	700- 900
7"	200-225	422-7	300-350	425-44	2000-2500
8"	250-300	422-8	200-225	430 10x25	400- 500
9"	275-325	422-9	250-300	431 10x25	400- 500
10"	300-350	422-10	275-325	437 13x27	600- 700
405-410-404-423-406		458-7	300-350	442 12x28	700- 900
ALL	275-325	458-9	200-225	452 14x33	1600-2000
506-8	275-325	459-8	275-325	479 10x30	800-1000
9	325-375	459-10	250-300	1201-25	500- 600
10	350-400	460-8	300-350	1203 10x25	600- 700
12	400-500	464-7	250-300	405	250- 300
508-7	250-300	464-9	200-225	410	300- 350
8	275-325		275-325	404	250- 300
10	350-400	403-404-407-410-419-406		423	300- 350
442 13x30	600-700	420-421-422-423-426-			250- 300
442 12x28	500-600	427-430			

BLUE/BLACK TEAPOTS . . . . Page 73
MOLD NUMBERS: (Same molds as Della Robbia)

1.	$350-400	5.	$225-275	241	$50- 75
2.	275-325	6.	225-300	242	75-100
3.	225-275			243	100-125
				244	125-150

BLUE/GREEN AND GOLD . . . . Page 74
MOLD NUMBERS:

Spittoon 615	$150-200	J & P	$800-1000
607	150-175		
Basin	200-250		
Toothbrush Holder	75-100		
Drinking Mug	50- 75		
Lg. Pitcher	200-250		

BURMESE . . . . Page 75

70B Male Candle	$250-400
71B Male Bookends	250-400
72B Male Wallpocket	275-375
75B Candleholder/B.E.	125-150
80B Female Candle	175-300
81B Female Bookends	175-300
82B Female Wallpocket	200-350
90B-10 Oriental Bowl	100-175

BUSHBERRY . . . . Page 76-77

1-3½	$100- 150	38-12	$325- 425	411-6	$ 200- 300
1-6	150- 225	39-14	500- 600	411-8	300- 350
1-10FB	225- 300	40-15	600-1000	412-6	150- 200
2T	250- 350	45	150- 225	414-10	150- 225
2C	75- 125	115-8	200- 250	415-10	150- 250
2S	75- 125	152-7	100- 150	416-12	200- 225
2-10	200- 300	153-6	100- 150	417-14	250- 300
3-8½	150- 200	154-8	150- 250	465-5	350- 450
3-15	600- 1000	155-8	150- 250	491-4	75- 125
9	200- 350	156-6	125- 175	548-4	75- 125
26	125- 200	157-8	200- 350	654-4	75- 125
28-4	100- 125	158-4	125- 225	657-3	75- 150
29-6	150- 200	282-4	100- 150	657-4	100- 175
30-6	100- 175	369-6	200- 350	657-5	150- 200
31-7	150- 225	370-8	200- 300	657-6	175- 250
31-8	175- 225	371-10	225- 300	JP657-8	1000-1500
32-7	200- 275	372-12	350- 400	JP657-10	1600-2000
33-8	175- 300	379-8	200- 275	658-5	325- 400
33-9	175- 300	383-6	100- 200	778-14	1500-2200
34-8	175- 225	384-8	125- 200	779-20	1000-1500
35-9	200- 300	385-10	150- 250	1147-2	100- 150
36-9	225- 325	411-4	100- 150	1148-4	150- 225
37-10	250- 350			1291-8	300- 350
1325	400- 600				

CAL ART . . . . Page 78

1507	$100-150

CAMEO . . . . Page 79
MOLD NUMBERS:

488-10-42	$1800-2200	#2-12	$1800-2200
488-13-42	2000-2600	489-6	200- 250
489-10	1800-2200	489-7	275- 325
489-12	2400-3000	489-8	325- 400
#2-10	1800-2200	489-9	375- 425
497-18-52"	3500-4500		

CAPRI . . . . Page 80-81

357-6	$ 40- 60	556-6	$ 75-100	598-9	$ 75-125
508-7	100-150	557-7	150-200	599-13	75-150
509-80	125-175	558	50- 75	C1003-8	100-150
510-10	150-200	563-10	100-150	C1004-9	125-175
525-5	40- 60	569-10	50- 75	C1009-8	100-150
526-7	50- 75	570-13	75- 100	C1010-10	70-100
527-7	40- 60	572-8	100- 150	C1012-10	150-200
528-9	70- 95	578-8	60- 80	C1013-5	200-250
529-9	60- 80	579-8	60- 80	C1116-10	150-250
530-12	75- 100	580-6	100- 150	C1017-12	150-200
531-14	125-175	581-9	125- 150	C1118	75-100
532-15	125-150	582-9	125- 150	C1119	125-200
533-10	50- 75	583-9	125- 175	C1120	150-200
534-16	125-175	586-12	150- 200	C1151	40- 60
552-4	40- 60	593-12	150- 200	WP	250-300
554-6	60- 80	597-7	40- 60		
555-7	40- 60				

CARNELIAN I . . . . Page 82-84
MOLD NUMBERS:

15-2	$ 50- 75	152-4	$100-150	1059-2	$150-200
15-3	75-100	152-5	100-150	1060-3	200-300
50-4	150-300	152-6	125-175	1063-3	150-200
50-5	200-350	152-7	150-200	1064-3	225-325
51-5	150-300	153-5	125-175	1065-4	225-300
52-6	150-300	154-6	150-200	1246-7	250-300
53-5	150-300	155-8	200-250	1247-8	300-350
54-8	175-325	156-12	250-300	1248-8	300-375
55-6	150-300	157-14	300-350	1249-9	325-400
56-5	150-300	331-7	150-200	1251-8	225-300
57-3	100-300	332-8	150-200	1252-8	225-325
58-3	100-150	333-6	200-300	1253-8	250-350
59-3	100-150	334-8	250-300	1311-10	300-375
60-6	150-300	335-8	225-325	1312-10	325-400
61-2	100-150	336-9	225-325	1313-12	325-400
62-3	100-150	337-10	300-350	1314-8	450-550
63-5	100-150	338-12	350-400	1315-15	450-550
64-2-5	150-200	339-15	450-500	1316-18	600-900
65-2-6	150-200	340-18	450-550		
1058-2	150-200				

PRICE GUIDE / INDEX

CARNELIAN II . . . . Page 85-86
MOLD NUMBERS:

15-2	$ 50-100	152-4	$200-300	1059-2	$300-400
15-3	150-300	152-5	200-300	1060-3	400-600
50-4	300-400	152-6	250- 350	1063-3	300- 400
50-5	300-500	152-7	300- 400	1064-3	400- 600
51-5	300-500	153-5	250- 350	1065-4	400- 600
52-6	300-500	154-6	275- 375	1246-7	400- 600
53-5	300-500	155-8	350- 450	1247-8	600- 700
54-8	350-500	156-12	500- 600	1248-8	600- 700
55-6	300-500	157-14	500- 700	1249-9	600- 800
56-5	300-500	331-7	300- 400	1251-8	400- 600
57-3	300-500	332-8	300- 400	1252-8	450- 650
58-3	200-300	333-6	400- 500	1253-8	450- 650
59-3	200-300	334-8	400- 500	1311-10	600- 700
60-6	250-550	335-8	400- 550	1312-10	600- 800
61-2	200-300	336-9	450- 600	1313-12	600- 800
62-3	200-300	337-10	600- 700	1314-8	900- 1100
63-5	200-300	338-12	700- 800	1315-15	900- 1100
64-2-5	300-500	339-15	700- 900	1316-18	1000-1800
65-2-6	300-400	340-18	900- 1100		
		1058-2	300- 400		
439-9	400- 500	450-14	2800-3500		
440-8	500- 600	456-20	3200-4200		
441-8	500- 600	457-24	2800-3800		
442-12	1000-1800	458-24	2800-3800		
443-12	1000-1500	459-28	3000-4000		
444-12	800-1200	460-28	3500-5000		
445-12	1200-1600	461-28	3500-5000		
446-12	1500-2000	WP7-8-9"	400- 500		
Frog	50- 150				

NOT IN PICTURE:

452-16	3000-3500
453-16	3000-3500
454-18	3200-3800
455-18	3200-3800

CERAMIC DESIGN 87-90
MOLD NUMBERS:

462-532-489		5"	$200-225	208-7	$325- 375
531-527		6"	225-275	209-6	250- 300
4"	125- 150	7"	250-300	210-4-8	350- 400
5"	150- 175	8"	325-375	211-3-6	300- 350
6"	175- 225	9"	350-400	212-10	600- 700
7"	200- 250	10"	450-500	213-3	175- 200
8"	275- 325	523 CERAMIC		213-4	200- 225
9"	300- 350	4"	150-175	213-5	225- 250
10"	400- 450	5"	175-200	214-4	200- 225
12"	600- 800	6"	200-225	214-5	225- 250
14"	650- 850	7"	225-275	215-4	200- 250
16"	750-1000	8"	300-375	215-5	225- 250
510-9"	325- 375	216-4	175-200		
4"	200- 250	10"	425-475	217-5	225- 250
6"	275- 325	527w/liner		218-3	150- 175
8"	425- 525	8"	400-500	218-4	175- 200
10"	625-825	532w/holder		218-5	200- 225
514-8"	450- 550	326-10	400-500		
4"	175- 225	9"	500-600	328-10	450- 500
7"	325-375	10"	600-700	330-11	600- 700
8"	400-500	12"	800-900	331-10	600- 700
10"	600-800	201-202-203-		334-14	750- 850
513-515-516		204-205-206		335-13	700- 800
4"	175-225	3"	125-150	336-18	800-1000
5"	200-225	4"	150-175	338-17	800-1000
6"	250-300	5"	175-200	1201	400- 500
7"	300-350	6"	225-250	1201-14	500- 600
8"	400-500	7"	250-300	1201-14	400- 500
9"	450-550	204		1202-15	500- 600
10"	600-700	3"	50- 75	CEMETERY VASE	
523 LILY-4"	75-100	10"	400-500		
4"	175-200	5"	100-125	12"	500- 600

IVORY CERAMICS

503-8	$325-375	505-7	$300-350	507-7	$325-375
503-9	400-450	505-8	325-375	507-8	400-450
503-10	750-850	505-10	750-850	507-9	400-450
504-7	300-350	506-8	325-375	508-7	300-325
504-9	400-500	506-9	400-450	508-8	325-375
504-10	750-850	506-10	750-850	508-10	750-850

CHERRY BLOSSOM . . . . Page 91

239-5	$350-400	623-7	$550- 600	627-9	$ 900-1200
240-8	350-400	624-8	550- 600	JP627-10	3000-4000
350-5	750-850	625-8	850- 950	627-12	1600-2100
617-3	350-400	626-10	850- 950	628-15	2500-3000
618-5	400-450	627-4	275- 325	1090-4	350- 400
619-5	350-400	627-5	325- 375	1270-8	1000-1400
620-7	350-400	627-6	375- 450	HB	700- 900
621-6	500-575	627-7	475- 525	LAMP	2000-2500
622-7	475-525	JP627-8	2000-2600		

CHERRY JUBILEE . . . . Page 92
Mug $150-200

CHLORON. . . . Page 93-94
MOLD NUMBERS:

3-16	$800-1000	24-4	$ 250- 300	333	$1000-1200
7-16	700- 900	25-5	275- 325	334	550- 600
10-8	$600- 700	26-2	$100- 125	335	$ 500- 600
11-9	450- 500	27-2	100- 125	336-18	1100-1300
12-10	500- 600	28-2	75- 100	337-15	1200-1500
13-3	225- 250	322-21	1300-1500	338-17	1200-1500
14-8	400- 500	323-19	1200-1400	339-12	2000-2500
15-8	400- 450	324	1000-1200	341-7	500- 600
16-6	375- 425	325	650- 750	342-2-9	275- 325
17-5	350- 400	326	400- 500	344-12	1100-1200
18-3	200- 250	327	750- 850	345-9	1500-1800
19-5	325- 375	328	600- 700	346-9	1500-1800
20-7	225- 275	329	650- 750	358-8	1200-1500
21-6	300- 350	330-11	400- 450	E61	1100-1300
22-8	350- 400	331	400- 500	E62	900-1100
23-8	375-425	332	1000-1200		

CHOCOLATE POT OR CHOCOLATE SETS . . . . Page 95
MOLD NUMBERS:

1st Row	All $300-350 ea.	3.	$375-425
2nd Row	All $300-350 ea.	4.	100-125 (Creamer)
3rd Row		5.	125-150 (Sugar)
1. $400-450			
2. 325-375			

CLEMENA . . . . Page 96

23	$150-225	749-6	$275-350	757-10	$400-450
112-7	250-300	750-6	250-300	758-12	500-600
122-7	300-400	751-7	275-300	759-14	700-800
123-7	250-300	752-7	275-300	954-10	350-400
280-6	300-350	753-8	350-450	1104-4	275-375
281-5	250-300	754-8	350-450	HB	350-450
282-8	300-350	755-9	325-400	WP	400-600
283-12	350-400	756-9	375-450		
746-6	200-300				

CLEMATIS . . . . Page 97-98

3-8	$400-450	111-14	$300-350	400-12	$100- 175
5T	250-275	111-15	275-350	445-4	100- 125
5C	75-100	112-12	250-325	445-4	100- 125
5S	75-100	114-15	400-500	455-5	100- 125
6-10	200-250	140-6	75-100	456-6	100- 150
14	250-300	146-6	75-125	457-8	150- 175
16-6	125-150	170-6	75-100	458-2	100- 125
16-8	225-275	186-6	100-150	458-10	200- 275
17-10	200-250	187-7	100-125	458-12	200- 275
18-15	300-350	188-6	100-125	459-10	150- 300
50	75-100	190-6	100-175	460-12	225- 275
101-8	125-150	191-8	125-175	461-14	275- 325
102-5	100-125	192-5	125-150	470-5	150- 225
103-6	100-150	193-6	100-175	667-4	100- 150
104-7	125-200	194-5	100-175	667-5	150- 200
105-7	100-175	195-5	100-175	668-5	175- 250
106-7	100-125	281-5	200-250	1158-2	100- 125
107-8	175-200	387-7	150-200	1159-4	100- 175
108-8	100-175	388-8	175-275	1295-8	175- 250
109-9	175-250	389-6	100-150	BE	250- 300
110-9	150-200	389-10	200-275	667-8 J&P	800-1200
111-10	250-275	391-8	125-175		

COLONIAL . . . . Page 99
MOLD NUMBERS:
Soap Dish $125-150

403

Colonial continued

Shaving Mug	100-125
Toothbrush Holder	125-150
Sm. Pitcher	150-200
Basin	200-225
Chamber Pot	275-350
Combinette Pot	375-425
Tall Pitcher	225-275

COLUMBINE . . . . Page 100

8-5	$300-350	27-14	$500-600	403-10	$125- 150
12-4	75-100	27-16	550-650	404-10	125- 150
13-6	75-100	30-8	100-150	405-12	150- 175
14-6	125-175	32-10	200-225	406-14	225- 275
15-7	100-150	42	150-175	464-5	275- 300
16-7	150-175	149-6	125-175	655-3	100- 125
17-7	175-225	150-6	125-175	655-4	125- 150
18-7	175-250	151-8	150-200	655-5	175- 200
19-8	125-175	355-5	150-225	655-6	225- 275
20-8	150-225	365-7	225-300	655-8 J&P	1000-1500
21-9	175-225	366-8	300-350	655-10"	1600- 2000
22-8	175-225	367-10	275-325	656-5	175- 250
22-9	175-225	368-12	325-375	1145-6	100- 125
23-10	275-375	399-4	100-125	1146-4	125- 175
24-10	200-275	400-6	150-175	1290-8	400- 475
25-12	450-600	401-6	100-125		
26-14	550-650	402-8	100-125		

CORINTHIAN . . . . Page 101-102

MOLD NUMBERS:

14-2	$ 50-100	235-10	$ 175- 225	
14-3	50-100	235-12	175- 275	
15-8	200-250	235-15	300- 500	
15-7	150-200	256-5	125- 150	
42	175-225	256-6	125- 150	
120-8	100-130	336-6	225- 275	
121-5	75-100	336-8	300- 350	
121-6	90-125	601-5	100- 150	
121-7	100-150	601-6	150- 200	
212-6	100-150	601-7	200- 250	
213-6	125-175	601-8	250- 350	
214-6	125-175	601-9	300- 400	
215-7	125-175	JP601-10	1200-1500	
216-7	125-175	JP601-12	2200-3000	
217-8	150-200	603-5	175- 225	
218-8	125-175	603-6	225- 275	
219-10	200-250	1048-8	325- 425	
220-12	250-300	1228-10	250- 350	
235-5	100-130	1229-12	350- 450	
235-6	100-130	1232-8	300- 350	
235-8	150-225	ASHTRAY	250- 275	

CORNELIAN COOKING WARE . . . . Page 103-104

1pt.	$ 60- 70	Pudding Dish 9"	$150-175
2pt.	80-100	10"	175-200
3pt.	100-125	12"	200-225
6pt.	175-200	Punch Bowl	350-400
Cracker Jar	$200-250	Soap Dish	125-150
Oatmeal Pitcher	60- 70	Shaving Mug	100-125
" " Bowl	50- 60	Brush Holder	125-150
Custard Cup	40- 50	Mouth Ewer	200-250
Shirred Eggs	50- 60	Lg. Ewer	325-375
Butter Dish	200-225	Basin	200-250
Fruit Dish	200-225	Chamber Pot	350-400
Mixing Bowls 7"	100-125	Combinette	450-550
" " 8"	125-150	E-1 Pitcher	90-110
" " 9"	150-175	E-2 "	100-125
" " 10"	175-200	E-3 "	125-150
" " 12"	225-275	E-4 "	200-250
" " 14"	300-350	E-5 "	250-300
Pudding Dish 4"	50- 60	Tobacco Jar	350-400
" " 5"	70- 80	D-2 Pitcher	150-175
" " 6"	90-110	D-3 Pitcher	175-200
" " 7"	100-125	Berry Set	550-650
" " 8"	125-150	Bread & Milk Set	150-175

COSMOS . . . . Page 105-106

39	$100-175	375-4	$175-250	950-8	$275-350
133-4	150-200	376-6	225-325	951-8	225-300
134-4	100-175	381-9	250- 350	952-9	225- 300
135-8	200-275	649-3	100- 150	953-9	225- 300
136-6	100-175	649-4	100- 150	954-4	125- 175
137-8	150-225	649-5	175- 250	954-9	200- 250
139-4	100-175	649-6	250- 350	954-10	250- 350
191-4	100-175	649-7	300- 375	955-10	275- 375
195-7	150-200	649-8 J&P	1200-1500	956-12	400- 500
357-10	300-350	649-10"	2000-2200	957-15	600- 900
358-12	450-550	650-5	225- 325	958-18	800-1200
361-5	275-375	905-8	225- 275	959-7	125- 175
369-6	125-175	944-4	100- 125	965-10	200- 250
370-8	150-200	945-5	100- 150	1136-2	150- 200
371-10	200-350	946-6	125- 175	1137-4	150- 200
372-10	200-250	947-6	150- 200	1285-6	400- 500
373-12	250-300	948-7	175- 250	1285-8	450- 550
374-14	275-375	949-7	150- 225	381-9-3-3	175- 200

CREMO . . . . Page 107

MOLD NUMBERS:

1.	$ 900-1100	7.	$1000-1200
2.	900-1100	8.	1000-1200
3.	1200-1400	9.	800-1000
4.	900-1100	10.	1100-1300
5.	800-1000	11.	1200-1400
6.	1000-1200	12.	1100-1300

CREMONA . . . . Page 108

MOLD NUMBERS:

72-4	$100-175	351-4	$150-200	358-10	$275-375
73-5	100-175	352-5	150-200	359-10	300-375
74-6	175-225	353-5	150-200	360-10	300-350
75	150-175	354-7	175-225	361-12	350-400
176-6	125-150	355-8	200-275	362-12	350-400
177-8	150-200	356-8	200-275	1068-4	175-275
178-8	175-225	357-8	250-300		

CROCUS . . . . Page 109

Left to Right: $450-500 $650-700

CUSPIDORS . . . . Page 110-111

MOLD NUMBERS:

PICTURE 1		PICTURE 2		PICTURE 3	
601	$175-225	612	$175-225	1. 909	$ 350- 400
602	175-225	608	175-225	2. 909	3000-3500
603	250-300	611	150-175	3. 909	400- 500
604	175-225	614	175-225		ROW 2
606	175-225		ROW 2	1. 621	175- 200
607	175-225	608	175-225	2. 615	175- 225
608	175-225	612	150-175	3. 626	175- 225
		613	150-175	4. 627	150- 175
614	175-225		ROW 3		
PICTURE 4		ROW 3		1. 627	150- 175
610	150-175	612	175-225	2. 601	175- 225
607	175-225	613	150-175	3. 626	175- 225
609	200-250	611	150-175	4. 607	150- 175
611	150-175				

DAHLROSE . . . Page 112

76-6	$175-250	365-8	$250-300	614-7	$ 200- 250
77-7	175-250	366-8	175-250	JP614-8	1200-1600
78-8	175-250	367-8	200-275	614-9	300- 400
79-6	150-200	368-10	275-375	JP614-10	2200-2800
179-8	125-175	369-10	300-400	614-12	1500-2000
180-8	175-225	370-12	400-500	1069-3	150- 200
343-6	300-350	375-10	250-300	1258-8	300- 400
363-6	100-150	375-14	300-400	1259-10	350- 450
364-6	175-225	614-6	175-200		

DAWN . . . . Page 113

4-5	$400-500	345-8	$250-300	831-10	$300-375
31-3-4	150-175	826-6	150-250	832-10	300-400
315-4	125-200	827-6	150-225	833-12	375-500
316-6	150-175	828-8	125-175	834-15	500-700
317-10	150-200	829-8	175-250	1121-2	125-175
318-14	175-225	830-8	200-250	1122-4	150-225
319-6	400-500	831-9	275-350		

PRICE GUIDE / INDEX

405

ELSIE, THE COW . . . . Page 133
Complete set in original box: $1000-1400

FALLINE . . . . Page 135
MOLD NUMBERS:

244-8	$350- 450	649-8	$ 700-1100
642-6	375- 525	650-6	500- 800
643-6	350- 550	651-8	600-1100
644-6	450- 650	652-9	800-1300
645-6	700-1200	653-12	1200-1800
646-8	600- 900	654-13	2500-3500
647-7	700-1000	655-15	2000-3000
648-7	600-1200	1092-3	400- 600

FATIMA/PROMOTIONAL ASHTRAYS . . . . Page 136
Fatima $100-150
Prom. Ashtrays 80-120

FERELLA . . . . Page 137
MOLD NUMBERS:

7"	$500-700	500-5	$400-700	509-8	$700-1000
15-2½	100-150	501-6	400-700	511-10	900-1100
15-3½	125-175	502-6	400-700	620-5	500- 600
87-8	400-700	503-5	500-750	1078-4	300- 600
210-4	400-600	504-5	450-800	1266-6	900-1200
211-8	600-800	505-6	500-800	212-12X7	750- 1000
497-4	350-450	506-8	500-850	Lamp	1200-1800
498-4	300-450	507-9	700-900		
499-6	500-800	508-8	600-800		

FERN DISH . . . . Page 138
MOLD NUMBERS:

BLENDED		SPONGE WARE	
6"	$100-150	7"	$125-150
7"	125-175	8"	150-175
8"	150-200	9"	175-200
207-6 w/liner	300-400		
E-11	250-350		

FLEUR DELIS . . . . Page 139
412-20 J&P	$600-800
6" Jar	225-250
7" Jar	250-300
8" Jar	300-350
Cuspidor	250-300

FLORANE . . . . Page 140
Pictured Bowl	$75-100
Pictured Bowl	75-125

FLORANE II . . . . Page 141
50-8	$100-150	71-4	$ 75-125	84-14	$150-175
51-10	125-175	72-5	90-125	90-4	55- 75
52-12	125-175	73-6	100-125	91-6	50-100
60-6	55- 95	79-7	75-100	92-6	50-100
61-9	75-100	80-6	75-100	93-7	50-100
62-8	70-100	81-7	85-125	94-8	90-120
63-10	65-105	82-9	100-150	95-10	50-100
64-12	95-125	83-11	100-150	96-10	90-120
97-10	100-150				

FLOOR VASES . . . . Page 142-143
ROZANE ROYAL

826-21	$3000-3500
832-20	2700-3200
863-21	3000-3500

FLORENTINE I . . . . Page 144-145
MOLD NUMBERS:

6	$ 75-125	229-6	$100-150	299-7	$ 100- 175
7	200-250	230-8	125-175	320-6	200- 250
17-3	75-125	231-8	140-185	320-18	400- 500
17-8	200-250	232-10	175-275	321-7	250- 300
40-4½	125-200	333-10	200-250	322-8	300- 350
41-6	175-225	234-12	250-300	602-4	100- 150
125-4	60-110	237-6	175-250	602-5	150- 175
125-5	65-115	237-7	250-300	602-6	200- 250
125-6	85-125	238-6	100-150	602-7	225- 275
125-7	100-150	252-6	100-150	602-8	300- 350
126-4	75-125	253-6	100-150	602-9	325- 375
126-5	75-125	254-7	150-200	JP 602-10	1000-1500
126-6	75-125	255-8	150-200	1049-8	175- 225

Florentine I continued
126-7	85-135	257-5	150-200	1050-10	275- 375
130-4	100-150	257-6	150-200	1230-10	300- 400
152½	40- 70	258-5	90-150	1231-12	350- 450
153½	45- 75	297-14	350-450	1238-8	300- 400
228-6	100-150	297-16	550-650	1239-7	300- 400
		298-18	400-500	1062-4	150- 200

Lamp 450-650

FLORENTINE II . . . . Page 146
MOLD NUMBERS:

6-4	$ 75-125	255-8	$125-175	602-8	$600- 700
40-4	125-150	321-7	250-300	602-9	325- 375
126-7	85-135	322-8	300-350	602-10	700-1000
130-4	100-150	339-5	150-175	763-20	550- 600
231-8	140-185	602-5	175-225	1062-7	200- 250
232-10	175-225	602-6	200-250	1062-4	100- 150
233-10	200-250	602-7	225-275	1238-7	200- 250
234-12	225-325				
Umbrella	450-550				
252-6	85-125				

FOREST (VISTA) . . . . Page 147-148
Picture 1		Picture 5	
18" vase	$2000-2500	20" Umbrella Stand	$2500-3500
10" vase	650-1000		
12" vase	750-1250		
15" vase	1400-2000		
Picture 2		Picture 6	
12"x5"x5" Window box	1200-2200	9½" Wall Pocket	1200-1800
Picture 3		Picture 7	
16" vase	1200-1800	18" vase	800-1200
3½"x7" bowl	300- 400	7½" basket	700- 900
12"	1200-2000	15" vase	1400-2000
		6 1/2" basket	500-1500
18" vase	1800-2200		
Picture 4			
12" vase	800-1200		

FORGET-ME-NOT . . . . Page 149
Dresser Set	$325- 375
4 pc. Coffee/Tea Set	800-1000
Cream Pitcher	75 each
#11 Creamer	100- 125
1 pt. Creamer	75- 100
#3 Creamer	75- 100 each
Candlesticks	150- 200 each

FOXGLOVE . . . . Page 150-151
2-10	$225-250	55-16	$600- 900	419-6	$ 125- 175
4-6	150-250	56-18	800-1100	420-10	200- 250
5-10	300-400	57-10	175- 250	421-10	150- 250
6-15	400-800	58-14	300- 400	422-10	175- 225
10	275-400	59-18	600-1000	423-12	200- 300
11-6	150-200	151-10	225- 325	424-14	275- 325
42-4	100-150	159-5	110- 175	425-14	300- 400
43-6	150-200	160-4	125- 200	426-6	200- 250
44-6	150-200	161-6	125- 200	466-5	250- 350
45-7	175-250	162-8	250- 350	659-3	100- 125
46	150-200	163-6	125- 200	659-4	100- 150
46-7	175-225	164-8	150- 225	659-5	125- 175
47-8	200-300	165-5	175- 225	659-6	175- 225
48-8	200-300	166-6	175- 225	659-7	125- 175
49-9	250-350	371-10	275- 325	JP659-8	900- 1200
50-9	200-300	373-8	225- 325	JP659-10	1400-1800
51-10	250-350	374-10	300- 350	660-5	175- 250
52-12	300-400	375-12	450- 550	1149	100- 150
53-14	500-700	418-4	150- 250	1150-4	175- 275
54-14	500-700	418-6	175- 250	1292-8	400- 500
54-15	650-950				
Tray 8"-8½"	175-225				
Tray 11"	250-300				
Tray 15"	300-350				

FREESIA . . . Page 152-153
4-8	$425-525	126-10	$200-250	464-6	$100- 150
6T	250-375	127-12	250-300	465-8	150- 200
6C	75-100	128-15	400-600	466-10	150- 200
6S	75-100	129-18	700-900	467-10	150- 200

Freesia continued

7-10	175-250	139-18	600-800	468-12	175-250
15	275-350	145	550-700	469-14	200-300
19-5	175-250	195-7	100-135	471-5	225-300
19-6	175-225	196-8	200-275	475-10	200-300
20-10	250-350	197-6	100-145	486-12	125-175
21-15	450-750	197-7	100-145	669-4	100-135
117-6	150-200	198-8	100-175	669-6	175-250
118-6	125-175	199-6	175-250	669-8	900-1500
119-7	125-175	200-7	150-200	670-5	175-225
120-7	125-175	346-5	100-150	965-8	150-200
121-8	150-200	390-7	175-250	1160-2	100-150
122-8	175-250	391-8	200-350	1161-4	100-150
123-9	175-250	392-10	300-450	1296-8	225-325
124-9	200-275	463-5	175-225	1392-8	175-250
125-10	175-200				

FUCHSIA .... Page 154

37	$175-250	359-5	$450-600	895-7	$225-275
127-6	150-200	364-4	125-175	896-8	275-350
129-6	150-200	645-4	125-200	897-8	225-300
248-5	200-250	645-4	200-250	898-8	300-400
345-3	150-200	645-5	250-300	899-9	300-400
346-4	150-200	645-6	200-300	900-9	325-425
346-5	175-225	645-8	1000-1200	901-10	375-475
347-6	200-300	645-10	1500-1800	902-10	325-425
348-5	175-250	646-5	375-450	903-12	600-800
8	175-275	871-6	250-300	904-15	800-1400
350-8	250-350	879-8	250-325	905-18	1200-2000
350-8 w/frog	450-600	891-6	175-275	1132-2	150-200
351-10	275-375	892-6	200-300	1133-5	275-375
351-10	275-375	893-6	200-300	1282-6	500-600
352-12	275-350	894-7	175-275	1322	500-700
353-14	350-450				

FUTURA .... Page 155-158

15-2	$150-200	387-7	$800-1000	422-6	$300-500
15-3	175-275	388-9	600-1000	423-6	300-500
81-5½x5	325-475	389-9	1000-1900	424-7	500-700
82-6	300-400	390-10	600-800	425-8	450-600
85-4	300-400	391-10	900-1200	426-8	800-1200
187-8	350-450	392-10	750-1050	427-8	800-1000
188-8	450-600	393-12	900-1400	428-8	400-800
189-4x6	550-650	394-12	1000-1400	429-9	900-1200
190-3x6	350-450	395-10	800-1200	430-9	900-1500
191-8	475-575	396-5	1200-1800	431-10	700-1000
194-5	600-1000	397-6	375-475	432-10	700-1000
195-10	800-1000	398-6	325-425	433-10	800-1200
196-12X5X3	475-675	399-7	425-625	434-10	2750-4550
197-6	475-675	400-7	1000-1800	435-10	1200-1800
198-5	475-700	401-8	500-800	436-12	3500-7000
344-5	400-500	402-8	600-1000	437-12	1000-1700
344-6	500-600	403-8	800-1200	438-15	1500-2000
376-15X4X6	1200-1500	404-8	1100-1500	616-6	400-600
380-6	400-550	405-7	900-1100	616-7	700-1000
381-6	400-550	406-8	700-900	616-8	700-800
382-7	500-750	407-9	900-1600	616-9	1000-1200
383-8	450-700	408-10	1000-1600	616-10	2500-5000
384-8	450-700	409-9	800-1200	1072-4	600-800
385-8	400-700	410-12	1100-1800	1073-4	350-650
386-8	1500-3000	411-14	1800-3200	1075-4	700-900
Frog	200-275	412-9	5000-9000	1261-8	550-900
421-5	300-500				

(Many molds with extremely rare color combinations will demand a much larger price.)

GARDEN LINE .... Page 159-160
MOLD NUMBERS:

Pots #610-611-612   Flower Pots #70-71-87-88

8"	$100-125	4"	$75-100
10"	150-175	5"	90-110
12"	200-250	6"	100-125
14"	300-350	7"	120-140
		8"	140-160

#10	12x14	$250-300	1 Bird Bath 23"	$400-500
#11	12x18	350-400	2 " " 26"	500-600
			3 " " 31"	600-700

GARDENIA .... Page 161-162

600-3	$ 75-100	621-6	$100-150	661-5	$ 300-350
600-4	100-125	622-8	150-200	662-8	200-300
600-5	125-150	625-10	150-200	666-8	250-325
600-6	200-225	626-6	125-150	668-8	100-150
600-8	650-750	627-8	125-175	669-12	100-225
600-10	1300-1500	628-10	125-180	681-6	100-125
601-6	100-150	629-10	150-180	682-6	100-125
603-10	600-650	630-12	175-200	683-8	125-200
605-8	350-450	631-14	200-225	684-8	150-200
606-10	450-600	632-14	175-200	685-10	175-225
608-8	200-275	641-5	125-150	686-10	125-200
609-10	200-300	651-2	100-125	687-12	275-325
610-12	275-375	652-4	125-175	688-12	200-275
616-6	125-200	656-3	100-125	689-14	450-550
617-10	175-225	657-3	100-150	690-16	800-900
618-15	275-375	658-8	125-150	606-8	1000-1500
Frog	100-125	658-10	150-200	606-10	1400-1800
		659	250-300		

GERMAN COOKING WARE .... Page 163-164

Coffee Pot	$325-375	Open Casserole	$100-125
Teapot	300-350	Pie Pan	80-100
Pitcher	100-125	Shirred Egg	50-60
Cream Pitcher	60-70	Bowl 5"	70-80
Custard or Ind. Bean	60-70	Bowl 6"	80-100
Cocortes 3"	60-70	Pudding Dish 3½"	50-60
Cocortes 3½"	70-80	Pudding Dish 4½"	60-70
Deep Dish Lg.	175-225	Pudding Dish 5½"	70-80
Deep Dish Sm.	150-200	Pudding Dish 6½"	80-100
Handled Cov. Casserole	150-200		

GERMAN FARM WARE .... Page 165

Coffee Pot	$250-300	Canning Jar	$100-125

GLAZE .... Page 166-167
MOLD NUMBERS:
JARDINIERE 419-420-421-422

	1419-1421-1427	Blue & Gold	
6"	$ 300-350	407-6	$ 150-175
7"	350-375	407-7	200-250
8"	400-450	407-8	225-275
9"	450-500	407-9	250-300
10"	475-525	407-10	300-350
403-10-26	450-550	407-11	350-450
		407-12-30	800-1100
Jardiniere & Pedestal		407-19-48	2000-2500
12x29	800-1000	410-12-22	400-500
14-23	1000-1500		
Glazed Asst.		Glazed & Gold Stippled	
7"	200-250	6"	150-175
8"	225-275	7"	200-250
9"	250-300	8"	225-275
10"	300-350	9"	250-300

GOLD TRACED .... Page 168
All priced at $150-200 each or $300-400 per pair

GOLD & WHITE TRACED .... Page 169
MOLD NUMBERS:

60-3¾	$200-250 pr.	344-12	$700-800
336-17	800-1000	347-15½	400-500
338-18	800-1000	351-5-6-13	350-400
343-5¾	300-350	362-12	400-500 pr.

GOLD & SILVER DECORATED 170-171
MOLD NUMBERS:

		J&P	
711-8½X11X26X26	$3500-4500	10X26	$1000-1500
712-9½X22½	1000-1600		
715-9X23	1000-1600		
717-10X23½	1500-2500		
717-10X24	1500-2500		

GOOD NIGHT CANDLESTICKS .... Page 172
Candlesticks $400-450

GREEN .... Page 173

		Jardiniere & Pedestal	
740-22	$1000-1200		
741-21	1000-1200	558-12-34	1200-1400
741-10-21	1000-1200	558-10-28	1000-1200

PRICE GUIDE / INDEX

HOLLAND . . . . Page 174

Tankard	$250-375	Combinette	$650-750
Mugs	175-225	Water Glass	125-175
Toothbrush Holder	175-225	Soap Dish	175-225
Chamber Pot	375-425	Washing Pitcher	400-450
Water Pitcher	275-325	Basin	300-350

HOME ART . . . . Page 175-176
MOLD NUMBERS:

Jardiniere & Pedestal		476-9-27	$ 800-1000	Umbrella Stand	
476-6x18½	$400-500	424-12-32	1200-1500	723-8X20	$500- 600
476-7X20½	500-600			723-21½	450- 500
476-8X23½	600-800	Jardiniere		724-20½	400- 500
476-9x26¾	800-1000	438-8	300- 350	910-10x22	1000-1500
476-10x29½	1200-1500	457-8	300- 350	715-9-23	1000-1600
476-12-37	2000-2500	462-7	250- 300	Flower Pot	
		476-3	100- 125		

HYDE PARK . . . . Page 177

Ashtrays	$25-75	Cigarette Humidor	$25-75

IDEAL PITCHERS . . . . Page 178
MOLD NUMBERS:

1-5 oz.	$ 50- 60	5-5 pt.	$150-175
2-¾ pt.	70- 80	6-7¼ pt.	200-250
3-1¾ pt.	100-125	7-15 pt.	225-250
4-3¼ pt.	125-150		

IMPERIAL . . . . Page 179
MOLD NUMBERS:

444-8"	$ 600- 700
9"	650- 750
10"	700- 800
12"	850- 900
424-12X32	1600- 2500

IMPERIAL I . . . . Page 180-181
MOLD NUMBERS:

29-8	$ 175- 250	163-18	$650-750	591-7	$225-275
30-8½	175- 250	251-6	125-175	591-8	325-375
31-9	175- 225	251-7	125-175	591-9	350-450
71-7	100- 150	252-7	150-200	591-10	500-650
71-8	100- 150	291-7	225-275	591-12	650-750
150-8	125- 175	333-6	225-300	759-20	650-750
151-8	125- 175	333-7	250-350	1221-7	250-350
152-8	150- 200	370-10	175-250	1222-9	275-325
156-12	175- 250	370-12	200-250	1223-10	300-400
162-18	550- 700	591-6	150-200	591-10 Jar. & Ped.	1200-1500

IMPERIAL II . . . . Page 182
MOLD NUMBERS:

#20	$175-275	467-5	$200-300	479-8	$500- 550
Ashtray	225-275	468-5	175-275	480-8	600- 700
199-4	300-400	469-6	275-375	481-8	700- 800
200-4	175-250	470-5	400-500	482-11	850-1250
201-4	450-500	471-7	300-375	483-10	750- 850
202-6	400-450	472-7	350-500	484-11	800- 900
203-5	500-550	473-7	550-600	1076-2	200- 275
204-8	275-375	474-7	325-400	1077-4	300- 400
205-8	400-450	475-9	400-450	1262WP	350- 450
206-8	700-800	476-8	500-600	1263WP	450- 550
207-8-12	350-450	477-9	500-600	1264WP	600- 700
466-4	300-375	478-8	500-550		

INDIAN . . . . Page 183

Tankers	$900-1200
Mugs	300- 400

IRIS . . . . Page 184

2	$600-700	363-12	$ 200- 300	921-8	$200- 250
5	250-300	364-14	225- 325	921-9	225- 325
30	150-200	647-3	75- 125	922-8	250- 300
38	125-175	647-4	100- 150	923-8	200- 350
130-4	100-130	647-5	200- 250	924-9	250- 350
131-6	100-175	647-6	300- 375	925-9	225- 300
132-8	125-200	JP 647-8	900-1200	926-10	300- 375
211-7	125-150	JP 647-10	1200-1800	927-10	300- 425
347-10	300-425	648-5	150- 250	928-12	400- 500
354-8	325-425	648-8	1000-1200	929-15	800-1200

Iris continued

355-10	375-600	911-6	125- 200	940-4	150- 200
357-4	150-200	914-4	100- 150	1134-3	100- 200
358-6	250-300	915-5	100- 140	1135-4	300- 400
359-5	150-200	916-6	125- 175	1284-8	500- 650
360-5	300-350	917-6	150- 250		
360-6	175-250	918-7	125- 200		
361-8	150-225	919-7	175- 225		
362-10	175-250	920-7	200- 225		

IRIS TURN OF THE CENTURY . . . . Page 185
MOLD NUMBERS:

J & P 12" X 36"	$1400-1800
450-7	300- 350
450-8	350- 450
450-9	400- 450
450-10	450- 550
450-12	550- 650
Umbrella 10x20	1000-1600

IVORY (OLD) . . . . Page 186
MOLD NUMBERS:

503-8	$325-375	506-10	$750-850	510-6	$275-325
503-9	400-450	507-7	300-350	510-8	425-525
503-10	750-850	507-8	325-375	510-10	625-725
504-7	300-350	507-9	400-450		
504-9	400-450	508-7	300-325	Flower Pots	
504-10	750-850	508-8	325-375	4"	175-225
505-7	300-350	508-10	750-850	5"	200-250
505-8	325-375	509-8	325-375	6"	250-300
505-10	750-850	509-9	400-450	7"	325-375
506-8	325-375	509-10	750-850	8"	400-500
506-9	400-450	510-4	200-250	9"	450-550
				10"	600-700

IVORY Page187-191
MOLD NUMBERS:

1	$300-550	301-10	$100- 150	734-7	$100- 125
2-4 pr.	125-150	302-14-6	125- 175	735-7	100- 125
3-4-5	175-200	303-13	150- 250	736-8	100- 150
5-7	75-125	311-7	80- 100	737-7	100- 150
12-4-8	100-125	314-14	110- 180	738-9	100- 150
14-4	125-175	315-4	80- 120	739-9	100- 150
15-3	25- 75	316-10	100- 170	740-10	100- 170
17	70-100	317-10	125- 175	741-10	100- 170
17-3	70-100	318-8	125- 175	742-12	150- 200
17-4	50- 75	335-8	125- 175	743-14	200- 275
24-3	50-100	337-10	150- 200	836-12	150- 200
24-5	50-100	341-5	80- 125	837-14	200- 250
24-8	75-125	345-8	100- 150	930-6	60- 100
28-9	600-700	346-9	100- 150	931-6	60- 100
44-8	40- 90	356-8	125- 150	932-7	50- 100
97-3-5	75-150	358-6	50- 100	933-7	70- 110
99-5	50-100	364-4x10	175- 225	934-8	100- 150
103-6	125-150	365-7	90- 120	935-8	100- 150
103-15	300-400	366-7	90- 120	936-8	100- 150
105-8	125-175	367-8	90- 120	937-9	125- 175
105-9-12	150-225	368-10	90- 120	938-9	125- 175
106-7	125-175	371-6	90- 120	939-10	125- 175
108-2-6	100-150	372-6	100- 150	940-10	125- 175
109-8	100-150	373-8	100- 175	941-10	150- 250
110-7	60- 90	374-8	100- 150	942-8	100- 150
111	125-175	378-3x10	100- 150	943-10	125- 175
115-7	70-100	467-5	70- 100	971-6	80- 120
119-6	80-140	548-4	50- 100	973-3-5	80- 120
119-10	135-175	549-4	75- 125	1063-3	80- 100
120-8x5	150-200	550-4	50- 100	1064-4	100- 150
126-6	80-110	570-4	50- 100	1065-4	100- 150
152-6	100-150	575-4	50- 100	1070-3	100- 150
158-5	80-100	575-5	100- 150	1093-4	100- 150
159-6	80-130	575-6	125- 175	1095	150- 175
161-7	80-130	575-8	175- 225	1096-4	150- 175
167-12	100-150	580-4	70- 120	1096-5	150- 175
168-10	100-150	580-5	100- 150	1098-4	90- 125
183-10x4	125-150	580-6	100- 150	1101-4	100- 150
183-9x4	100-130	585-4	80- 100	1103-4	90- 110
196-12x5x3	100-150	586-8	100- 150	1111-4	100- 125
209-10	125-175	617-10JP	800-1000	1112-5	250- 300
222-12	150-200	630-4	50- 100	1114-2	100- 150

ory continued

36-3	60-100	679-6	50- 100	1115-6	300- 350
38-5	60-100	694-7	80- 120	1116-6	700- 800
49-12	100-125	695-8	75- 150	1122-5	100- 150
59-6	100-125	696-8	100- 150	1273-8	175- 200
60-8	70-100	697-8	100- 150	1315-15	225- 275
66-8	100-150	698-9	100- 150	3635-5	75- 100
66-12	110-150	699-9	100- 150	3645-5	75- 100
67-6x12	125-165	701-10	100- 175	3646-6	70- 100
72-10	70-100	702	150- 175	A602-8	400- 500
73-12x5x2	110-160	722-14	200- 250	A602-10	600- 800
74-6	100-125	733-6	50- 100	A764-10	250- 300
75-12x8	90-120			Sign	1200-1500
77-8x12	80-120				

IVORY TINT .... Page 192-193

Stein Sets

Mugs	$100-125
Tankers	300-350
Sugar & Creamer	125-150
Tea Set 3 pc.	250-300
Tobacco Jar	200-250
Fern Dish	250-300
Powder Jar	200-250
Wall Pocket	400-500
Dresser Set	325-350
Mug, Small	150-175
Mug, Large	175-200

IXIA .... Page 194

4	$125-150	610-9	$ 500- 525	858-8	$ 200- 300
25-3	100-125	640-4	125- 150	859-9	200- 250
25-5	100-125	640-5	175- 200	860-9	250- 275
26-4	125-175	640-6	250- 300	861-10	275- 325
27-6	250-300	640-7	325- 425	862-10	300- 350
28-12	225-275	640-8JP	1000-1500	863-10	350- 400
29-7	150-175	641-5	250- 300	864-12	375- 425
30-7	150-175	835-6	125- 150	865-15	550- 750
30-9	175-225	852-6	125- 150	1125-5	100- 125
31-9	175-200	853-6	125- 150	1126-4	175- 225
32-12	200-300	854-7	150- 200	1127-4	275- 300
33-14	250-325	855-7	175- 200	1128-5	325- 400
34-14	300-350	856-8	200- 225	HB	500- 550
46-10	200-325	857-7	200- 275	Lamp	500- 750
57-5	325-375	857-8	200- 275	640-10	1500-2000
87-6	200-225				

JEANETTE .... Page 195

Only price available $1100-1500

JONQUIL .... Page 196-197

MOLD NUMBERS:

3-4½	$175-250	328-9	$550- 650	542-5	$275- 325
4-5½	275-325	523-3	175- 275	543-6	300- 350
5-6½	400-600	524-4	150- 250	544-9	300- 400
6-7	325-375	525-5	200- 300	621-4	150- 200
7-6	450-500	526-6	250- 325	621-5	175- 225
8-10	275-375	527-7	250- 300	621-6	350- 500
19-8X6X3	275-375	528-8	250- 325	621-7	375-675
20-10X6X3	325-400	529-8	300- 400	621-8	400-800
23-6	275-375	530-10	650- 750	621-9	500-1000
23-7	350-450	531-12	800-1200	621-18X10 J&P	
24-8	450-700	538-4	175- 275		2500-3500
25-6	450-550	539-4	175- 275	1082-4	250- 300
26-8	350-450	540-6	250- 350	Frog 2"	50- 100
27-8	450-500	541-7	350- 450	Frog 3"	75- 150

Juvenile Ware

Picture 2 (left to right)
Top Row: (1) $400-500 (2) $300-350 (3) $175-200 (4) $300-350 (5) $150-175
Mid. Row: (1) 450-500 (2) 125-150 (3) 500-600 (4) 400-500 (5) 400-500
Bot. Row: (1) 500-600 (2) 135-160 (3) 400-500

Picture 3 (left to right)
Top Row:
(1) $135-150 (2) $100-125 (3) $100-125 (4) $110-120 (5) $125-150 (6) $125-150
2nd Row:
(1) $500-600 (2) $400-500 (3) $400-500 (4) $400-500 (5) $450-550 (6) $450-500
3rd Row:
(1) $135-160 (2) $110-125 (3) $100-125 (4) $110-130 (5) $125-150 (6) $125-150
4th Row:
(1) $200-225 (2) $175-200 (3) $125-150 (4) $150-175 (5) $175-200 (6) $175-200

Jonquil continued

Picture 4 (left to right)
Top Row:
(7) $125-130 (51) $75-100 (1) $300-350 (2 Egg) $325-375 (2 Mug) $150-175
(1 Soap) $250-275
2nd Row:
(3 Mug)$175-200 (1 Soda) $225-275 (1 Mug) $200-250 (6 Cup/Saucer) $175-200
(4-5¾) $100-125 (22-6¾) $125-150
3rd Row:
(5-6½) $100-125 (1-7½) $125-150 (1-7½) $125-150 (5-6½) $100-125
(6 B&M) $100-150
4th Row:
All B&M (4) $125-150 (4) $150-175 (1) $125-150 (1) $125-150 (3) $135-160
(3) $150-175 (8) $135-150 (8) $125-150 (5) $135-160 (2) $130-160 (2) $100-125
(7) $135-160 (7) $125-150
5th Row:
(3-8¼) $150-175 (9 B&M) $150-175 (9 B&M) $150-175 (Ewer) $400-500
(Basin) $300-350 (Chamber Pot) $400-500 (Chamber Pot) $300-350

KETTLE AND SKILLET SET .... Page 201

Set Price: $150-200   In box add $50 more
1797 - 1798 - 1799

LAMPS 202

7001	$1000-1200
7003	700- 900
7005	700- 900
7007	400- 500
7009	800-1000
7011	1100-1300

LANDSCAPE 203

Tea Set 3 pc.	$300-350
Ceramic Planter	
203-4	150-175
203-5	175-225
203-6	225-250
10" Coffee Pot	325-350
Custard Cup	75-100
4" Tumbler	150-175

LAROSE .... Page 204-205

MOLD NUMBERS:

14-2	$ 50-100	240-7	$175- 250	604-9	$ 400- 500
14-3	70-120	241-8	200- 275	604-10	1400-1600
43-4	160-210	242-9	250- 350	605-5	175- 250
127-5	125-175	243-10	260- 375	605-6	200- 250
127-6	100-150	259-5	150- 200	605-6w/s	225- 275
127-7	125-175	259-6w/l	150- 200	761-20	800-1000
128-5	125-175	338-6	250- 300	1051-4	175- 250
128-6	125-175	338-7	300- 400	1052-8	250- 350
128-7	130-180	604-5	125- 175	1233-7	325- 425
236-4	150-225	604-6	200- 250	1234-8	350- 450
237-5	150-225	604-7	275- 325	1235-11	400- 500
238-5	150-225	604-8	900-1200		
239-6	175-250				

LAURAL .... Page 206

250-6	$200-275	673-8	$275-375
667-6	250-350	674-9	300-400
668-6	350-450	675-9	300-400
669-6	200-300	676-10	300-400
670-7	275-375	677-12	400-500
671-7	200-300	678-14	650-900
672-8	325-425		

LEMONADE SET .... Page 207

Dutch	
Tumbler	$ 200- 250
Pitcher	250- 300
Set of Mugs & Pitcher	1200-1500
Conventional	
Lemonade Set	
Tumbler	60- 80
Pitcher	225- 275
Set of 6 Tumblers & Pitcher	600- 700

LIGHT ART .... Page 208

MOLD NUMBERS:

457-4	$125-150	457-8	$350-400
457-5	150-175	457-9	400-500

Light Art continued

457-6	225-275	457-10	500-600
457-7	275-325	457-12	700-900

LODGE LINE .... Page 209

Eagle Mug	$125-150
Tanker	400-500
Elk Mug	100-125
Tanker	300-400
Knight of the Pythias Mug	200-250
Tanker	600-700

LOMBARDY .... Page 210
MOLD NUMBER:

15-2½	$ 50- 100	350-10	$400- 500
15-3½	60- 120	613-6	250- 300
175-5	175- 200	613-7	325- 375
175-6	200- 225	613-8	400- 500
175-7	250- 275	613-9	500- 600
342-5	800- 900	613-10	700- 800
342-6	1200- 1500	613-12	800-1000
350-6	200- 225	1256-8	275- 325
350-8	325- 375	1257-8	275- 325

LOTUS .... Page 211

L3-10	$200-250	L6-9"	$100-150
L4-10	250-300	L7-10"	200-250
L5-3"	100-125	L8-7"	275-300
		L9-4"	100-125

LUFFA .... Page 212

Row One		Row Two	
258	$175-275	688-8	$325-475
1097-4½	150-250	687-8	300-450
1272-8	500-600	686-7	275-400
17-4½	75-125	685-7	225-325
257	125-225	684-6	200-275
		683-6	175-225
		235-6	100-175

Row Three

693-15	$ 700-1200		
692-14	425- 600		
691-12	420- 720		
690-9	250- 400		
689-8	225- 375		
631-4	125- 200	631-8	J&P $1200-1500
631-5	200- 250	631-9	450- 600
631-6	250- 300	631-10	J&P 1800-2400
631-7	275- 350	771-10-15	900-1400

LUSTRE .... Page 213-214
MOLD NUMBERS:

5-8	$150-200	84-10	$125-175	296-6	$200-250
6-10	150-200	85-10	125-175	297-8	250-300
7-10	150-200	85-12	175-200	298-8	350-400
8-6	100-150	86-8	100-150	299-9	350-400
15-2	45- 90	86-10	150-200	300-14	400-500
15-3	65- 95	86-12	175-200	307-9	400-500
34-8	100-125	87-7	125-175	308-9	450-500
35-10	75-125	169-6	100-125	309-9	350-400
76-5	80-110	170-7	110-160	310-9	400-500
77-5	80-110	171-8	125-150	311-9	400-500
78-6	90-120	172-9	125-175	312-13	450-500
79-6	90-120	173-10	150-200	1019-8PR	125-175
80-7	100-150	175-7	100-125	1020-10PR	200-250
81-7	100-150	175-8	150-200	1021-12	325-375
82-4	100-125	176-12	175-250	1023-5	125-150
83-5	125-150	177-12	200-275	1024-6	150-200
84-6	100-150	178-14	200-300	1025-8	200-250
84-7	125-175	179-14	250-350	1026-10	250-300
84-8	125-175	294-6	300-350	1027-10	250-300
		295-6	200-250	1028-12	325-375

MAGNOLIA .... Page 215-216

2-8	$400-600	95-12	$200- 275	389-8	$ 125- 200
3-3	100-200	96-12	350- 450	446-4	125- 200
4T	300-400	97-14	325- 450	446-6	130- 190
4C	75-125	98-15	400- 600	447-6	120- 180
4S	75-125	99-16	500- 900	448-8	150- 200
5-10	175-225	99-19	600-1000	449-10	150- 225

Magnolia continued

13	225-300	100-18	700-1100	450-10	150- 250		
13-6	150-200	179-7	125- 175	451-12	175- 275		
14-10	200-300	180-6	100- 150	452-14	200- 250		
15-15	400-600	181-8	150- 225	453-6	150- 225		
28	100-175	182-5	100- 150	454-8	150- 250		
31-8	150-200	183-6	100- 150	459-10	100- 175		
41-10	200-300	184-6	100- 150	469-5	175- 275		
44-8	100-175	185-8	125- 225	665-3	65- 100		
49	65-100	186-4	125- 175	665-4	75- 125		
86-4	75-100	186-6	75- 100	665-5	115- 150		
87-6	100-175	383-7	125- 200	JP 665-8	800-1200		
88-6	100-175	384-7	125- 175	JP 665-10	1000-1500		
89-7	100-175	384-8	200- 275	666-5	175- 250		
90-7	100-175	384-10	225- 300	1108	100- 150		
91-8	175-275	385-10	250- 300	1156-2	75- 150		
92-8	175-250	386-12	325- 375	1157-4	100- 200		
93-9	175-275	387-6	175- 225	1294-8	225- 325		
94-9	175-275	388-6	120- 180	1327	300- 500		

MATT COLOR .... Page 217
MOLD NUMBERS:

22	$ 70-120	608-6	$ 60-100
236-3	50-100	609-6	75-125
236-4	50-100	624-4	60-100
364-5	125-175	625-5	100-125
548-4	50-100	Gate	100-150
549-4	50-100	HB	150-250
550-4	75-125	WP	125-200
607-4	50-100		

MATT GREEN .... Page 218-222
MOLD NUMBERS:

No. 1 Vase 319-6	$ 150- 175	501-503-506-508			
12"	500- 600	7	$ 225- 250	4	$ 200- 300
16"	800-1000	8	250- 300	5	300- 400
18"	1100-1300	12	400- 500	6	400- 500
24"	1800-2000	320-6	100- 200	7	500- 600
No. 2 Vase		8	200- 300	8	$ 650- 750
12"	$ 300- 400	12	350- 400	9	800- 900
16"	500- 600	321-5	125- 150	10	1100-1300
18"	800-1000	7	200- 250	12	1300-1500
24"	1200-1500	8	250- 300	502-6	275- 325
No. 3 Vase		10	$ 300- 350	8	$ 500- 600
12"	$ 400- 500	Round Bowl		10	800- 900
16"	700- 800	456-5	200- 250	504-7	550- 650
18"	900-1100	6	325- 375	9	900-1100
24"	1500- 1800	7	450- 550	10	1200-1500
No. 4 Vase		8	$ 600-700	505-7	$ 400- 450
12"	$ 400- 500	9	750- 850	8	500- 600
16"	700- 800	10	1000-1200	10	600- 700
18"	900-1100	12	1200-1400	507-7	400- 450
24"	1500-1800	14	1500-1700	8	500- 600
313-6	125- 150	Footed Jardiniere		9	550- 650
7	150- 200	457-4	125- 150	458-3	45- 50
8	225- 250	5	150- 175		55- 65
314-6	75- 100	6	250- 300	549-4	95- 110
7	125- 150	7	350- 400	5.4-6	100- 125
8	150- 200	8	500- 600	5.5-8	125- 150
9	225- 250	9	650- 750	5.6-9	150- 200
Fern Dish w/liner		10	800- 900	5.7-12	250- 300
314-6	75- 100	12	1000-1200	5.8-15	450- 550
7	125- 150	Jardinieres		5.10-18	600- 700
8	150- 200	462-463 7	125- 150		
9	225- 250	3	75- 100	3645-5	200- 250
Hanging Basket		4	100- 125	3656-5	200- 250
314-4		5	125- 150	3675-6	300- 350
5	250- 300	6	150- 200	3684-4	200- 250
6	400- 500	7	275- 325	Jard. & Ped	
7	650- 750	8	400- 550	456-10-27	
315-7	325- 375	9	550- 600		2000-2500
316-6	125- 150	10	650- 750	456-12-31	
7	150- 200	12	800- 900		3500-4500
8	225- 250	468-5	200- 250	963-49-½	
317-6	150- 200	6	325- 375		400- 500
7	225- 250	7	450- 550	Hanging Basket	
8	250- 300	8	600- 700	102-4	250- 300
318-6	125- 150	9	750- 850	5	300- 350
7	150- 200	10	1000-1200	6	400- 500
8	225- 250	12	1200-1400	7	650- 750

PRICE GUIDE / INDEX

Normandy continued

609-7	275-325	Umbrella Stand 600-1000
609-8	300-350	Sand Jar 500- 800
609-9	350-400	

NOVA . . . . Page 242

90-4	$50-100	94-8	$ 75-125
91-6	60-100	95-10	100-150
92-6	60-100	96-10	100-150
93-7	75-125		

NOVELTY STEINS . . . . Page 243

All $225-300

NURSERY . . . . Page 244

"Little Bo Peep"
"Tom, The Piper's Son"
"Little Jack Horner"   All for $250 to $350 each
"Little Miss Muffet"
"Tom Thum"

OPAC ENAMELS . . . . Page 245

MOLD NUMBERS:

4"	$150-175	8"	$ 600- 700
5"	200-250	9"	750- 850
6"	325-350	10"	1000-1200
7"	450-550	12"	1200-1400

ORIAN . . . . Page 246

272-10	$175-275	736-8	$150-250	742-12	$300-450
273-12-5-4	200-250	737-7	200-275	743-14	400-550
274-6	200-250	738-9	200-275	744-15	500-700
733-6	150-200	739-9	200-275	1108-4	175-250
734-7	125-200	740-10	200-300	1276-8	600-700
735-7	140-240	741-10	300-400	WP	600-800

ORISIS . . . . Page 247

1pt.	$100-150
2pt.	150-250
3pt.	250-300

PASADENA PLANTERS . . . . Page 248

L2B	$ 90-130	L20-10	$100-150	L29-7	$ 75-125
L10-8	60-120	L21-12	100-150	L30-3	75-125
L11-10	75-150	L22-4	100-150	L31-4	75-125
L12-12	100-150	L23-5	125-175	L32-5	100-150
L13-16	125-175	L24-3	100-150	L33-6	100-150
L14-4	50-100	L24-6	125-175	L34-8	100-150
L15-5	75-125	L25-6	75-125	L35-10	100-150
L16-7	75-125	L26-7	50-100	L36-4	100-150
L17-9	100-150	L27-5	50-100	L37-5	75-125
L18-6	50-100	L28-6	100-150	L38-6	75-125
L19-8	100-150	L28-6	100-150	L38-6	75-125

PAULEO . . . . Page 249

To rare to put a value on

PEONY . . . . Page 250-251

2-3	$100-150	69-15	$475-575	431-10	$ 175- 200
3P	300-325	70-18	525-725	432-12	200- 225
3C & S	75-125	115-5	100-175	432-14	200- 225
3-10	275-325	119-4	75-100	433-14	250- 275
4-10	225-300	167-4	100-175	434-6	125- 175
5-10	225-300	168-6	150-200	435-6	125- 175
7-6	100-175	169-8	150-225	435-8	150- 200
8-10	225-350	170-6	100-175	435-10	200- 250
9-15	400-475	171-8	150-200	436-10	175- 275
11	225-275	171-10	125-175	454-8	200- 250
27	125-175	172	125-200	467-5	175- 275
47	100-125	173-6	100-150	651-4	200- 250
57-4	75-100	276-6	100-175	661-3	75- 125
58-6	100-175	376-6	150-175	661-4	75- 125
59-6	100-150	377-8	150-200	661-5	150- 175
60-7	125-175	378-10	225-325	661-6	200- 275
61-7	125-175	379-12	325-375	JP 661-8	1200-1500
62-8	175-250	386-6	150-200	JP 661-10	1500-1800
63-8	150-200	387-8	125-175	662-5	150- 200
64-9	175-275	389-10	150-200	1151-2	100- 125
65-9	175-250	427-4	100-150	1152-4	125- 175
66-10	225-275	427-6	150-175	1153	200- 250
67-12	275-350	428-6	125-175	1293-8	225- 325
68-14	375-425	429-6	100-175	1326-7	225- 375
		429-8	125-175	8" Tray	100- 200
		430-10	125-200		

PERSIAN . . . . Page 252-253

MOLD NUMBERS:

Jardiniere

315-8	$450-500	Planterw/liner #523		10"	$800-1000
462-5	200-250	4"	$250- 300	HB #315	
462-6	250-300	5"	325- 425	4"	300- 400
462-7	300-350	6"	450- 500	5"	300- 400
462-8	400-500	7"	550- 650	6"	400- 500
462-9	450-550	8"	650- 750	7"	500- 600
Candlesticks	225-250	9"	700- 850	8"	600- 700
Jar. & Ped.	462-10x27½	1500-2000			
	462-12x33	2000-2500			
Picture	2500-3500				

PINECONE . . . . Page 254-259

1-4¾	$400- 700	415-9	$ 500- 800	704-7	$ 250- 375
1-5-8	700- 900	416-18	1200-1800	705-9	300- 400
2	400- 600	421-6	150- 250	706-8	300- 350
2-3	150- 175	421-6-8	200- 250	707-9	400- 500
5	450- 550	422-8	250- 325	708-9	800-1200
20-4	150- 250	426-6	225- 275	709-10	500- 700
21-5	175- 275	427-8	275- 375	711-10	500- 700
25	150- 250	428	250- 350	712-12	400- 600
32	175- 250	428-8	200- 300	713-14	700-1000
33	200- 300	429-10	350- 450	745-6	225- 350
73	300- 400	430-12	300- 450	745-7	350- 500
109-10	550- 650	431-15	325- 425	746-8	250- 350
112-6	200- 300	432-12	375- 475	747-10	350- 650
112-7	200- 300	433-12	375- 475	748-6	250- 350
113-8	275- 350	441-4	200- 250	776-14	2000-3000
114-8	350- 500	441-10	325- 425	777-20	2300-3800
121-7	200- 350	445-7	200- 300	797-10	425- 600
122-6	175- 275	451-4	300- 400	804-10	300- 400
124-5	225- 325	454-7	250- 350	805-12	600- 800
126-6	225- 275	455-6	150- 200	806-12	600- 800
127-8	150- 200	456-6	175- 250	807-15	800-1000
128-8	225- 325	457-7	250- 325	838-6	200- 300
261-6	250- 350	458-5	350- 500	838-8	200- 300
262-10	350- 500	461	350- 400	839-6	200- 350
263-14	350- 450	462	375- 475	840-7	300- 400
270-9	350- 450	466	400- 600	841-7	300- 400
276-9	250- 350	468-8	200- 400	842-7	325- 375
278-4	250- 325	468-12	350- 450	842-8	300- 400
279-9-6	200- 350	469-8	250- 350	843-8	400- 500
279-9	275- 325	469-12	350- 450	844-8	300- 450
288-7	400- 600	472-6	300- 400	845-6	300- 400
320-5	150- 225	472-8	375- 450	845-8	300- 500
321-9	375- 575	473-8	300- 400	846-9	450- 650
322-12	350- 550	478-7	225- 325	847-8	175- 250
323-15	400- 600	479-7	200- 300	847-9	350- 500
324-6	500- 700	480-7	150- 225	848-7	300- 400
338-10	350- 550	485-10	500- 750	848-10	400- 500
339-14	550- 750	488-8	200- 300	849-10	500- 600
345-6	125- 175	490-8	350- 450	850-14	600- 900
352-5-3-2	800-1200	491-10	500- 750	851-15	700- 900
353-11	400- 600	492-12	800-1200	888-6	150- 250
353-12	400- 600	493-12	350- 450	906-6	200- 300
354-6	150- 250	497	150- 250	907-7	300- 400
355-8	175- 275	498	250- 350	908-8	300- 500
356-5	150- 250	499	125- 225	909-10	350- 500
379-9-3-3	400- 600	632-2	150- 250	910-10	500- 700
380-10-5	1200-1500	632-4	200- 275	911-12	700-1000
388-10	600- 700	632-5	200- 300	912-15	2000-2800
400-4	125- 175	632-6	300- 400	913-18	2000-2500
401-6	250- 350	632-7	400- 500	917-6	250- 350
402-8	800-1400	632-8	550- 750	960-4	250- 350
403-10	900-1200	632-9	600- 900	964-2	200- 250
405-8	900-1200	632-10	900-1200	1073-4	250- 350
406-6	300- 375	632-12	1500-2000	1099-4	275- 400
406-10	800-1000	633-5	300- 450	1106-4	500- 700
408-6	300- 500			1123	200- 300
409-8	350- 500			1123-2	200- 275
410-10	375- 550			1124-4	500- 800
411-10	400- 500			1127	500- 700
414-5	175- 275			1273-8	350- 450
				1283-4	1000-1500
1321	500- 700			1283-9	800-1200

PRICE GUIDE / INDEX

Pinecone continued

Jardinieres & Pedestals:

Plate	$ 400- 600
02-8	1600-2400
32-8	2000-4000
32-10	2500-5000
32-12	3500-7000

Rare Planter Bookends:

59	$ 750-1000
Punch Bowl	800-1200
Plate	400- 600

POPPY . . . . Page 260

5	$175-200	363-4	$ 100-125	869-7	$150- 225
34-4	150-250	366-6	150-175	870-8	175- 250
35-6	200-225	368-7	150-175	871-8	200- 275
36-3	100-150	370-8	150-175	872-9	175- 275
36-5	110-160	642-3	100-125	873-9	175- 275
36-7	125-200	642-4	100-150	874-10	275- 375
36-8	150-200	642-5	150-200	875-10	350- 450
36-10	150-200	642-6	250-300	876-10	375- 475
37-6	125-175	642-7	300-350	877-12	400- 450
77-8	150-250	642-8 JP	1200-1500	878-15	450- 650
38-5	110-160	642-9 JP	1500-2000	879-18	800-1200
38-10	175-225	642-10 JP	1750-2000	880-18	600-1000
39-12	250-300	643-5	150- 250	1123	200- 250
40-14	250-325	675-10	250- 300	1129	200- 250
41-7	375-400	865-8	125- 175	1130-5	250- 275
46-6	150-200	866-6	100- 150	1135-5	250- 300
47-10	350-475	867-6	125- 175	1281-8	450- 550
48-12	400- 550	868-7	150- 200		
58-5	350- 400				

PRIMROSE . . . . Page 261-262

2-4	$150-200	634-8	$ 425- 525	766-6	$ 200- 300
25-6	125-175	634-9	500- 600	766-8	200- 300
60-5	150-200	634-8 J&P	1000-1200	767-8	225-325
34-4	125-175	634-10"	1500-1800	768-9	225- 300
35-5	150-200	634-12"	1800-2000	769-9	225- 350
35-6	150-200	636-5	200- 250	770-10	250- 300
36-9	150-200	760-6	125- 175	771-12	325- 525
37-12-7	175-250	760-12	225- 275	772-10-14	250- 350
41-10	300-400	761-6	125- 225	772-14	500- 700
54-5	300-350	762-7	150- 175	773-10-21	1000-1800
81-10	325-425	763-7	150- 200	1105-4	225- 325
34-4	100-150	764-7	175- 225	1113-5	300- 500
34-5	150-175	765-8	200- 275	1277-8	350- 450
34-6	200-250				
34-7	325-375				

QUAKER . . . . Page 263

Jugs	$175-200
Tankers	500-600
Humidors	375-425
Tea Set	300-400
Dresser Set	350-400

RAMEKIN . . . . Page 264

OLD NUMBERS:

04-3 pt.	$175-200
Special	150-175
93 1/2 Oval 8"	150-175
94 1/2 Oval 9"	175-225
74-7	150-175

RAYMOR . . . . Page 265-266

50	Cup	$ 25- 35
51	Saucer	10- 25
52	Dinner Plate	20- 30
53	Salad Plate	20- 30
54	Bread & Butter Plate	12- 17
55	Lug Soup	22- 32
56	Individual Covered Ramekin	40- 50
57	Covered Sugar	40- 50
58	Covered Cream Pitcher	40- 50
59	Stand Only for Sugar & Creamer	40- 50
57-158-159	Together	100-150
60	Vegetable Bowl	20- 40
61	Salad Bowl	35- 45
62	Individual Corn Server	20- 28

Raymor continued

163	Platter	50-100
164	Chop Platter	55- 75
165	Divided Vegetable Bowl	50- 75
166	Handled Fruit Bowl	90-110
167	6 pc. Condiment Set	200-275
168	Salt Shaker	15- 40
169	Pepper Shaker	15- 40
170	Vinegar Cruet	40- 60
171	Oil Cruet	40- 60
172	Covered Jam or Relish w/spoon	40- 75
173	Condiment Stand Only	40- 75
174	Teapot	200-250
175	Teapot Trivet	50- 60
176	Lg. Coffee Pot and Stand	350-450
177	Celery & Olive Dish	75-100
178	Steak Platter with Well	100-150
179	Handled Coffee Tumbler	50- 60
180	3 pc. Cheese & Relish set	100-150
181	Covered Butter Dish	55- 75
182	Relish & Sandwich Tray	75-125
183	Medium Casserole	55- 85
184	Medium Casserole Trivet	30- 50
185	Lg. Casserole	125-175
186	Lg. Casserole Trivet	45- 65
187	4 qt. Bean Pot	100-150
188	Bean Pot Trivet	35- 55
189	Water Pitcher	150-250
190	Gravy Boat	30- 75
191	Pickle Dish	24- 44
192	Lug Fruit	14- 25
193	3 qt. Bean Pot	100-135
194	2 qt. Bean Pot	75-100
195	Individual Bean Pot	40- 60
196	4 qt. Handled Casserole	140-170
197	2 1/2 qt. Handled Casserole	100-150
198	1 1/2 qt. Handled Casserole	60- 80
199	Individual Casserole	45- 75
200	Shirred Egg	40- 60
201	Double Stacked Warmer	60-100
202	Bun Warmer	200-300
203	Ashtray	75-100

RAYMOR MODERN ARTWARE . . . . Page 267

Mixing Bowl	10-6	$ 50- 75	Teapot 14P		$200-250
	11-8	75-100	Sugar 14S		35- 50
	12-10	125-150	Creamer 14C		35- 50
Pitchers	15-5	75-100	Fruit Bowl 13-11		150-175
	16-6	125-150			
	17-7	150-200			

RAYMOR GOURMET . . . . Page 268

Mixing Bowls

9-1 qt.	$ 50- 75	Bean Pots	
10-1 1/2 qt.	75-100	18-2 1/2 qt.	$150-200
11-3 qt.	100-150	19-5 qt.	100-150
12-6 qt.	150-200		
		Casseroles	
Pitchers		20-2 qt.	$150-200
14-1 pt.	$ 75-100	21-5 qt.	175-225
15-1 qt.	100-125	22-2 1/2 pt.	100-150
16-1 1/2 qt.	150-175		
17-2 1/2 qt.	200-250		

ROMAFIN . . . . Page 269

To rare to put a value on

ROSALIE . . . . Page 270

Umbrella Stand	723-21	$ 800-1000	Toilet Set		
Spitoon	5"	300- 400	Toothbrush Holder	$	175- 200
Jar & Ped		2000-2800	Chamber Pot		500- 800
			Pitcher		400- 600
Jardiniere			Combinett		800-1000
	6"	$100-150	Drinking Cup		125- 150
	7"	150-200	Soap Dish w/lid		150- 200
	8"	200-250	Lg. Pitcher		400- 700
	9"	250-300	Basin		400- 500
	10"	300-400			

Rozane Line continued

R110-6	150-200	300-6	350- 400		
WP	250-300	367-10	500- 600		
1	350-400	588-5	125- 175		
2-8	225-275	588-6	175- 250		
16F	150-200	588-8	300- 400		
102-12	200-300	588-10JP		1200-2200	
250-6	250-350	756-9-19	700-1200		
251-5	200-250				

ROZANE-CRYSTALIS . . . . Page 287
MOLD NUMBERS:

C12	$2500-3000	C20	$2300-2800
C13	2000-2500	C22	2500-3000
C14	2300-2800	C23	2200-2600
C15	1500-1800	C24	2000-2500
C16	2000-2500	C25	1800-2000
C17	2000-2500	C26	2200-2600
C19	2300-2800	E64	2000-2500

ROZANE-DELLA ROBBIA . . . . Page 288-295
MOLD NUMBERS:

D1	$2000-2200	4-15	$9000- 11000	36-11	$8000-10000
D2	2200-2500	5-7	4000- 5000	37-14	8000-10000
D3	2000-2200	6-12	7000- 8000	38-6	3500- 4000
D4	1300-1500	7-8	5000- 6000	39-7	2500- 3000
D5	2000-2200	8-10	6000- 7000	40-7	8000-10000
D6	1800-2000	9-10	4000- 5000	41-9	8000-10000
D7	2000-2200	10-9	7000- 8000	42-6	6000- 7000
D8	2200-2500	11-10	7000- 8000	43-11	10000-12000
D9	1800-2000	12-10	6000- 7000	44-5	2500- 3000
D10	2200-2500	12-16	15000-20000	45-9	4000- 5000
D11	1800-2000	13-18	30000-35000	46-9	7000- 8000
D12	2200-2500	14-15	9000-11000	47-16	15000-20000
D13	2200-2500	15-14	7000- 8000	48-10	6000- 7000
D14	2200-2500	16-12	7000- 8000	49-14	18000-22000
D15	2000-2500	17-12	10000-12000	50-3	2000- 3000
D16	1300-1500	18-12	7000- 8000	51-6	2000- 2200
D17	1800-2000	19-9	7000- 8000	51-7	2500- 2800
D18	1300-1500	20-16	20000-25000	51-8	3000- 3500
Teapots		21-13	8000-10000	52-16	10000-12000
1	1400-1600	22-6	3000- 3500	53-14	4000- 5000
2	1400-1600	23-6	2200- 2500	54-7	5000- 6000
3	1400-1600	23-7	2800- 3000	55-13	15000-20000
4	2000-2500	23-8	3300- 3600	56-4	3000- 3500
5	1400-1800	24-11	14000-16000	57-5	1500- 1800
6	2000-2400	25-8	3000- 3500	58-10	6000- 7000
7	1400-1800	26-6	1500- 2000	59-7	4000- 5000
8	1400-1800	27-9	4000- 5000	60-4	1500- 1800
9	1400-1800	28-19	20000-28000	61-20	20000-25000
10	1500-2000	29-9	7000- 8000	62-10	7000- 8000
11	1500-2000	30-19	35000-40000	63-13	12000-15000
12	1500-2000	31-9	3000- 4000	64-3	8000-10000
		32-10	3000- 3500	65-11	8000-10000
1-18	18000-22000	33-17	15000-20000	66-11	8000- 9000
2-16	15000-20000	34-6	3500- 4000	67-17	14000-16000
3-6	2500- 3000	35-7	4000- 4500	68-11	10000-12000
		69-13	35000-40000		
		70-7	7000- 8000		

ROZANE-EGYPTO . . . . Page 296-300
MOLD NUMBERS:

E10	$600-700	E34	$ 150- 200	E46	$1500-2000
E11	400-500	E35	350- 425	E47	600- 700
E12	500-600	E36	400- 500	E48	450- 550
E15	400-450	E37	1200-1500	E49	450- 550
E17	350-400	E38	250- 350	E50	600- 700
E19	325-375	E39	175- 225	E51	800-1200
E20	275-350	E40	350- 450	E52	275- 350
E21	300-400	E41	500- 600	E53	250- 300
E29	300-375	E42	150- 250	E56	225- 300
E30	150-200	E43	300- 400	E57	150- 200
E31	175-225	E44	200- 250	E58	1000-1400
E32	200-275	E45	800-1200	E59	1000-1500
E33	250-300	E68	1800-2400		
Picture (not shown on plates)			3000-3500		

ROZANE-FUDJIYAMA/FUDGI . . . . Page 301
MOLD NUMBERS:

R3	$2200-2600	R15	$2500-3000	971	$1800-2200

R5	2200-2600	892	1800-2000	972	1500-1800
R6	1500-2000	893	3000-3500	973	2200-2600
R12	1800-2200	961	2000-2500	974	2200-2600
R14	2200-2600	970	2000-2500	975	1200-1500
		982	1500-2000		

ROZANE-HAND DECORATED . . . . Page 302
MOLD NUMBERS:
Vases Jardinieres

807-12¾	$350-400	438-438 (A-B-C-D)	
822-16	500-600	7"	$275-300
893-12¾	300-350	8"	300-350
900-6	225-275	9"	350-400
956-8½	275-325	10"	400-500
961-10½	350-400	12"	500-600

ROZANE-HOLLYWOOD WARE . . . . Page 303
MOLD NUMBERS:

R1-7	$200-225	878-7	$225-250	977-6	$150-175
R2-6	175-200	886-5	175-200	979-7	200-225
R3-11	300-325	921-11	550-700	980-5	150-175
R9-4-9	275-325	940-9	450-550	981-5	125-150
R22-3	200-225	969-12	400-550	984-5	125-150
268-9	225-250	973-11	400-550	990-4	175-200
804-2	125-150	976-7	175-200	994-4	100-125
877-7	200-225	995-4	100-125		
		999-7	175-200		

ROZANE-MARA . . . . Page 304-305
To rare to put a value on

ROZANE-MONGOL
To rare to put a value on

ROZANE-OLYMPIC . . . . Page 309

7"	Pitcher	$4000- 4500	
14"	Footed Vase	7000- 8000	
13"	Vase	4500- 5000	
20"	Vase	9000-10000	
11"	Tanker	4000- 5000	
11"	Footed Urn	5000- 6000	(2 Handles)
	Mug	1200- 1500	

ROZANE-PATTERN . . . . Page 310
MOLD NUMBERS:

1	$100-125	8-10	$125-175	398-4	$ 75-150
1-6	100-150	9-10	150-175	398-6	175-200
2 Frog	75-110	10-12	175-200	398-8	250-300
2	175-225	11-15	275-325	407-6	100-150
2-6	75-150	44	100-150	408-8	100-150
3-8	110-130	144-3	100-150	409-12	125-175
4-8	125-150	395-9	100-150	410	150-200
5-8	100-150	396-10	100-150		
6-9	110-150	397-14	125-175		
7-9	110-160				

ROZANE-ROYAL . . . . Page 311-322
MOLD NUMBERS:

R1-7	$ 300- 400	813-10	$ 400- 500	928-9	$ 350- 450
R2-6	300- 400	814-10	450- 500	931-14	1600-2000
R3-10	350- 450	815-20	2000-2400	932-17	1400-1800
R4-9	375- 475	816-15	800-1200	933-13	1200-1600
R5-10	400- 500	818-12	550- 750	949-15	1000-1400
R7-12	400- 450	821-9	500- 600	950-7	300- 400
R8-12	400- 425	822-16	1000-1400	953-30	4000-5000
R9-16	1000-1400	823-6	225- 250	954-21	1800-2200
R10-20	2000-2600	826-21	2700-3200	955-18	1800-2200
R11-19	1800-2400	827-9	700- 900	956-8	350- 450
R12-8	350- 450	828-8	600- 800	957-15	1200-1600
R13-6	300- 400	831-10	750- 850	958-11	325- 425
R14-8	350- 450	832-20	2200-2700	959-7	225- 350
R15-11	500- 700	837-12	575- 625	961-10	300- 400
R16-7	350- 450	843-7	250- 275	962-14	800-1200
R17-8	450- 550	845-11	700- 800	964-16	800-1200
R18-3	300- 350	850-24	3000-3500	965-6	225- 325
R19-5	300- 400	854-16	1000-1400	966-14	700- 900
R20-6	325- 425	855-14	600- 700	967-10	500- 700
R21-3	300- 400	858-16	1000-1200	968-10	600- 700
R22-3	300- 400	861-16	1800-2200	969-12	500- 600
R23-5	350- 450	863-21	2500-3000	970-10	350- 450
R25-12	350- 450	864-8	1600-2200	971-9	300- 400

PRICE GUIDE / INDEX

Rozane-Royal continued

R27-19	1700-2400	867-10	350- 450	973-11	500- 700
R28-10	500- 600	868-9	350- 450	974-11	350- 450
R29-14	1000-1500	870-11	500- 675	975-6	250- 375
R31-6	300- 375	879-10	450- 550	976-7	300- 400
R32-15	1200-1600	881-6	300- 400	977-6	350- 450
R33-11	300- 400	882-9	3000-4000	978-8	300- 400
R34-11	300- 450	883-6	300- 400	979-7	300- 400
R35-8	300- 450	884-16	1000-1600	980-5	300- 375
R36-5	275- 375	886-5	300- 400	981-5	300- 350
R37	325- 425	887-16	1000-1400	982-8	350- 450
R38-3	300- 400	889-7	350- 450	983-8	300- 350
R39-6	300- 400	890-12	450- 550	984-5	300- 400
R40-6	300- 400	891-14	1000-1400	985-10	1000-1500
R41-5	300- 400	892-8	300- 400	986-9	450- 550
R42-17	1500-2000	893-12	500- 700	987-8	400- 650
R43-7	300- 400	895-8	350- 450	988-6	400- 500
R44-9	400- 500	896-8	400- 500	989-5	350- 450
R45-11	375- 475	897-5	1200-1500	990-4	350- 450
R46-10	350- 450	898-13	650- 750	991-3	325- 425
R47-9	350- 450	900-7	300- 400	992-5	350- 450
R48-9	350- 425	903-9	275- 350	993-8	500- 600
R49-5	250- 350	904-11	400- 500	994-4	300- 400
R50-4	250- 350	905-10	500- 600	995-4	300- 400
R51-8	325- 425	906-8	300- 500	996-8	300- 400
R52-11	700- 900	908-5	300- 450	997-7	300- 400
804-2	250- 350	911-6	275- 375	998-6	300- 400
807-12	500- 700	921-11	500- 800	999-7	300- 400
812-13	700-1000				

ROZANE-SURPRISE PACKAGE .... Page 323
MOLD NUMBERS:

R5-10	$500-700	R44-9	$400-500	867-10	$400-500
R8-12	500-750	R45-11	375-475	890-12	650-950
R15-11	500-700	807-12	500-600	893-12	600-700
R17-8	400-500	814-10	400-500	900-6	300-400
R19-5	350-450	821-9	600-700	905-10	500-600
R28-10	400-550	823-6	300-450	921-11	550-750
R33-11	350-450	830-12	600-800	956-8	350-450
R34-11	400-500	843-7	550-650	974-11	400-475
				987-8	500-700

ROZANE-UNTRIMMED .... Page 324

1st Row: (left to right)

(1)	$125-200	(2)	$100-175	(3)	$125-200
(4)	100-150	(5)	100-150	(6)	125-250
(7)	250-300	(8)	200-300	(9)	275-400

2nd Row: (left to right)

(1)	$250-300	(2)	$250-300	(3)	$275-325
(4)	275-350	(5)	250-350	(6)	350-500
(7)	300-400	(8)	300-475		

3rd Row: (left to right)

(1)	$375-475	(2)	$400-475	(3)	$400-475
(4)	375-475	(5)	350-450	(6)	475-600
(7)	500-650				

ROZANE-WOODLAND .... Page 325-327
To rare to put a value on

RUSSO .... Page 328
MOLD NUMBERS:

15-2	$ 55- 80	260-6	$ 75-150	698-9	$150-225
15-3	55- 80	260-12	125-225	699-9	175-250
107-8	100-150	337-10	250-350	700-10	175-250
108-6	125-200	694-7	150-250	701-10	175-250
109-8	125-200	695-8	75-125	702-12	200-300
259-6	75-150	696-8	100-200	703-15	300-450
		697-8	150-200	1098	150-200

SAVONA .... Page 329
MOLD NUMBERS:

13-4	$200-300	186-8	$200-250	375-10	$300-350
14-4	100-175	207-6	100-200	376-10	325-400
15-2	45- 85	209-10	250-350	377-11	375-425
15-3	45- 85	222-12	300-400	378-8	400-450
102-6	100-175	371-6	150-250	379-12	450-500
119-6	150-200	372-6	150-250	1070-3	150-200
183-10	175-225	373-8	300-400	1071-4	200-250
184-12	250-300	374-8	300-400	1260-8	500-600
185-6	150-200				

SIGNS .... Page 33

9"x4"	$1500-1800
Moderne	1600-2000
Script	1800-2500
Little Print	1200-1500
Little Block Print	1500-1800

SILHOUTTE .... Page 331

708-6	$150-200	731-14	$150-200	779-5	$100-150
708-8	150-200	737-7	275-375	780-6	100-150
709-8	150-200	740	200-275	781-6	100-150
710-10	200-350	741-4	100-150	782-7	75-125
716-6	100-175	742-6	300-450	783-7	250-350
717-10	200-300	750	100-150	784-8	250-350
721-8	75-150	751-3	150-250	785-9	200-300
722	100-150	756	100-150	786-9	200-300
726-6	75-125	757	100-150	787-10	400-500
727-8	100-150	758-9	75-125	788-12	175-250
728-10	100-150	761-4	250-400	789-14	450-850
729-12	100-175	763-8	400-500	791	100-150
730-10	100-175	766-8	300-500	796-8	100-150
731-10	100-175	768-8	75-125	799	150-200
		769-8	100-150		

SILHOUTTE-NUDES

6" Fan Vase	$ 650- 850
8" Fan Vase	400- 600
296-10 Cylinder Vase	800-1200
298-11½ Vase	700-1000
Wall Pocket	500- 800
Lamp	1000-1500

SMOKER SETS .... Page 332
MOLD NUMBERS:

1B	$800-1000	4B	$500-700	7B	$300- 400
2 Ash	125-150	4 Ash	125-150	8A	600- 800
2B	350-450	5B	300-350	8B	400- 600
3	400-500	5C	150-175	9A	800-1200
3A	300-350	6A	200-300	10A	400- 600
3C	150-175	6B	200-300	10B	300- 450
3S	400-500	7A	400-600		

SNOWBERRY .... Page 333-336

1A	$100-175	1CC8	$125-175	1TP	$ 325- 425
1BE	250-300	1CS1	100-150	1UR8	125- 200
1BK7	150-250	1CS2	100-150	1V6	100- 150
1BK8	175-275	1FB-10	200-300	1V15	400- 600
1BK10	225-275	1FH6	100-200	1V18	600- 900
1BK12	250-300	1FH7	100-200	1V1-7	100- 150
1BL1	100-130	1HB5	200-300	1V1-8	150- 200
1BL8	100-200	1J4	125-175	1V1-9	150- 200
1BL10	150-200	1J5	100-150	1V1-10	175- 250
1BL12	250-350	1J6	200-275	1V1-12	200- 300
1BL14	250-350	1J8	450-500	1V1-15	400- 500
1BL1-6	100-125	1P8	450-550	1V1-18	600- 900
1BL1-10	125-175	1PF5	75-125	1V2-7	100- 150
1BL1-12	200-300	1PS5	175-200	1V2-8	125- 175
1BL2-6	100-150	1RB5	100-150	1V2-9	140- 240
1BL2-10	150-250	1RB6	110-160	1V2-10	150- 250
1BL2-12	200-300	1S	75-125	1V2-12	300- 400
BV	100-125	1TK6	125-200	1V2-18	650- 800
1BV7	100-150	1TK7	140-220	1WP8	200- 300
1C	75-125	1TK10	200-300	1WX8-2	200- 300
1CC6	100-140	1TK15	475-675	1JP8	1600-2000

SPECIAL .... Page 337-338
MOLD NUMBERS:

886-5	Mug	$200- 250	886-12		$200- 350
884-15	Tanker	800-1200	890-12		600- 900
718-9x21	Vase	500- 600	964-16		800-1400
452-14	Jardiniere	500- 600	965-6	Mugs	250- 300
719-9x21	Umbrella Stand	500- 800	966-14		500- 800
429-A-26 ½	Jar & Ped	1000-1500			
429-B26 ½	Jar & Ped	1000-1500			
429-c-26 ½	Jar & Ped	1000-1500			

STORK .... Page 339
MOLD NUMBERS:

Flower Pots		Jar & Ped	
335-5½	$ 75-100	408-15	$ 350- 450

416

Stork continued

335-6½	100-125	408-20	500- 700
335-7½	125-150	408-25	1000-1400
335-8½	150-200	Umbrella Stand	
335-9½	200-250	705-8x18	450- 500
335-10½	250-300		

SUNFLOWER .... Page 340
MOLD NUMBERS:

208-5	$600- 800	490-8	$ 800-1300	619-12	$3000- 4200
485-6	500- 700	491-8	1200-1600	619-12 JP	7000-12000
486-5	500- 700	492-10	1100-1700	770-20	4000- 7500
487-7	500- 700	493-9	900-1200	1265-7	800- 1200
488-6	600- 900	494-10	1500-2200	HB	1200- 1800
489-7	900-1500	619-10	5000-8000	WP	1200- 1800

SYLVAN .... Page 341-342
MOLD NUMBERS:

S33-7-6	$450-550	225-6	$ 200- 250
S34-5-5	350-450	325-4	300- 400
S35-5-2-7	275-325	325-5	400- 500
S35-4-4	200-250	325-6	400- 500
S36-2-5	150-175	325-7	500- 600
S37-1-4	150-175	325-8	600- 700
S38-2-2-8	225-275	325-10	650- 750
S40-1-5	150-175	361-11½-6½	300- 350
S41-2-3-7	200-250	361-14-8	400- 500
S42-3-6-12	300-400	361-16½-8½	500- 600
225-4	125-150	Vase	500- 600
225-5	150-175	568-12-33 J&P	3000-4500
Flower Vase	175-200		

TEA SETS .... Page 343-344
Priced Per Set
Picture 1
#3 Ceramic

C-D-E	$400-500

Picture 2

Dutch	300-350
#2 Dutch	300-350
#3 Dutch	300-350
#2 Landscape	350-400
#3 Landscape	300-350
#4 Ceramic	300-350 3 pc.

Picture 3

Sugar & Creamer	125-150 each
Teapot, Sugar & Creamer	300-350

TEASEL .... Page 345

36	$125-200	349-10	$ 350-400	885-8	$150- 200
342-4	125-175	644-4	125-175	886-9	225- 275
342-5	100-175	644-5	150-200	887-10	250- 350
343-6	175-250	881-6	150-200	888-12	275- 375
344-6	150-250	882-6	175-225	889-15	275- 375
345-12	225-275	883-7	175-250	890-18	700-1100
348-6	150-225	884-8	150-250	1131	200-225

THORNAPPLE .... Page 346-347

3-5	$300- 350	355-5	$300- 400	813-7	$150-250
29	200- 250	356-4	900-1200	814-7	175-250
30	200- 250	365-7	200- 300	815-7	175-250
127-6	115- 135	382-14	350- 450	816-8	200-275
262-5	125- 150	638-4	125- 150	817-8	200-250
304-4	125- 150	638-5	175- 200	818-8	200-250
305-6	275- 325	638-6	250- 275	819-9	225-275
306-5	125- 200	638-7	325- 375	820-9	250-300
307-6	125- 250	638-8	325- 425	821-10	300-350
308-4	125- 150	638-9	525- 625	822-10	275-350
308-7	150- 200	638-10	725- 825	823-12	325-425
308-12	275- 375	638-12	800-1000	824-15	575-675
310-10	225- 275	639-5	250- 300	825-5	100-175
311-12	275- 325	774-8-12	300- 375	825-15	450-650
312	275- 425	774-12	800- 900	1117-2	200-225
313	325- 425	808-4	125- 200	1118-4	175-225
342-10	325- 425	809-5	150- 225	1119-5	325-375
343-12	500- 575	810-6	150- 225	1120-5	475-575
Jard. & Ped		811-6	175- 250	1280-6	350-500
838-8	1200-1500	812-6	125- 200	1280-8	500-600
838-12	2500-3000				

TOPEO .... Page 348
(Blue Topeo Add 25% more)

Blue	666-15	$2000-2500
Blue	665-14	1400-1600
Blue	664-12	600- 650

245-6	$200-250	658-7	$275-300	663-10	$400- 475
246-2	125-175	659-8	300-350	664-12	500- 600
246-3	150-200	660-8	300-375	665-14	600- 800
656-6	125-200	661-9	300-400	666-15	800-1000
657-6	200-275	662-9	300-400	1093-4	300- 350

TOURIST .... Page 349
Picture #1: (left to right) $5000-5500, $1750-2000, $4000-4500
$1250-1500, $1250-1500, $3000-3500, $3500-4000

Picture #2: (left to right) $3000-3500, $2500-3000, $2500-2800

Not pictured: Three sizes of window boxes - Lg. $4000-4500, Med. $2500-2800
Sm. $1750-2200, J&P $8000-18000

TOURMALINE .... Page 350
MOLD NUMBERS:

A65-6	$125-200	A429-9	$200-225	612-7	$125-175
A152-6	100-150	A435-10	250-300	613-8	150-225
A152-7	125-225	A444-12	275-325	614-8	175-250
A200-4	100-150	A517-6	100-175	615-9	150-250
A308-7	150-200	238-5	125-175	616-10	200-250
A332-5	175-275	241-12	150-200	1089-4	150-175
A425-8	150-200	611-6	150-175		

TUSCANY .... Page 351
MOLD NUMBERS:

66-5	$125-175	174-12	$200-300	348-10	$300-375
67-4	125-175	341-5	150-225	349-12	350-400
68-4	150-200	342-6	200-300	1066-3	100-175
69-5	150-200	343-7	200-300	1067-4	125-200
70-5	150-200	344-8	225-325	1254-7	300-350
71-6	160-220	345-8	225-325	1255-8	350-400
171-6	125-175	346-9	250-350	Sm. Frog	55- 85
172-9	150-200	347-10	250-375	Lg. Frog	75-100
173-10	175-300				

UNIQUE .... Page 352

Coffee Pot	$350-450
Teapot	300-350
Chocolate Pot	300-400

VASE ASSORTMENT .... Page 353
MOLD NUMBERS:

Assortment #60		Assortment #24		Assortment #60	
101	$175-275	200	$275-325	102	$200-250
104	150-250	201	325-400	103	275-375
106	225-325	203	225-275	105	200-300
108	200-250	204	175-200	NIP 107	200-300
111	150-200	205	150-175	108	250-350
112	175-225	206	200-225	110	275-375
Not in picture		202-6½	$100-150		

VELMOSS I - SCROLL .... Page 354
MOLD NUMBERS:

14-8	$150-200	196-6	$225-275	335-6	$ 450- 550
115-5	125-175	197-8	250-350	600-5	200- 250
115-6	125-175	198-8	250-350	600-6	225- 275
115-7	125-200	199-8	250-350	600-7	275- 300
116-5	125-175	200-8	250-350	600-8	300- 400
116-6	125-200	201-10	350-400	600-9	400- 500
117-6	125-200	202-10	350-400	JP 600-10	1800-2600
118-6	150-200	203-10	350-400	1044-8	300- 400
193-5	175-225	204-10	350-400	1045-10	400- 500
194-6	175-275	205-12	450-550	1226-11	450- 550
195-6	225-275	254-6	200-250	1227-12	500- 600

VELMOSS II .... Page 355
MOLD NUMBERS:

115-7	$175-275	266-12	$275-375	719-9	$300-400
116-8	250-350	714-6	175-275	720-10	350-450
117-8	200-275	715-7	150-250	721-12	400-500
119-10	350-450	716-7	175-250	722-14	500-800
264-5	175-275	717-8	200-275	1100-4	150-250
265-6	200-275	718-8	250-350	1274-8	400-700
266-5-8	200-275				

VENETIAN . . . . Page 356

SET 1		SET 3	
7" Baking Dish	$150-175	7" Baking Dish	$150-175
9" " "	175-200	9" " "	175-200
11" " "	200-225	11" " "	250-300
SET 2		SET 4	
7" Baking Dish	$150-175	7" Baking Dish	$150-175
8" " "	160-170	8" " "	160-180
9" " "	225-275	9" " "	175-200
11" " "	200-225		
6 Custard Cups with Wire Lift	$200-250		
9" Pudding Dish	250-275		

VICTORIAN ART POTTERY . . . . Page 357
MOLD NUMBERS:

132-4	$250-300	260-8	$375- 425
133-6	350-400	261-8	700- 800
256-6	275-325	262-10	500- 600
257-7	300-350	263-10	600- 700
258-7	300-350	264-9	900-1000
259-7	300-350	265-12	800-1000

VOLPATO . . . . Page 358-359
MOLD NUMBERS:

2-5	$125-175	103-8	$150-200	207-6	$125-175
3-8	200-250	104-10	150-200	208-8	175-225
5-10	300-350	105-14	200-250	209-10	200-250
12-8	150-200	119-6	100-175	599-6	225-275
13-10	200-250	120-8	200-250	1039-8	200-275
97-4	100-150	188-5	100-150	1040-8	350-450
98-5	100-150	189-7	150-200	1041-10	350-450
99-5	100-150	190-9	250-300	1042-10	350-500
100-6	110-180	191-10	225-275	1043-12	500-600
101-6	115-185	192-12	300-350	1046-10	300-350
102-6	110-180	206-6	150-200	1047-12	400-500
Window Box	$100-125				

WATER LILY . . . . Page 360-361

1-8	$450-650	82-14	$425-575	440-8	$ 125- 175
10-6	150-200	83-15	450-625	441-10	125- 175
11-10	225-325	84-16	500-700	442-10	150- 200
11-20	275-350	85-18	700-900	443-12	200- 300
12	250-350	172-9	250-350	444-14	250- 350
12-15	450-550	174-6	150-225	445-6	125- 200
48	100-150	175-8	200-275	463-5	75- 125
66-3	75-100	176-6	150-200	468-5	225- 325
66-5	75-100	177-6	100-150	538-8	200- 350
71-4	100-150	178-8	175-225	663-3	75- 125
72-6	150-175	179-7	175-225	663-4	100- 150
73-6	150-175	380-8	175-275	663-5	150- 200
74-7	150-200	381-10	225-325	663-8JP	1000-1500
75-7	150-200	382-12	250-350	663-10JP	1500-2000
76-8	175-225	387-10	250-300	664-5	200- 250
77-8	175-225	393-12	250-350	999-15	700-1000
78-9	175-250	437-4	80-100	1139-6	75- 125
79-9	175-250	437-6	150-175	1143	125- 150
80-10	200-300	438-8	175-275	1154-2	125- 175
81-10	200-300	439-6	100-175	1155-4	175- 225
81-12	275-375				

WHITE ROSE . . . . Page 362-363

1	$150-250	389-6	$ 100- 150	979-6	$100-150
1-5	75-150	390-8	100- 150	980-6	100-150
1C	75-125	391-10	175- 275	981-6	100-150
1S	75-125	392-10	175- 275	982-7	125-175
1T	250-300	393-12	225- 325	983-7	140-200
7	250-350	393-14	225- 325	984-8	200-350
41	125-175	394-14	225- 325	985-7	225-325
143-6	100-175	463-5	225- 325	985-8	200-300
144-8	125-200	642-4	100- 150	986-9	200-300
145-8	150-200	653-3	75- 150	987-9	200-250
146-6	100-175	653-4	100- 175	988-7	175-350
147-8	100-175	653-5	125- 200	988-10	275-375
184-4	125-175	653-6	250- 350	990-10	200-300
309-8	125-225	653-7	275- 375	991-12	350-500
326-8	150-225	653-8 J&P	800-1200	992-15	400-500
350-8	200-250	653-10	1200-1700	993-15	350-450
353-3	100-150	654-5	175- 225	994-18	550-700
362-8	225-300	918-6	150- 200	995-7	100-150

White Rose continued

363-10	275-375	922-15	400- 475	1141-4	100-200
364-12	300-500	933-7	100- 200	1142-4	100-175
378-10	275-375	933-15	300- 400	1143	300-400
381-10	275-375	938-7	150- 250	1288-6	300-400
382-9	150-200	969-6	150- 200	1289-8	375-475
387-4	120-170	974-6	100- 150	1324	275-375
388-7	225-300	978-4	100- 150		

WINCRAFT . . . . Page 364-367

2CS	$100-125	241-6	$125-150	272-6	$100-150
208-8	175-250	242	125-175	273-8	100-150
209-12	175-250	250P	250-350	274-7	125-150
210-12	200-250	250C	75-125	275-12	250-350
216-6	100-150	250S	75-125	279-18	400-500
216-8	100-175	251PR	75-125	281-6	75-125
217-6	75-150	252PR	100-150	282-8	125-150
218-18	350-550	253	250-350	283-8	100-150
221-8	75-100	256-5	100-150	284-10	175-250
222-8	100-150	257-6	125-150	285-10	175-250
225	100-150	259-6	125-175	286-12	150-200
226-8	100-150	261	200-250	287-12	175-250
277-10	100-150	263-14	275-350	288-15	350-450
228-12	125-175	265-5	100-150	289-18	425-525
229-10	100-150	266-4	225-325	290-10	350-450
229-14	125-175	266-8	150-250	1050	100-150
230	125-175	267-5	150-250	1051	100-150
231-10	125-175	268-12	200-300	1053-8	100-150
232	125-175	271P	250-350	1054-8	125-175
233	125-175	271C	75-125	HB	200-300
238-8	150-200	271S	75-125		
240	100-175				

WINDSOR . . . . Page 368
MOLD NUMBERS:

10X3	Ov Bowl	$400- 500	224-10	$400-500	549-7	$ 700- 900
10-3	Rd Bowl	400- 550	329-4	500-700	550-7	700- 900
12"	Rd Bowl	450- 550	330-5	700-800	551-7	700-1000
7"	Fern	1000-1400	331-8	700-900	552-8	700-1000
9"	Fern	900-1100	545-5	400-600	553-9	900-1200
16"	Fern	2800-3200	546-6	600-850	554-10	1000-1400
7"	Rd Vase	1800-2200	547-6	600-800	1084-4	400- 600
15"	Frog	125- 200	548-7	600-800		

WISTERIA . . . . Page 369
MOLD NUMBERS:

242-4	$400-550	631-6	$500- 750	639-10	$ 700-1000
243-4	400-550 nip	632-5	400- 650	640-12	1500-2000
243-5	400-550	633-8	550- 750	641-15	1500-2800
243-12	500-650 nip	634-7	700-1100	1091-4	500- 700
610-7	400-600 nip	635-8	600- 800	HB	600- 900 nip
623-5	400-600 nip	636-8	700-1000	WP	1000-1600 nip
629-4	400-600	637-6	600- 900	Candle	600- 800 nip
630-6	450-650	638-9	650- 950	J&P	4000-7500 nip

ZEPHYR LILY . . . . Page 370-371

5-8	$450-650	137-10	$200- 250	471-12	$175- 250
7C	75-100	138-10	250- 350	472-5	225- 325
7S	75-100	139-12	275- 375	472-6	100- 140
7T	300-350	140-12	300- 400	473-6	100- 140
8-10	200-250	141-15	500- 800	474-8	150- 200
16	225-275	142-18	700-1100	474-14	200- 250
22-6	150-200	201-7	125- 175	475-10	150- 200
23-10	225-275	202-8	125- 175	476-10	150- 200
24-15	400-600	203-6	100- 150	477-12	150- 225
27	100-150	204-8	150- 200	478-12	150- 200
29	125-175	205-6	150- 250	479-14	200- 300
130-6	75-150	206-7	175- 250	671-4	150- 200
130-10	120-180	391-7	125- 175	671-6	175- 275
131-7	100-200	393-7	150- 250	671-8JP	900-1500
132-7	125-175	394-8	175- 275	672-5	175- 225
133-8	150-200	395-10	275- 375	1162-2	100- 150
134-8	175-275	398-7	190- 290	1163-4	175- 225
135-9	200-250	441-10	150- 250	1237	150- 250
135-12	200-275	470-5	100- 175	1393-8	150- 250
136-9	150-250	471-6	175- 275		

PRICE GUIDE / INDEX

UMBRELLA STANDS, SAND JARS,
 JARDINIERES & PEDESTALS . . . Page 372-395
MOLD NUMBERS:
Jardinieres:

Plate 1					
454-4	$125-150	533-7	$200-225	407 A-B-C	
533-4	125-150	419-8	250-300	All	$275-325
537-4	125-150	537-8	250-300	405 A-B-C-D-E-F	
533-4	125-150	479-8	250-300	All	275-325
454-4	125-150	445&447 R-Y-G		411 A-B-C-D-E	
537-5	150-175	8"	300-400	All4	300-350
454-5	150-175	9"	400-500	410 A-B-C-D	
12"	550-600	10"	450-550	All	275-325
537-5	150-175	419 A-B-C-D			
Row 2		444&446 R-Y-G		All	275-325
473-6	175-200	8"	350-450	403 A-B-C	
533-5	150-175	9"	400-500	All	200-250
419-6	175-200	10"	450-550	409 A-B-C-D-E-F	
533-5	150-175	12"	550-650	All	350-450
454-5	150-175	446-447-448-450-451		422 A-B-c	
537-4	125-175	7"	300-350	All	200-250
Row 3		8"	350-400		
454-6	175-200	9"	400-500	Sand Jars:	
547-7	200-225	10"	450-550		
533-6	175-200	12"	550-650	764-11-14	300-350
537-7	200-225	1421-1419-1427		769-11-14	500-600
479-8	250-300	6"	175-200	768-12-14	500-600
Row 4		7"	200-225		
547-7	200-225	8"	225-250		
		9"	275-325		

UMBRELLA STAND

Plate 1		Plate 5		Plate 7	
715-A&B-23	$1000-1600	715-9x23	$1000-1600	710-10-22	$600-700
725-A&B-23	1200-1600	715 R&Y	1000-1600	709-11-23	600-700
Plate 2		Plate 6		Plate 10	
716-8-23	600- 900	707-9-23	300- 700	750-21	1500-1800
713-9-23	1000-1600	720-9-22	500- 750	723-21	2000-2800
Plate 3		Plate 9		740-22	1000-1200
711-8x11x26	1500-1800	718-9-21	900-1400	Plate 11	
717-10x24	900-1400	703-9-22	600- 700	716-8-23	600- 900
Plate 4		721-8-21	1500-2500	714-8-23	1000-1600
717-10-23	1500-2500	Plate 8		Plate 12	
712-9-22	1000-1600	705-8x18	1000-1400	729-A&B	550- 650
		708A&B	400- 600	727-A&B	400- 600

JARDINIERES & PEDESTALS:
(Explanation of numbering: 1st number represents the mold, 2nd is the jardiniere size and 3rd is the height.)

Plate 1		Plate 7&8		Plate 15	
457-5	$ 75- 100	440-15x12x45	1400-1800	508-10x34A,B,C&D	
457-6	100- 125	Plate 9			600-1000
Plate 2		477-6x12	300- 400	Plate 16	
405-10	200- 250	475-6x14	400- 500	1427-22"	600-1000
422-9	200- 250	477-7x18	500- 700	Plate 17	
411-8	150- 200	475-7x18	500- 700	478-10x30	1200-1800
419-7	150- 200	477-10x30	1200-1800		
429-10	800-1000	475-9x25	800-1200	475-10x30	1500-2000
1203-10	600- 800	479-8x24½	1500-2200	Plate 18	
427-9	600- 800	475-8x21½	1500-2200	534-10x30A	1200-1800
421-9	500- 800	Plate 10		534-10x30B	800-1400
Plate 3		427-9X22	800-1400	534-10X30C	700-1200
442-7½	225- 275	421-10x25	700-1000	Plate 19	
442-8½	250- 300	486-11x26	900-1200	J&P 10"	1000-1400
442-9½	275- 325	Plate 11		J&P 12"	1400-2000
442-10½	300- 350	410-38	1000-1600	Jar 7"	225- 275
442-14x30	1400-2200			Jar 8"	250- 300
442-12x28	1200-1600	410-22	700-1400	Jar 9"	275- 325
				Jar 10"	300- 350
Plate 4		Plate 12		Plate 20	
All three J&P's		558-12x34	800-1400	744	900-1500
Plate 5		558-10x28	1000-1200	Plate 21	
		558-12x34	1200-1400	440-15x12x45	1800-2800
403-25	800-1500	Plate 13		433-13x39	1000-1500
410-22	800-1600	Left to Right		Plate 22	
411-22	800-1400		1200-1600	416-28	700-1000
411-37	1200-1800		1000-1400	422-29	800-1200
Plate 6			800-1200	Plate 23	
439-13x34	700-1400	Plate 14		425-15x44	2000-3000
414-14x33	1000-1200	495-10x30	1400-2200	Plate 24	
		A	1400-2000	B	1400-2000
495-6x12	250-400	496-6x12	200- 350	Plate 25 (left to right)	
		495-10x30	1400-2200	1.	50- 100
				2.	50- 75
				3.	75- 125

Collectors Guide to
FRANKOMA POTTERY
1933 through 1990
Identifying Your Collection including Gracetone

by Gary V. Schaum

This is a reference and price guide to the fine wares Frankoma produced from 1933 to the 1990's. Not only is the regular line examined, but the Gracetone lines are included as well. Included is a detailed history of the company and its designers, full color photographs and original catalog pages, marks, reference numbers, years of production all making the identification a simple task.

The author Gary Schaum was very pleased to have Joniece & Donna Frank, daughters of John & Grace Lee Frank help with the publishing of this fine book.

8 1/2" x 11" • 200 pages • full color
$29.95+$3.00 shipping

To order mail check or money order to:
**L-W BOOK SALES • PO Box 69 • Gas City, IN 46933
or call 1-800-777-6450 for VISA or MASTERCARD orders**

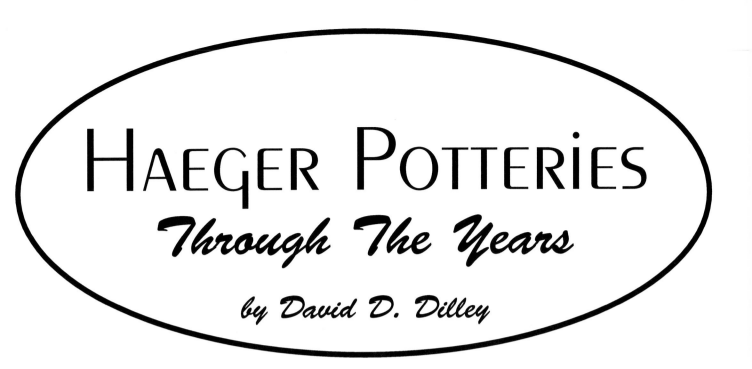

NOTES